The United States and the Americas

Lester D. Langley, General Editor

This series is dedicated to a broader understanding of the political, economic, and especially cultural forces and issues that have shaped the Western hemispheric experience— its governments and its peoples. Individual volumes assess relations between the United States and its neighbors to the south and north: Mexico, Central America, Cuba, the Dominican Republic, Haiti, Panama, Colombia, Venezuela, Peru, Ecuador, Bolivia, Brazil, Paraguay, Argentina, Chile, and Canada.

The United States and the Americas

Bolivia and the United States

Kenneth D. Lehman

Bolivia and the United States: A Limited Partnership

The University of Georgia Press

Athens and London

© 1999 by the University of Georgia Press
Athens, Georgia 30602
All rights reserved
Set in 10 on 14 Palatino by G & S Typesetters, Inc.
Printed and bound by Maple-Vail
The paper in this book meets the guidelines for
permanence and durability of the Committee on
Production Guidelines for Book Longevity of the
Council on Library Resources.

Printed in the United States of America

03 02 01 00 99 C 5 4 3 2 1
03 02 01 00 99 P 5 4 3 2 1

Library of Congress Cataloging-in-Publication Data

Lehman, Kenneth Duane, 1947–
    Bolivia and the United States : a limited partnership /
Kenneth D. Lehman.
        p.   cm. — (The United States and the Americas)
    Includes bibliographical references and index.
    ISBN 0-8203-2115-x (alk. paper). — ISBN 0-8203-2116-8
(pbk. : alk. paper)
        1. United States—Relations—Bolivia.   2. Bolivia—
Relations—United States.   I. Title.   II. Series.
E183.8.B6L44   1999
303.48'273084—DC21   99-22737

British Library Cataloging-in-Publication Data available

Contents

Bolivia: Current Political Boundaries

Based on a map from *Bolivia: A Country Study,* ed. Rex A. Hudson and Dennis M. Hanratty (Washington, D.C.: 1991), xxii.

Preface

In one of their songs, Los Kjarkas, a popular Bolivian folk group, ask why destiny has placed so many obstacles in Bolivia's path. The song recounts the story of the Spanish conquest and the frustration of incomplete independence, and then laments Bolivia's loss of a seacoast to Chile in the War of the Pacific.[1] Each year Bolivians remember that loss on 23 March, the day in 1879 that the one unequivocal Bolivian hero of the war, Eduardo Abaroa, died at Calama Bridge. To Bolivians, Abaroa's brave but lonely stand against an advancing Chilean army—his defiant curse and then his death—symbolize both the pride and the frustration of Bolivian nationhood.

As this volume will demonstrate, Bolivians are a justifiably proud people—not least because groups like Los Kjarkas produce some of the most hauntingly beautiful music in the world—yet the sense of Bolivian national frustration runs deep in popular culture and historical myth. It goes beyond the loss of a seacoast. "Bolivia, a tragic country," wrote Fernando Diez de Medina, one of its most literary sons, "is sustained by the opposition of the elements that comprise it. . . . Bolivia is the culmination of South American confusion. It is the land that least knows itself."[2] Alcides Arguedas, arguably Bolivia's greatest writer, called his people sick—"un *pueblo enfermo*." More recently, a Bolivian scholar contemplating how to teach his country's history to young students confessed, "I think we should invent an official history for ourselves that would serve us better than the real one! Everything we learned in school about Bolivia has to do only with defeats."[3]

These frustrations are the product of a history that contrasts sharply with the North American experience. While Bolivia was suffering as many revolutions as years of existence, losing half its territory, and alternating between economic stagnation and neocolonial dependency on a single primary export, the United States was establishing a working democracy, leapfrogging across a continent, and developing into an industrial, financial, and military power. Such success fosters confidence and nurtures powerful national myths. Americans see themselves as a vanguard nation and people—a "city on a hill"—whose success, measured in material well-being and progress, derives from freedom, self-determination, and liberty of the individual. It is a success Americans naturally wish to share with their neighbors.

On the other hand, Bolivia's history of military defeat, economic stagnation, and growing international dependency has inculcated Bolivians with very different national myths and a profound, even fatalistic, awareness of limits and loss. If Americans are steeped in a self-confident assurance that "anything is possible," Bolivians, for good reasons, tend to assume just the opposite. Explaining why the church on Plaza Murillo in La Paz was never finished, a Bolivian recently told visiting journalist Eric Lawlor: "We complete nothing in this country. . . . Even our revolution was abandoned. We dislike conclusions. In our hearts, we expect things to turn out badly. And why not? Doesn't our history confirm it?"[4]

In history, mythology, power, and culture, Bolivia and the United States are distinct and very distant, and this inevitably shapes the relations between them.[5] The "United States," as I use that name in this work, is a powerful nation-state keenly aware of its strength relative to Bolivia. It is both an economic center that profits from a stable world capitalist system and a regional hegemon interested in maintaining hemispheric order for its own self-interest. Thus the United States is deeply conservative. On the other hand, "America" is a more nebulous cultural entity—a weltanschauung built on dreams, hopes, ideologies, and myths that intermittently captivate and repel Bolivians. "America" believes in itself and thus believes it has a responsibility to export its dreams and myths as well as its technology and its political and economic system. America is imperialistic yet at the same time profoundly revolutionary.[6]

Bolivia, too, is both a nation-state and a shared weltanschauung, though the term *Bolivia* has no meaningful alternative and I will not attempt to create one. It is a nation-state with real, if limited, power, and genuine, if often frustrated, interests. It exists within a world economic system that accentuates its dependency, and within a regional hegemonic system that severely constrains its sovereignty. Bolivia is also a symbiotic cultural entity—indigenous and Spanish, elitist and populist, modern and traditional. Bolivians are a people both attracted to and repelled by modernity, wishing for change yet fearing it, and deeply resenting dependency and weakness yet accepting them as inevitable and natural.

International relations are inevitably relations of culture as well as of power, and to treat them otherwise is to miss much of their nuance and a significant portion of their substance. Anthropologist Clifford Geertz, who is justifiably cautious when defining culture, quotes Max Weber in saying "that man is an animal suspended in webs of significance he himself has spun." Culture, Geertz adds, is that web.[7] The web analogy is useful because it illustrates why culture lies somewhere between the irrelevant and the determinative. Like a web, culture is both product of its creator and subject to infinite and constant revision. Yet, once created, the web subsequently tends to define and circumscribe the perceptual universe of its architect. Culture is too mutable to be a determinative structure and too significant to be no more than an epiphenomenal shadow of material reality; it is, according to Geertz in another of his writings, a discourse, a system of interpretative symbols by which humans order and give meaning to their environment.[8]

With different histories and national mythologies and with dramatically different endowments of power and wealth, the United States and Bolivia have spun distinct cultural webs that affect their discourse. A number of observers have argued that to the degree the United States possesses a "national character" or defining culture, it is one rooted in presuppositions of "boundlessness," "freedom," "abundance," and "limitless good."[9] Historian Fredrick Pike notes that Americans historically have assumed that they played a positive-sum game in which all could be winners if they played by the rules. American political ideology, economic values, and social ethics celebrate the individual and his/her quest to be masterless. To be masterless is to be neither exploited nor to exploit, but rather to create expanding economic opportunity, pluralistic democracy, and a commonwealth of societal harmony free of tyranny as one pursues individual self-interest and wealth.[10]

This paradox underlying American political, economic, and social ideology makes little sense to Bolivians, whose colonial experience, reinforced by subsequent history, leads them to assume that one either exploits or is exploited within overlapping political, economic, and social hierarchies. In Bolivia, the quest is not to be masterless—for such is an illusion—but rather to be a master. But since few can become complete masters of their situation, most instead search for security within the hierarchy by forming asymmetrical patron-client bonds. One is either dominant or dependent, although the harsh Darwinian features of this apparently continuous struggle to define a pecking order are mitigated by paternalism, brokering mechanisms, and myths of reciprocity. It is an arrangement, Pike notes, rooted in expectations of "limited good": a belief that wealth, goods, and resources are relatively fixed and that one person's gain is another's loss. If North Americans historically have believed that individual freedom leads to order and progress, Bolivians sense that it can lead nowhere but to exploitation and chaos. And if North Americans have faith that pluralism in an environment of constantly expanding possibilities results in the kind of balanced stability celebrated by Adam Smith's economic theories or James Madison's Federalist 10, Bolivians historically assume that a plurality of competing interests can lead only to anarchy.[11]

Other works on Bolivia, written from a variety of theoretical and disciplinary perspectives, corroborate the validity of Pike's attention to the hierarchical and patron-client features of Bolivian culture, but also reveal competing sets of values that complicate the picture. In her study of Bolivian tin miners, June Nash argues that miners combine Marxist, indigenous, and Catholic belief systems and practices with little sense of dissonance. So, too, they employ rival logics of action: the logic of class that has made them distinctively and undeniably militant when conditions are right, and the logic of dependency that leads them to seek security through patron-client bonds when militancy is deemed counterproductive on practical grounds.[12]

Pierre Lavaud adds that if Nash is right about miners, who historically have constituted one of the most militantly class-conscious sectors in Bolivian society, the logic of dependency is even stronger among other groups. Lavaud's own work supports earlier studies by political scientists James Malloy, Christopher Mitchell, and Laurence Whitehead, who describe the lingering influence of dependency on revolutionary politics in Bolivia. After the 1952 revolution, Bolivian political sectors were among the most mobilized in Latin America, but, limited by economic stagnation and international weakness, much of the political logic of revolutionary mobilization continued to be the quest for security and jobs through cliental networking and clinging to the rising political star. Finally, my own work on the Bolivian revolution and U.S. assistance to the revolutionary regime after 1953 suggests that the leaders of the Movimiento Nacionalista Revolucionario (MNR) recognized and used Bolivia's dependency to forge a reciprocal if asymmetrical bond with a powerful U.S. patron.[13]

The causes and consequences of dependency have been bitterly debated in recent years. Marxist-oriented theories of the 1960s and 1970s stressed international and domestic power relations and structures of exploitation and dependency but ignored ways in which dependency had been internalized culturally. Recent neoliberal interpretations (dubbed "neoconservative" inside the United States) refute the validity of external dependency and exploitation as explanatory variables but resurrect concepts of psychological dependency and its cultural manifestations to explain why Latin America remains poor.[14]

This volume tries to take dependency seriously at all its levels. Overlapping systems of culture and power shape U.S.-Bolivian relations, and the relationship between these two countries can best be understood by paying attention to both simultaneously. Through much of their early histories, little tied the two countries to each other; however, there have been periods when Bolivia became important to the United States. During World War II, for example, Bolivia provided the only secure supply of tin in the hemisphere. In the 1950s and early 1960s Bolivia's nationalist revolution threatened regional stability and U.S. cold war hegemony. And today, cocaine produced from Bolivian coca has become an American scourge. When circumstances have increased the coincidence of their vital interests, the two nations have formed an informal partnership rooted in mutual self-interest, but one in which the United States clearly dominates.

These have been partnerships in which clear disparities of wealth and power have been reinforced by cultural assumptions to create patron-client bonds. Culturally these are bonds between a people who understand their weakness yet fiercely resent it and a people who see themselves as special, as a model worth emulating, and have little natural propensity to mistrust the purity of their own motives. These periods of unequal partnership generally have begun with common interests and genuine, if asymmetrical, friendship, but almost inevitably they have ended in frustration followed by imposition on the part of the patron, and by submission, resentment, and finally resistance on the part of the client. The history of U.S.-Bolivian relations illustrates the real as well as mythical bonds that link even the most distant and different of neighbors, yet at the same time it provides an abundance of evidence to show how factors of culture and power complicate true partnership.

Acknowledgments

It is more than a cliché that when one embarks on a project of this sort, one incurs many debts. My first and greatest debt is to the people of Don Lorenzo, Bolivia, for it was they who gave me my own personal introduction to how disparities of wealth and power and differing cultural perceptions affect even the friendliest discourse. When I first went to Bolivia in 1971, I knew next to nothing about the country. I knew that Ché Guevara had died there a few years before, and, like many North Americans, I would soon learn—perhaps erroneously— that Butch Cassidy and the Sundance Kid suffered a similar fate there early in the twentieth century.[1]

I was in Don Lorenzo for reasons having little to do with prior knowledge, understanding, or even interest in Bolivia and much more to do with a typically American blend of idealism and arrogance. I went to Don Lorenzo to teach, to encourage development and community solidarity, and generally to do some good. I suppose that over the next two years I did a bit of each, but far more important was what Don Lorenzo did to and for me. My experiences there initiated a process of discovery that continued through the research for my doctoral dissertation, motivates this book, and almost certainly will absorb my attention for the rest of my life.

Don Lorenzo is not large or wealthy in a conventional sense, but it possesses a wealth of history and tradition. According to its inhabitants, it was the original site of the Spanish settlement of Santa Cruz de la Sierra. If true, this makes the tiny village of less than one hundred families some fifty years older than Jamestown. It was in Don Lorenzo that I first began to understand that as a result of my cultural upbringing I saw and understood things very differently from *lorenzeños*. It was there, too, that I came to understand how the reality of power and perceptions of power qualify and distort even friendly relationships. I had many friends in Don Lorenzo, but, although our relations were non-coercive, they were never relations of equals. I was a volunteer, but my monthly personal allowance for toothpaste, movies, and restaurant meals during periodic trips to the city was greater than the normal monthly income of many lorenzeño families.

I had outside contacts, knowledge, and resources that they lacked, although they were by no means powerless. If my umbilical cord to the outside world had been severed, I would have been in serious trouble. Lorenzeños, on the other hand, had a sure knowledge and understanding of their own environment that provided them with an almost unfailing internal compass to determine when gringo ideas made no sense. They saw that what I most had to offer was new resources and connections, and with their gifts of food and hospitality they sought bonds of genuine if asymmetrical reciprocity with this strange intruder in their midst—bonds of patron and client. It was not a relationship that I sought, nor was it one with which I, as an American, was comfortable. In Don Lorenzo I began to understand the degree to which I shared that distinct American weltanschauung blending idealism and arrogance, and there I came to see the equally paradoxical Bolivian mix of friendly eagerness and fierce, resistive pride that forever maintained a certain distance in our relationship.

It would be a cognitive error of the first order if I were to project my own experiences large upon the pages of history, yet it would be equally a mistake to ignore them in a futile quest for objectivity. After spending five years in Bolivia, I do not claim objectivity. I am within one culture, but I will describe facets of another to readers who largely share my own web of understandings. Because I have not helped to spin the Bolivian cultural web, many of its patterns remain exotic to me. Through the eyes of a stranger, differences are often magnified and the similarities are sometimes missed. The differences constantly stimulate analysis, but just as constantly evade complete understanding. Perhaps as confusing is the issue of power. It is much easier to see the power of the strong and the powerlessness of the weak than it is to appreciate and understand the foibles and illusions that accompany strength and the enduring resistance that gives dignity to weakness. This work will not resolve the paradoxes laid out here, but it will remain aware that they exist. For making *me* aware that they exist, I thank the lorenzeños.

Other debts are too numerous to acknowledge in full, but I thank the University of Texas, the Eisenhower World Affairs Institute, the Tinker Foundation, the Virginia Foundation for Independent Colleges, and Hampden-Sydney College for helping to finance my research. Several individuals assisted this project in significant ways. I sincerely thank colleagues here at Hampden-Sydney who read all or parts of the manuscript and helped me to express myself more clearly: Ron Heinemann, David Harms, John Eastby, Scott Colley, and George Bagby. The readers assigned by the University of Georgia Press to review the manuscript gave many useful suggestions and helped me avoid some embarrassing errors. Series editor Lester Langley was a model of supportive, patient, and insightful counsel to this first-time author. Courtney Denney helped guide me through the intricacies of the production phase, and Mindy Conner helped me to see all those little mistakes and possible improvements that are so easy to miss when one is deeply involved in a project. Of course, any errors or deficiencies this work still possesses are fully my own responsibility.

I thank all the people who taught me to love and value history. First I must give special credit to my parents, Harold and Ruth Lehman, who, well into their eighth decade, remain active historians and writers. My history mentors since high school also deserve mention: the names of John Krall, John Lapp, and Al Keim spring to mind. At the University of New Mexico, Ed Lieuwen and Peter Gregory first interested me in examining U.S.-Bolivian relations. At the University of Texas at Austin, Alan Knight and Jonathan Brown helped me hone my research and writing skills, and Robert Divine taught me the intricacies of U.S. diplomatic history. Finally, I owe a big debt to graduate student colleague Seth Fein, whose serendipitous tip led me to Lester Langley and a publisher for this project.

On a more personal note, I thank the Mennonite Central Committee for giving me the chance to live and learn in Don Lorenzo; my parents for their loving support as well as their example through the years; my three college professor brothers, whose scholarship and friendly com-petition spur me on; and my children, Susan, Michael, and Christian, who have helped me keep my priorities straight. Finally I thank my wife, Jackie—the only person as happy to see this project concluded as I am—you have helped make this book possible in countless ways, and I dedicate it to you.

Bolivia and the United States

1 Most Different of Neighbors

The first great age of anticolonial uprisings against European imperialism began in Great Britain's mainland colonies in 1776 and ended ambiguously in 1825 on the high plains of the Spanish colony that became Bolivia. This contrast symbolizes the profound differences that placed the United States and Bolivia near opposite poles of a spectrum of colonial patterns in the New World. The New World served two primary functions to the Old: it provided exploitable resources to be developed and expropriated to benefit a Europe in transition from feudalism to capitalism, and it served as an escape valve to release some of the social, economic, political, and religious tensions accompanying that transformation. The Spanish colony that was to become Bolivia fulfilled almost exclusively the first function, while the British colony that was eventually to become the United States largely fulfilled the second.

This chapter must cover too much material to deal effectively with nuance and complexity; instead it describes the impact of those patterns on significant North American and Bolivian national myths. As Eldon Kenworthy has observed, myth and history are not opposites: myth is, rather, a distinct narrative depiction of history that simplifies and generalizes complexities into paradigmatic and usable "truths." There is a great deal of validity to Fredrick Pike's assertion that people who seek to make sense of the past "live more by myths than facts."[1]

Contrasting Bases of Colonial Wealth

Spaniards first came to the Andean region that became Bolivia more than three quarters of a century before the English settled Jamestown or Plymouth. When Diego de Almagro and his men joined Francisco Pizarro late at Cajamarca and thus failed to receive a full share of Incan treasure from Atahualpa's ransom, they pushed on south, looking for wealth they could call their own. In 1535 Almagro passed through the Bolivian highlands on his way to Chile and claimed it for the king of Spain. Disappointed in Chile, Almagro returned to clash with Pizarro in a bloody struggle that cost him his life. Francisco Pizarro passed Almagro's claims to the highland region south of Lake Titicaca to his half-brother Gonzalo. In 1538 Gonzalo Pizarro established a settlement at Chuquisaca (modern Sucre), attracted not only by the pleasant valley and friendly natives, but also by active preconquest silver operations at nearby Porco. The Spaniards originally called that region Charcas, after the Indians who lived around Chuquisaca, but the name most common at the close of the colonial period was Alto Peru—Upper Peru.[2]

The natives of Upper Peru had long been sedentary. Advanced civilizations had lived there well before A.D. 600, when the city of Tiahuanaco on the southern shore of Lake Titicaca emerged as a major ceremonial and trade center for the entire central Andean high plains (*altiplano*). More than 350,000 people inhabited the Tiahuanaco heartland, perhaps as many as 115,000 in the capital and its satellite cities alone. The Tiahuanacans were able to sustain a population far in excess of what the region supports today by constructing raised planting beds separated by ditches that not only irrigated the beds but also insulated the crops from the frigid altiplano nights. With this ingenious system guaranteeing ample food supplies, Tiahuanaco established direct control over the western and southern shores of Lake Titicaca and exerted administrative and trade hegemony over a much larger zone.[3]

During Tiahuanaco's decline, between A.D. 1000 and 1100, power became localized in traditional kinship groups called *ayllus*. Each ayllu exploited one of the wide variety of ecological niches at the different Andean altitudes and established trade links with outlying areas.[4] The region comprised the Incas' southern province of Kollasuyo, although the Incas never completely subdued the dozen or so kingdoms of Aymará speakers south of the lake. To control them, the Incas created settlements of transplanted Quechua speakers from the Cuzco area around the perimeter of the Aymaras in places such as Cochabamba. Today Quechua and Aymará are still the first languages many Bolivians learn.[5]

The Spaniards brought profound changes to Upper Peru. Gonzalo

Pizarro introduced the *encomienda* system, which granted tributaries to individual Spanish conquerors and brought natives formally into semifeudal domination by the Spanish invaders. Then, in 1545, Spanish explorers from Chuquisaca discovered a massive outcropping of ore—three hundred feet long, thirteen feet wide, and 50 percent pure silver—in a cone-shaped mountain near Porco. That mountain, which became simply and descriptively known as El Cerro Rico (the rich hill), was the source of more than half the silver produced in the New World during the next century. The Cerro Rico produced enough wealth to trigger European inflation, alter patterns of international trade, finance a generation of Catholic Spanish wars against the rising Protestant challenge, cover Spain's mounting trade deficits with the Orient and later northern Europe, and make the name of Potosí—the city founded at the base of the *cerro* in 1546—synonymous throughout Europe with wealth. In 1558, King Philip II created the semiautonomous Audiencia of Charcas in Chuquisaca to provide closer royal oversight of the crucial mining region, and by 1611 Potosí's population of 160,000 made it the largest city in the New World and perhaps the third most populous city in all Christendom.[6]

The crown claimed subsurface rights and levied the royal fifth on silver produced at Potosí, but the mines were privately owned by Spaniards, who contracted and/or coerced encomienda Indians into providing the necessary labor. During the first decades after the discovery of the silver lode, Indians and Spaniards alike came to Potosí to burrow like moles along the rich veins of ore. The refining process employed preconquest technologies and remained in the hands of natives, who built and operated wind ovens called *guayras* that out-performed European bellows at Potosí's 14,350-foot altitude.

By the 1560s the richest ores had played out and preconquest refining methods no longer maintained the flow of silver to which Spanish monarchs had become accustomed. A concerned King Philip II formed a special investigative committee to improve colonial administration and restore the flow of wealth to Spain. One of its members, Francisco de Toledo, was named viceroy of Peru, and the policies he implemented during his tenure (1569–81) laid the foundation of the Spanish colonial system in Upper Peru. To extract silver from increasingly complex ores, the viceroy introduced the amalgamation, or *patio*, smelting process first used in Mexico in 1554. The patio system utilized mercury in a chemical bonding process to separate silver from impurities, a process made feasible by the discovery of mercury deposits farther north at Huancavelica in modern Peru.[7]

To provide labor for the mines and the newly industrialized smelting operations, Toledo adapted an existing native system of corvée labor called the *mita*, which required Indian communities near Potosí to provide draft labor on a rotating basis. To bring the communities more completely under Spanish control, Toledo repressed a series of rebellions that had begun in 1565 and captured and killed the last Incan ruler, Túpac Amaru. Toledo next tried to reconsolidate the native population, decimated by European diseases, by congregating the survivors in villages, or *reducciones*. Each *reducción* was given a mita quota, with local enforcement assured by a new crown official in each community—the *corregidor de indios*. Toledo also reorganized and improved the city of Potosí by creating a royal mint, rationalizing the tax system, and developing the water supply necessary for the patio process. Because of Toledo's reforms, the king's share of the silver from Potosí rose tenfold between 1570 and 1585 and stayed at that level for the next sixty years.

Silver and Indians were Upper Peru's twin sources of wealth, and Viceroy Toledo's policies allowed both to be more efficiently exploited to the benefit of Spain and local Spanish mine owners. Potosí was a boomtown with all the unbridled energy and opportunism of any boomtown at any time in any place. Yet it was also distinctively colonial—swarming with accountants, assayers, and other royal officials whose responsibility it was to guarantee that the mother country and its monarch received their share. Stripped to its essentials, the Spaniards' task was simple: monitor production of silver, claim the royal fifth, assure its safe passage to Spain, and create a commercial system that would guarantee that much of the remaining four-fifths also flowed back to Spain. To that end the crown required that all silver be minted with the official royal seal before it could circulate, and carefully controlled and monitored the supply of mercury to provide a crude measure of actual silver production.

The king's share of minted silver was carried to the coast by carefully controlled pack trains and loaded on ships for Callao; from there it went to Panama, whence it was transported by well-guarded fleets to Spain. The fleets returned twice a year carrying Spanish goods that were sold at inflated prices by the king's chartered merchant house in Seville.

Governmental oversight was hierarchical, with all authority, in theory, emanating from the crown and flowing downward to local crown representatives. At the local level, the Spanish retained traditional Andean relations of production so that Indian communities might regularly be milked of their surplus through mechanisms like the mita.[8] Each reconstituted community in sixteen provinces around Potosí provided one-seventh of its adult male population at a given time to work in the mines. This meant a total mita labor force of between thirteen and fourteen thousand workers, who with their families added a floating population of about forty thousand to Potosí.

Mita workers spent four months in Potosí, working inside the mines every third week and spending the intervening weeks selling their labor to raise funds for their subsistence. The burden on a given individual was, in theory, perhaps no more onerous than that earlier imposed by the Incas—four months of forced labor every seven years. But it was a system open to myriad abuses. The nature of the mita as a forced migratory labor system meant that mining entrepreneurs had no incentives to limit exploitation of their workers. Because work was forced, the entrepreneur did not worry that harsh conditions would drive away potential workers. And because he did not own the workers, he did not risk losing a valuable capital investment by overexploitation. Nor, unlike feudal serfdom, was he concerned with reproduction and maintenance of the labor force, because a *mitayo's* basic subsistence support came not from wages but rather from his home community and the sale of his labor during off weeks.[9]

Workers on mita assignments were given the most odious tasks— primarily carrying out ore on their backs through steep, winding shafts too low for standing. Often they spent their entire week in the mines, working day and night and sleeping when and where they could. To discourage slacking, owners set stiff production quotas that the mitayo had to meet before he was released from his obligation. As time passed and the mines became less profitable, the incentives to exploit the mitayos increased, as did the implicit subsidy that native communities provided the mining entrepreneurs. These subsidies became increasingly fundamental to turning profits by the late seventeenth century. Without them, according to historian Enrique Tandeter, much of the production in the area would have been abandoned.[10]

Overseeing the system at the local level were the corregidores de indios, who saw that each community fulfilled its assigned role in the colonial system. Corregidores occupied the bottom rung of the bureaucratic hierarchy, and they were badly underpaid and open to graft. A favorite abuse was the *repartimiento de mercancías,* a compulsory sale of Spanish goods to Indian communities at substantial mark-ups, with the corregidor serving as both local salesman and law-enforcing official.[11]

In short, well before the English had permanently settled in the New World, Potosí and the surrounding area of Upper Peru had become almost a paradigmatic case of an exploited colony in which wealth was transferred from Indian communities and the Cerro Rico to local elites and the mother country. Although half a world distant from Spain, Potosí was in many ways at the very heart of the Spanish colonial system, and Magnus Mörner observes that Potosí's silver was essential to Spain's valiant if ultimately doomed efforts "first to obtain and then to defend West European hegemony."[12]

From the perspective of their mother country, the British mainland colonies in North America were neither so valuable nor so efficiently organized as Spain's Upper Peru. Founded almost a century after Charcas in an area without gold, silver, or exploitable natives, the colonies appeared to hold little of commercial value other than a noxious weed of dubious utility or morality known as tobacco. The colonists, first in Virginia and then in Massachusetts, were products of ferment on their home island, a ferment marked by rising population, a Protestant challenge to Roman Catholic hegemony with resulting religious conflicts, and an economic shift toward capitalism. Those who initially came to the colonies were, more often than not, the misfits and refuse of England. Occasionally an entrepreneurial young gentleman on the make or a second son of the landed gentry made his way across the Atlantic, but most of the early colonists were either landless and desperate indentured servants, convicts forced to the colonies against their will, or religious troublemakers seeking to create their "city on a hill." Colonists who did not arrive in families quickly formed them—bulwarks of civilization in a forbidding wilderness.

Yet it was the wilderness that drew them in increasing numbers. The New World liberated both Englishman and Spaniard from the dogma, the hierarchy, and the social class system of Europe. There is general truth to Fredrick Pike's assertion that Spaniards came to the New World to escape their inferior position in the existing feudal system and re-create a new form of it here, while many English settlers came to escape feudalism itself.[13] The English mainland colonies had few exploitable resources beyond the land—fertile land that appeared wild and underutilized to Europeans, who did not understand the ways in which the natives carefully managed it. Rivers opened the way to the interior and contributed to the colonists' avaricious assault on the frontier. The wilderness took on mythical powers, taking vestigial feudal elements of order and place and slowly grinding them away, and in the process transforming Europeans into Virginians, Carolinians, and Pennsylvanians.

The differences in basic cultural patterns between the British mainland colonies and the Spanish South American colony that was to become Bolivia were established early in the colonial period. Upper Peru, a colony geared toward exploitation, was organized hierarchically and corporately beneath the watchful eye of the crown; natives were incorporated into the system, although at its base. To the north, each generation of North Americans invaded and tamed a new slice of the wilderness, pushing the natives aside as they went. Every step took the colonists further from the already less-than-vigilant eye of the English crown and contributed to an emerging sense of individual autonomy. In such an environment, developing myths of mobility, liberty, and plenty inculcated a sense of special American energy and virtue.

Colonial Paradoxes

It would be highly inaccurate to paint the contrasts between the Spanish and British colonial systems too starkly, however. There were ironies to the North American myths. The expanding freedom rested on a contradictory base of slavery and was rooted in the exploitation of the land and the obliteration of its native inhabitants. The American dream was a white man's dream at this point, and the colonists had not yet completely shaken a European sense of both hierarchy and place. While religious sectarianism led slowly to religious tolerance for other sects, it did not yet extend to Catholics, Africans, or natives.

If the reality of the British colonies did not always conform to developing myths, neither was Upper Peru so completely and efficiently exploited as a superficial study of Spanish colonial institutions might indicate. The reality in both places was far more complex and interesting. Illustrating the problems facing Spain as it sought to exploit its silver-producing Andean colony were the far from simple logistical problems of getting silver from Potosí to the coast. The first load of silver left Potosí in March 1549: 7,771 bars carried by pack train requiring two thousand llamas and a thousand Indians to safeguard the treasure. The trip to the coast took more than six months, by sea to Panama took several weeks, and across the isthmus and through what eventually became pirate-infested seas to Spain, several additional months.[14]

Added to the logistical problems of moving and safeguarding the flow of silver were myriad other challenges: the tendency of low-paid crown officials to cheat, the abundant opportunities to cheat that their great distance from Spain gave them, and the time-honored principle of *obedezco pero no cumplo* ("I obey but do not comply") that limited the coercive power of royal decrees emanating from a metropolis thousands of miles and many months distant. Added to these control problems were smugglers, pirates, and the simple fact that the king had hundreds of competing priorities. To combat these problems, Spain created over-lapping bureaucracies—watchers to watch the watchers—and initiated review and oversight mechanisms such as the *visita* (an official inspection tour by a trusted crown official) and the *residencia* (a formal review process at the beginning and end of the tenure of every royal official). It was ungainly and far from efficient, but as effective a system to exploit the wealth of the New World for the benefit of the Old as any that could be devised in that age.

Yet another factor limited the smooth operation of the exploitation system: it inevitably undermined its basic unit, the native community. The Europeans brought diseases that decimated the Indian population of Upper Peru. Mita and tribute demands on the local community further depleted the ranks of Toledo's original tributaries and their descendants, and provided the indigenous population with an irresistible incentive to formally disaffiliate from the home community and join the relatively rootless *forastero* or *yanacona* groups. Forastero was a new category, referring to the sector of the native population in a given community who were not descendants of the original Toledan tributaries, or *originarios,* and thus were not subject to community obligations. Yanaconas were landless workers no longer tied to the communities, but rather to Spanish employers or landlords. Until the eighteenth century, neither forasteros nor yanaconas were subject to the mita or tribute. Many who went to Potosí as mitayos remained to sell their labor and fill more permanent and skilled positions in the mines, thus becoming yanaconas. Others moved out of the mita zone and became forasteros. Recent research hints that this did not mean a rupture between migrant and home community. Absent Indians continued to send resources back to their original community chieftains, or *kurakas.* In 1683 Viceroy Palata tried to get an accurate count of people where they actually resided in order to force forasteros and yanaconas to share more fully with originarios the burdens of the colonial system, but at the middle of the next century, his reforms had still not been fully implemented.[15]

The looseness within the Spanish colonial system also becomes apparent when one examines the role of the church. Spain did not tolerate religious deviance in Upper Peru, but neither was Catholic hegemony complete. As in other Spanish colonies, the one true church played a complicated if integrative role. Roman Catholicism absorbed and subordinated native beliefs in a syncretistic blend that made the church an instrument of ideological control as well as, paradoxically, a haven for the maintenance of indigenous beliefs. As an institution, the church levied a variety of taxes and other exactions on the indigenous community and was yet another tool of Spanish exploitation; nevertheless, the church also defended the natives' basic humanity, and on occasion, specific priests supported Indian rebellions.

In short, Upper Peru was never the stable hierarchical society, geared for exploitation, it was designed to be. If Spaniards attempted to recreate feudalism in the New World, simple market forces also provided ample opportunities for entrepreneurship and mobility. Potosí lay on a barren and windswept plain more than fourteen thousand feet above sea level. Little could be produced locally to feed the immense floating population of the city, meaning that the mining center became a powerful market hub that stimulated commercial trade networks over a wide radius from southern Peru to northern Argentina. Drawing grain crops from nearby valleys; coca from the semitropical *yungas* east of the Andes; and meat, mules, wine, and sugar from northern Argentina, Potosí encouraged the economically venturous and stimulated an expanding pool of mobile free labor despite the best efforts of crown officials to maintain colonial structures of extraction.[16]

When Potosí's production halved between 1600 and 1650, and halved yet again by the end of the century, the population of the city fell commensurately, to seventy thousand by 1700 and to thirty thousand by 1750. Both the carefully constructed imperial system and Potosí as a market pole eroded. However, the century was less a time of local depression than of economic restructuring, diversified production, and a more complex if localized trade. Hacienda growth leveled out and Indian communities strengthened, the result of the resurgence of the native population, the reduction of exploitative pressures on the community, and the expansion of trade networks as the Potosí locus weakened.[17]

Between 1650 and 1750, Upper Peru and the English mainland colonies went in different directions. Upper Peru turned inward as the unifying ties to the mother country weakened, thus encouraging regionalism, increasing local autonomy, and shifting the social and economic relations of production. During this same period, the ties between the British colonies and England strengthened as England finally arrived at a semblance of internal order after the 1660 Restoration. The various English colonies became increasingly integrated into an emerging North Atlantic economy. Historian John Murrin notes that during this century, the "main counterpoise" to increased regional diversity "came not from any commonly shared 'American' experience but from the expanding impact of empire."[18] It was this contact with metropolitan England that brought the colonies closer to each other as together they grew closer to England, and it was the growing links within the colonial system that increased commercial and other contacts between the colonies.

Independence

It is ironic, although perhaps not surprising, that the culmination of this century of growing connection between England and its North American colonies was independence. The French and Indian War (Seven Years' War) brought colonists and the mother country together in common cause, but it also definitively illustrated the nature of their existing relationship as well as the maturing identity that set off Americans from Englishmen. Close proximity during that war convinced many colonists that they were no longer British but something else— something better. Their success against the French led the colonists to feel powerfully vindicated in their faith in voluntaristic institutions while the undisciplined colonial militias convinced London authorities that colonists were incapable of their own defense. The war led the colonists to demand greater autonomy at the same time that it convinced the crown to tighten political control over the colonies so as to defray the costs of the war. The goals of the new king, George III, and the purpose of Lord Grenville's tax program were political in the sense that they were designed to strengthen the eroding lines of authority between metropolis and colonies. Economic ties were already strong.[19]

The clashes with England that followed were a product of forces too complex to properly analyze here. They include the influence of Enlightenment ideology on colonial elites; a variety of complaints about taxes and increasing debts to British merchants; a resulting nostalgia for a mythical era when the colonists were more self-sufficient; an emerging sense of colonial identity, which the British seemed bent on thwarting; and, perhaps most important, the perception of increased outside meddling by a people accustomed to self-rule. Although historians have shown that class and race conflicts lurked beneath any common cause the colonists shared, the American Revolution did not develop into class or race warfare. Louis Hartz has observed that "social revolution" theory provides few analytical insights into the causes or results of the revolution.[20] The goals of American independence were narrowly political and essentially conservative even if its results were profoundly radical. It was, as Cecilia Kenyon has noted, "a petty rebellion [transformed] into a symbol for the liberation of all mankind."[21] With its demands for release from colonial bonds; its faith in voluntarism, individualism, and republicanism; and its willingness to experiment with new forms of federalism to embrace a large population spread over a diverse and extended area, the North American conflict marked the beginning of a great age of revolution.

Independence, when it finally came to Upper Peru, was a much more convoluted affair that lasted more than sixteen years and combined deep class tensions, underlying fears of race war, regionalist resentments against outside agitators, and the conservative desire of local elites to retain as much of their traditional privileges as possible when the Spanish colonial system was in shambles. To paraphrase Kenyon, when the age of revolution came to its ambivalent end in Upper Peru, issues of the "liberation of mankind" resolved themselves in pettiness. A coterie of erstwhile royalists finally tipped the balance toward independence when Simón Bolívar's armies threatened and it became clear that they could expect no help from Spain.

The origins of the independence process in Upper Peru are not unrelated to the rebellion in North America. All through the eighteenth century, increasing amounts of smuggled silver escaped Spanish control and flowed directly to northern Europe while European contraband flowed back into the Spanish colonies. Spain's weakening hold on its Latin American empire became clear during the Seven Years' War when the British seized Havana and threatened Buenos Aires. Charles III, like his fellow "Third" in England, had come to power during the war and resolved to strengthen the lines of authority between colony and crown. But Charles of Spain also had to restimulate mechanisms of colonial extraction. Lester Langley comments that while "the British had elected to redefine empire; the Spanish elected to reconstruct it." Ultimately, both failed.[22]

In 1776, with the British diverted by their developing crisis in North America, Charles decided to make a preemptive move against Britain's ally Portugal and drive the Portuguese from their smuggling stronghold on the east bank of the Río de la Plata. The commander of that successful seizure was made viceroy of a new viceroyalty with its seat in Buenos Aires. To assure an enlarged financial base, the new viceroyalty of La Plata was given jurisdiction over Upper Peru and its mines.[23]

That same year, Spain's colonial secretary, José de Gálvez, sent Antonio de Areche as *visitador general* (inspector general) to Peru to inaugurate the sorts of fiscal and other administrative reforms that Gálvez himself had implemented in New Spain. Areche stepped into a volatile situation. The creation of La Plata cost Lima an important source of revenues that compounded the effects of its loss of jurisdiction over northern South America early in the century when the Viceroyalty of New Grenada was created. Official flows of Potosí silver now joined the illegitimate flow of smuggled metal toward the Atlantic, disrupting existing trade lines and threatening the livelihood of Peruvian muleteers. Their unrest spread to Indian communities that were suffering increased tribute exactions as well as the increased abuse of the repartimiento de mercancías as Lima merchants sought to recover profits lost in other markets and local corregidores felt the squeeze created by Peru's economic depression. In 1778, Spain joined France and the rebellious North American colonies against England, and the Spanish crown ordered Areche to increase revenues for the war. To that end, the visitador raised the *alcabala,* or sales tax, from 4 percent to 6 percent and hinted that tribute requirements might henceforth be required of mestizos as well as Indians.[24]

Peru's viceroy, Manuel Guirior, warned that these moves were a recipe for rebellion and counseled Areche against them, but the visitador interpreted Guirior's advice as insubordination and had him recalled to Spain. Then, on 4 November 1780, the day before Guirior's replacement officially took office, José Gabriel Condorcanqui executed the corregidor of the village of Tinta near Cuzco and set in motion the rebellion the former viceroy had feared. José Gabriel, a mestizo who traced his lineage on one side to Incan royalty, changed his name to Túpac Amaru in commemoration of the last Inca emperor and quickly raised an Indian and mestizo army that also drew support from disgruntled Creoles (American born but of Spanish descent). At its height in early 1781, the rebellion involved some 100,000 rebel troops whose goal, like that of their contemporaries in North America, was independence.[25]

Túpac Amaru knew of the struggle in North America and was aware that Spain was now involved. The British temporarily forced the port of Buenos Aires to close, further disrupting trade, and by late 1780 English fleets threatened the western coast of South America. Areche had been preparing and fortifying Lima against a possible attack, but now he turned his attention to the more pressing problems in the highlands and quickly raised an army of Spanish regulars and loyal Indians. José Gabriel Túpac Amaru was captured in April 1781 and executed a month later.

Trouble had been brewing in Upper Peru even before the Túpac Amaru uprising, and as the rebellion was brought under control near Cuzco, it broke out with renewed ferocity farther south. In February 1781 a revolt in the mining town of Oruro revealed the growing rift between Indian and non-Indian rebels. At the outset, Creole mining entrepreneurs led a broad-based uprising against Spanish officials. Then Indians from outlying villages descended on Oruro to demand redress of their own long list of grievances. To regain control, the Creole leader,

Jacinto Rodríguez, issued a series of decrees that promised land reform and the end of tribute and tithes, and that required all non-Indians to wear Indian garb. The decrees reveal the strength of the Indian rebels at that juncture as well as the degree to which the colonial world was on the verge of turning upside down. Indians who had once seemed submissive and in the worst case only passively resistant to colonial demands now exhibited a fierce desire for revenge that frightened Creole leaders, who had assumed that they could manipulate native discontent to further their own ends. Before the rebellion in Oruro played out, it evolved from an independence movement to class conflict, and then to impending caste and race war. Rodríguez finally reforged an alliance of Spaniards, Creoles, and mestizos, and the rioting Indians were expelled from the city.[26]

The events in Oruro presaged the growing racial caste split in the rebellion. At about the same time, Julián Apasa, a coca trader, and his heavily Aymaran army laid siege to La Paz for almost four months. Driven back, Apasa—who had renamed himself Túpac Katari—joined forces with remnants of Túpac Amaru's army and again attacked La Paz. By now Creole support for the rebellion had completely vanished, and the Creoles joined the Spanish to launch a full-scale war of attrition against Túpac Katari's army. In November 1781, the Aymaran rebel was captured, tortured, and drawn and quartered, and the rebellion in the two Perus finally ended, leaving between 100,000 and 140,000 dead. When calm was restored, the Spaniards not only liquidated the leaders of the rebellion but also attempted to obliterate its ideological underpinnings. They proscribed titles of indigenous nobility and such symbols of Incan nationalism as the writings of Garcilaso "El Inca" de la Vega, the use of Quechua, and the practice of pre-Columbian ceremonies.[27]

But the crown also responded with reforms. Areche was removed from office for failing to restrain the rebellion, the office of corregidor was abolished—at least in theory—and the crown restricted the repartimiento de mercancías. Increased Spanish administrative and military presence in the region exacerbated Creole tension but at the same time held it in check. Further serving to mute anti-Spanish agitation among

Creoles in Upper Peru was the realization that more tied them to Spain than to the Indian rebels who had so destabilized their world. Herbert Klein states that postrebellion reforms successfully restored the economy, rebuilt new trade networks, and soon made the Túpac Amaru rebellion "a distant memory in the minds of the population of Upper Peru."[28] But it was a nagging memory; a dormant volcano rumbled beneath Creole society in Upper Peru that in many ways defined the nature of independence when it came almost a half century later.

The years between 1781 and 1809, crucial to both the United States and Upper Peru, took those two regions in very different directions. A month before Túpac Katari was drawn and quartered, the thirteen British mainland colonies forced the British to surrender at Yorktown. In the years that followed, the new United States more than doubled its territory at the postwar peace conference, established a functioning constitutional government after one failed attempt, and found its feet under conditions of general European war. By remaining neutral, the United States took advantage of the European conflict to double its size yet again and further diversify its economy.

Meanwhile, Upper Peru was reabsorbed into the Spanish empire, its colonial features reinforced and strengthened. While postinsurrection reforms corrected some abuses, they also increased both the peninsular presence and the efficiency of colonial exactions. Bourbon reforms led to a temporary resurgence in mining, but the boomlet was less a response to new exploration, investments, or technologies than to continuing crown subsidies, increased exploitation of mitayos, and the reworking of existing mine tailings.[29]

Then, in 1797, Spain again went to war with England. English gunboats disrupted Spanish trade, cutting off the supply of mercury to Upper Peru from Europe needed to supplement dwindling supplies from Huancavelica. The mercury shortage combined with the declining quality of recoverable ore in mine tailings precipitated a general mining crisis. Compounding the crisis was a drought that reduced water supplies essential for refining operations in Potosí and caused crop failures, famine, and disease that disrupted the supply of mita laborers. At war and desperate for funds, Spain tightened the screws on its colonies. Despite the drought and the mining collapse, income from Indian tribute rose 24 percent and total treasury income from Upper Peru rose 18.5 percent during the first decade of the nineteenth century.[30] The overlapping pressures of economic depression and increased levels of colonial exploitation made the Creoles of Upper Peru unhappy, but the memories of the 1781 insurrection remained sufficiently vivid to keep them subordinate to the crown. They might have remained subordinate indefinitely were it not for events in Spain itself. In March 1808, under pressure from France, Charles IV abdicated, and Napoleon seized Ferdinand VII and imposed his own brother Joseph on the throne of Spain. Popular and regional protests spread through the Iberian peninsula and destabilized the already volatile colonies.

In July 1809, the people of La Paz seized the local governor and bishop and declared their independence from Spain. Although short-lived, the rebellion in La Paz was the first relatively unambiguous declaration of independence by an American colony of Spain, and it served notice of the coming sixteen-year struggle that would encompass almost all of Hispanic America. The end of that struggle also came in Upper Peru when, on 1 April 1825, renegade royalist Pedro Olañeta was defeated at Tumusla and the last important bastion of Spanish colonialism disappeared from mainland South America. During the interim, all the complicating factors that made Bolivian independence a far more convoluted affair than U.S. independence become apparent.[31]

The declaration of independence at La Paz followed an earlier legal skirmish in Chuquisaca between the president of the Audiencia, who favored loyalty to the Spanish junta ruling in the name of Ferdinand, and the Audiencia judges, who believed that in the absence of a legitimate king, power reverted to the locality. This conflict among royal officials was joined by Creole students at the University of Saint Francis Xavier, who backed the judges for their own reasons. Saint Francis Xavier, the third university established by Spain in the New World, drew students from all over the southern half of South America. In 1767, when the Jesuits were ousted by the crown, Saint Francis shifted its emphasis from theology to law, and in 1776 the local audiencia created the Real Academia Carolina for postgraduate studies in law. The Academia became a center of Creole nationalism where, despite royalist proscriptions, students read Garcilaso, the *History of Ancient Mexico* by Jesuit radical Francisco Clavigero, and the writings of the French philosophes. One young student, Vicente Pazos Kanki, a descendent of native nobility, championed Thomas Paine and provided one of the first Spanish translations of *Common Sense.* To freethinkers like these, the absence of a legitimate monarch sparked demands for regional autonomy, making the students allies of the ultraconservative Audiencia judges.[32]

But the La Paz uprising revealed the undercurrents of class and ethnic tension that would frustrate and limit Creole nationalism in Upper Peru. The La Paz declaration was triggered by the visit of a student emissary from Chuquisaca, but events in La Paz quickly took a more radical turn. The official manifesto, proclaimed on 27 July 1809, granted Indians the same rights as Creoles and mestizos and said nothing about loyalty to Ferdinand. The rebellion quickly fractured along class and ethnic lines and was easily crushed by imperial forces from Lima with the support of local Creoles.

For the next several years, the fate of Upper Peruvian independence lay in the hands of foreign invaders and local guerrilla chieftains. A year after the revolt in La Paz, and after the dissolution of the Junta of Seville by Napoleon's armies, Creoles in Buenos Aires ousted the viceroy and issued an ambiguous declaration of autonomy in the name of Ferdinand. Resolved to retain control of Upper Peru and its vital mines, Buenos Aires sent an army under Jacobin general Juan José Castelli, who attempted not only to reintegrate Upper Peru into Argentina, but also to instigate social reform that would, at least theoretically, erase colonial lines of caste. Castelli insisted that at least one Indian deputy be chosen from each Upper Peruvian province, and promulgated his proclamations in Quechua as well as Spanish so as to stir the native population to revolt. Castelli's decrees triggered Creole memories of the worst days of the 1780–81 insurrection, and that along with his mass executions of royalists won him little support among the Upper Peruvian elite. Castelli's army was driven from the region in mid-1811, a year after his invasion. Two subsequent Argentine invasions drew little or no local support. The incursions from Buenos Aires only emphasized the territorial and jurisdictional conflicts that complicated matters in South America and reveal the priority most Creoles gave to maintaining social order.

Despite crown decrees that tied Upper Peru to Buenos Aires, the great rebellion of 1781 made the region's lingering cultural and historical connections to Lower Peru obvious. When the Viceroyalty of Lima took the lead in restoring order after the July 1809 uprising in La Paz, Upper Peru again found itself de facto under the jurisdiction of Lima and its powerful viceroy, José Fernando Abascal. Guerrilla actions by local caudillos kept parts of Upper Peru—the so-called *republiquetas*— outside royal control but further compounded the disintegrative, regionalist tendencies of the independence struggle.

By 1817 Ferdinand VII was again on the throne of Spain and royalists were firmly in control of Upper Peru. A fourth Argentine army had been repulsed, and only 9 of a onetime high of 106 regional rebel caudillos remained active. The final stages of Upper Peruvian independence would be determined by events in Spain and by Bolívar's armies from Colombia.

Ferdinand's inept rule after his restoration led to a liberal uprising in Cádiz in early 1820 that again fractured Spain. The royalist stronghold in Lima divided between those favoring Ferdinand and those favoring the liberal reformers in Cádiz, and the schism opened the way for Simón Bolívar's armies. Meanwhile, the ebb and flow of royalist, Argentine, and guerrilla forces in Upper Peru; the assaults each made on the treasury at Potosí; and the vacillations of policy in Spain itself left the Upper Peruvian elite exhausted and confused and served to further crystallize their desire to be left alone. These same factors also allowed a cadre of erstwhile royalists to seize the initiative when it became clear that Bolívar's armies were destined to prevail in Lower Peru. Led by men such as Casimiro Olañeta, who went from fervent support for Ferdinand to advocating independence in a matter of weeks, Creoles now shifted en masse as they became convinced that independence accompanied by autonomy from both Buenos Aires *and* Lima would best increase their influence and power within an otherwise unchanged economic and social order.[33]

On 9 February 1825 Antonio José de Sucre, the commander of the Colombian forces in Upper Peru, decreed that an assembly be held to determine the fate of the region. Bolívar was himself convinced that an autonomous Upper Peru was not viable, but despite his concerns, the assembly on 6 August 1825 declared Upper Peru independent. Appealing to the Liberator's vanity if not his better judgment, the assembly named the new nation the Republic of Bolívar, designated Bolívar as their first president, and invited him to write a constitution. Bolívar served briefly as president during his triumphant tour of the region in early 1826, then named Sucre as his successor.

The constitution the Liberator presented revealed his growing pessimism concerning the prospects of liberal republicanism in newly independent South America. It combined standard republican features like an elected representative assembly and division of powers with paternal elements designed to maintain order, preserve continuity, and provide focus. Bolívar proposed a third chamber of congress made up of "censors," men elected for life whose role was to safeguard order and serve as the republic's moral compass. He also proposed a patriarchal lifelong president who would choose his own successor and serve, in a country without a formal nobility or royalty, as "a fixed point . . . about which leaders and citizens, men and affairs, can revolve."[34] The U.S. Constitution was to provide such a fixed point, but in the Republic of Bolívar, the life-term-president provision fostered ill-disguised local resentments that made Bolívar's constitution a point of contention rather than a focal point.

In fact, as Bolívar well understood, there was little to provide focus to the new republic, its name now shortened to Bolivia. The first and second presidents were Colombians, and only the presence of Colombian troops kept the new republic from further fracturing. In the aftermath of independence, a few residents of the eastern lowlands sought to have that area annexed into monarchist Brazil rather than continue under a government in the highlands, and one of Bolivia's most able early presidents, Andrés de Santa Cruz, worked energetically to forge Bolivia and Peru into a single federation.[35]

British observers believed that Bolivia was a useful buffer between its more powerful neighbors, but Simón Bolívar himself was inclined, as was Santa Cruz, to see a natural connection between the two Perus. "We must set an example of joining Bolivia and Peru in a federation," Bolívar wrote to Sucre soon after he left Bolivia and the seductive allure of its adoring throngs. "Bolivia cannot remain as she is, because the Rio de la Plata and the Emperor of Brazil [will] eventually bring about the destruction of that Republic."[36] The Liberator was mistaken; Bolivia survived, although neither as a tightly focused entity nor as a buffer. Over the course of the next century, when neighbors coveted a chunk of Bolivia, they took it. Bolivia's survival owed less to its significance as a buffer than to the general stagnation of the area. Neither Bolivia's neighbors nor the European powers displayed much interest in the heart of South America in the years immediately following independence.

Imagined Community

As a nation, Bolivia was yet to be fully invented. Its boundaries, both real and mythical, were unclear; its sovereignty was limited; and the bonds of what Benedict Anderson calls "imagined community" were still weak.[37] Of course, the new nation continued to possess Potosí, long a chief jewel of the Spanish crown and the object of an ongoing tug-of-war between Lima and Buenos Aires. But that city was now a mere shadow of its former greatness. The population of the once largest city in the Americas had plummeted to nine thousand by 1827, and most of its mines had been abandoned during the independence struggle. The mita was also a casualty of the wars of independence, banned first in 1813 by Castelli's invading army, a decision seconded by the Spanish Cortes meeting in Cádiz at about the same time. The ban was not closely enforced, but with the arrival of Sucre's liberating army and new decrees ending the mita, the almost 250-year-old institution was moribund. Without the mita, crown assurances of secure supplies of mercury, and credits from the Royal Bank, mine owners lost the subsidies that had kept their enterprises solvent through much of the eighteenth century. By 1819, mining activity was one-tenth what it had been a decade before, and activity had decreased even more by the time Upper Peru gained its independence. At mid-century, José María Dalence recorded ten thousand abandoned mines in Bolivia. Because Bolivia's mines had become so dependent on state subsidies, observes Enrique Tandeter, "the collapse of the colonial state in Upper Peru dragged silver production down with it."[38]

Official British envoy Joseph Barclay Pentland, who visited Potosí soon after independence, ventured that Potosí would soon return to its former greatness with the help of British capital. "I do not know a country which offers to the foreign miner the same advantages as those possessed by Bolivia," he wrote in his 1827 report to the Foreign Office.[39] British speculative capital briefly flowed into Bolivia in 1824–25, but London agents were overly optimistic about the salutary impact of a little machinery and European expertise and ignorant of Bolivian conditions. Twenty-six companies were formed to exploit South American mineral resources, but only two sent men and equipment to Bolivia, and none actually went into operation. Almost as soon as it developed, the speculative bubble burst, taking the companies in Bolivia and the London stock exchange with it. Sucre's supposed comment was that "*los señores ingleses* must have been reading the history of El Dorado with a little more credulity than it deserves." By then, silver production was half what it had been in the late eighteenth century; only after the mid-nineteenth century would the mines slowly recover.[40]

Even Pentland was cautious about the prospects for foreign trade, noting that there was not one foreign commercial agent in all of Bolivia. The trails linking Bolivia's population centers to the sea were very difficult, Pentland noted, and could be traversed only by mules or llamas. Not a single carriage road or wheeled vehicle existed in the entire country.[41] Towering peaks and bleak deserts sealed the altiplano from the Pacific, and nine-tenths of Bolivia's territory drained instead to the distant Atlantic. The only navigable rivers in the country flowed eastward and northward through thousands of miles of empty and virtually unexplored frontier before reaching the ocean. Geographer J. Valerie Fifer observes that even now, "mileage alone gives little indication of the true sense of physical and mental separation which has always existed between Altiplano settlements and the sea."[42]

Bolivia was not yet technically landlocked. By the principle of *uti possidetis* (literally, "as you now possess") Bolivia comprised the territory of the colonial Audiencia of Charcas. None of the Audiencia's borders had been clearly delineated, a matter of minimal importance in the colonial era but now crucial in an age of independent and competing nation-states. Bolivia's claims to a Pacific coastline were nebulous at best, and one fact was indisputable—the most accessible colonial port of entry, Arica, had never been part of the Audiencia of Charcas and now lay in Peruvian hands. It was assumed by President Sucre and many Bolivians that Peru would cede the coast from Arica southward to Bolivia, but Bolívar himself was opposed to tampering with existing boundaries, and Lima proved unwilling to relinquish its claim despite continuous Bolivian entreaties.[43]

Instead of a natural port, then, Bolivia inherited a stretch of desolate shoreline beginning some two hundred miles south of Arica. This coastal panhandle lay distant from, and at an oblique southwesterly angle to, Bolivia's population centers. Of Bolivia's leading towns, only Potosí was closer to the Pacific via Bolivian territory than via Peruvian territory. The only existing port on the Bolivian coast in 1825 was Cobija, a town with a secure harbor but perched on a narrow ledge without an adequate water supply and backed by mountains so uniform that the tiny port was difficult to spot from the sea. The difficult journey from Cobija to Bolivia's population centers tripled the price of imported goods and kept Arica the key port of entry until after mid-century, when railroads farther north switched the bulk of Bolivia's foreign trade to the Tacna-Mollendo route—a route that also traversed Peru. With the vigorous promotion of President Santa Cruz, Cobija became the point of entry for almost one-third of Bolivia's foreign trade in the early 1830s, but twenty years later a U.S. envoy stated that nine-tenths of all Bolivian imports again came through Peru.[44]

More important than the geographical isolation that shut off Bolivia from European markets was the deterioration of local trade networks that accompanied the wars of independence. No longer did goods flow freely to and from northern Argentina or southern Peru, areas incorporated into the larger Upper Peruvian trade network throughout the colonial period. To raise revenues, the new South American republics adopted protectionist policies whose dampening effect on interregional trade was compounded by sporadic conflicts. In 1825, while at war in the Banda Oriental (later Uruguay), Buenos Aires blockaded the River Plate. Shortly afterward, when Argentina was slow to recognize Bolivian independence, Bolivia slapped a duty of 40 percent on all merchandise arriving from the south. Meanwhile, Bolivia's ongoing conflict with Peru meant that trade through Arica, when it moved at all, was subject to duties ranging from 45 to 92 percent.[45]

The costs of isolation were high. Pentland reported to the British Foreign Office that during 1825–26 Bolivia paid Peru duties amounting to $820,000 (the peso then being roughly equivalent to the dollar) on articles of foreign manufactures while another $300,000 in duties went to Buenos Aires. Since the value of Bolivian exports to Lower Peru did not exceed $150,000, Bolivia was forced to meet the balance with specie payments. Of Bolivia's total foreign exports of $3,613,750 in 1826, $3,420,000 was in silver and gold, with the balance in tin, cinchona bark to make quinine, wool, and assorted low-value products.[46]

The situation had improved little by 1856, when U.S. officials estimated that 2.9 million pesos out of a total of 4 million in total exports was in silver, gold, and silver coin. Dalence's careful statistical study shows that by 1846, production of precious metals lagged behind the value of imports by more than 14 million pesos, leading to the exhaustion of reserves of precious metals.[47] In a literal sense, Bolivia was exporting capital to meet negative balances of trade.

Despite these problems, in 1827 Pentland felt confident of Bolivia's prospects based on the facts that foreign debt was low, the reformed tax system had removed the colonial burden on the indigenous population, and the Sucre administration was honest and competent: "To General Sucre, Bolivia is mainly indebted for the commanding position which she now holds, and for the peace and tranquility which reign throughout her territory, contrasting forcibly with the anarchy and disorder that surround her."[48]

But Bolivia's isolation, the collapse of mining, and the paucity of alternative exports provided powerful pressures that pushed the new republic inward and its economy back toward subsistence. These economic trends contradicted the liberal goals of Bolívar and Sucre, both of whom were determined to destroy colonial vestiges and release the productive potential of private self-interest. During his brief sojourn in Bolivia, Bolívar attacked the property base of the colonial order by passing a series of decrees designed to stimulate production through more efficient use of land. During the interim while he was president, the Liberator published laws stipulating, among other things, the end of the mita and all caste distinctions and the division of community land among its members.[49]

When Sucre received the mandate from Bolívar in December 1825, he responded with a series of reforms that rationalized administration, reduced the power of the church, improved education, and attempted to bring financial stability to the country. His administrative reforms had limited effect. The best-trained and -educated Spanish bureaucrats deserted at independence, leaving only the negative legacies of bureaucratic centralization and a tendency—heightened when postindependence stagnation limited other opportunities for advancement—to look to the government as a primary source of jobs and social mobility. Sucre's educational reforms impressed contemporaries and modern scholars alike. William Lofstrom states that they brought "more tangible progress in four years than Spain had brought in two and one-half centuries."[50] Included in the reforms were mining schools to increase technical training and a program of free elementary education for the major cities. Ultimately these educational innovations died in their infancy, victims of economic stagnation and mounting financial problems.

Sucre's ecclesiastical reforms had a more lasting impact. The upper clergy remained royalist to the bitter end, and many fled in the aftermath of independence, weakening the institution and facilitating

Sucre's plan to subordinate church to state. He assumed direct control over the collection of tithes and ordered all monasteries with less than twelve inhabitants to close. By 1826 the number of monasteries in Bolivia had fallen from forty to twelve, the number of convents had likewise been trimmed, and the total clergy had been reduced by one-third. Sucre also completed the consolidation of church credits begun under the Consolidación de Vales Reales and disentailed church-held properties. When Sucre left Bolivia in 1828, the church was unquestionably subordinate to the republican government; much of its former power was gone, and anticlericalism would have little subsequent force in Bolivian politics.[51]

In destroying the church's economic power, however, Sucre also destroyed the institution that had, for centuries, regulated the flow of capital. The immediate returns to the state from confiscated church wealth were rapidly spent to maintain remaining church personnel, pay state debts, and carry out educational reforms. As its deficits mounted, the Sucre administration issued floating bonds, but with no established banking institutions to replace the church, the bonds quickly lost value. To preserve the value of the bonds, Sucre allowed holders of devalued paper to use it to purchase public properties and redeem *censos* (church-held mortgages), thus providing a structural incentive to land and debt speculation by a tiny well-connected elite. The distortions this policy wrought in state-citizen relations, argues Thomas Millington, linger in Bolivia to this day.[52]

Sucre probably had few alternatives. Bolivia's swollen military establishment (mostly Colombians), its conflicts with its neighbors, its lack of dependable export revenues, its mining crisis, and its paucity of financial capital or banking institutions kept the economy weak. Meanwhile, a new single direct tax of three pesos, to be paid semiannually by all Bolivian males aged eighteen to sixty, proved unenforceable, and by mid-1826 government revenues were declining rapidly. Indian tribute was reinstituted late that year, and by the end of the decade, tribute provided 60 percent of government revenues, versus only 25 percent of total royal revenues during the colonial period.[53]

Sucre's reforms directly attacked the basis of long-standing social stratification in Bolivia. His educational and social innovations were aimed at removing colonial barriers of caste. But such reforms ran counter to the conservative self-interest of Bolivian elites, who feared an upheaval from below and sought to maintain colonial order. Sucre's reforms also ran counter to the reality of Bolivia's economic stagnation and added to the fiscal problems of the new state. Increasingly opposition to Sucre's program focused on Bolivians' resentment of occupying troops and a Colombian president in office for life. In April 1828 an unsuccessful coup and assassination attempt left Sucre with the first wound he had suffered during his long and illustrious military career. When Peruvian forces joined dissident Bolivians to demand that he leave, Sucre resigned in disgust and returned to Colombia. However enlightened his project, Sucre's reforms had failed to take root. Marxist commentator Miguel Bonifaz paraphrases Mark Twain in aptly remarking that "despite the imposition of republican forms, rumors of the death of colonialism in Bolivia were highly exaggerated." [54]

After a brief chaotic interlude, the able Andrés de Santa Cruz came to power. A mestizo from La Paz, Santa Cruz had been a royalist officer until 1821, when he switched sides and joined the rebellion. From 1829 to 1839 he brought order and stability to Bolivia and revised both the civil and commercial laws in line with the Napoleonic codes. Essentially, however, the order Santa Cruz brought to Bolivia was based on recognition of colonial continuities. Santa Cruz reached a modus vivendi with the church and discontinued most of the internal reforms of his predecessor. Returning to a mercantilist position, Santa Cruz raised tariff barriers and reduced mining taxes to stimulate the internal economy. He issued debased silver coins called *pesos febles* to pay government obligations. The pesos febles also reduced some of Bolivia's balance of payments problems because they were used to pay customs requirements in Peruvian ports. Indian tribute also compensated for lost revenue and continued to provide more than one-half of Bolivia's total government receipts. The dependence on tribute meant that Sucre's efforts to incorporate natives into national life were also terminated. As had been the case during the colonial period, Indian communities as corporate identities were protected as vital sources of revenue. Bolivian historian José Fellman Velarde charges that, in this sense, Santa Cruz was "the grand architect of the semi-feudal Bolivian state."[55]

Santa Cruz was eventually ousted, but not because of domestic unhappiness with his shift away from enlightened liberal policy. His opposition instead came from outside. The president was closely linked by both his father and his early military career to Cuzco, making him as much Peruvian as Bolivian. By 1836, he felt sufficiently secure in Bolivia to embark on a more ambitious plan to unite Peru and Bolivia into a single confederation composed of Bolivia, south Peru with Cuzco as its capital, and north Peru with Lima as capital. Argentina and Chile feared the potential strength of the confederation, but Santa Cruz successfully fought off their attempts to destroy it. In January 1839, however, a second Chilean expedition, backed by disgruntled north Peruvians unhappy at Lima's loss of influence within the confederation, defeated Santa Cruz at the Battle of Yungay and the experiment was over.[56]

Two years later Peru attempted to bring large portions of Bolivia back under the Lima's control, but at the Battle of Ingavi on 18 November 1841 Bolivians dealt the Peruvians a decisive defeat. Ingavi has a paradoxical significance to Bolivians. It reconfirmed Bolivia's existence and is sometimes described as the date of Bolivia's true independence—this time not of Colombian doing. But Yungay and Ingavi also marked the end of Bolivia as an important contender for power in South America and brought to a close the period of relative political stability achieved under Sucre and Santa Cruz. The country entered nearly a half century of political chaos and continuing economic stagnation that thwarted any emerging sense of "imagined community."

Although their histories have vague parallels, the United States and Bolivia as newly independent republics continued to represent the opposing boundaries of a range of New World experiences. Their different histories created different perceptions, different cultures, and significantly different national mythologies. Bolivia and the United States were not only the most different of neighbors, they were also the most distant.[57]

2 Most Distant of Neighbors

Bolivia was the last country in South America to be visited by a diplomatic or consular agent of the United States. In his 1848 letter of instruction to the first chargé d'affaires, Secretary of State James Buchanan insisted that the delay resulted not from ill will or disinterest, but rather from the lack of ports that kept Bolivia locked in the interior of South America. Because of Bolivia's isolation and distance from the United States, trade between the two countries was "trifling." U.S. seamen visiting Cobija in the 1830s found the tiny port and the exotic land it served "as remote from the United States as Tibet."[1] Now that the United States had its own ports on the Pacific, Buchanan expected this situation to change. He instructed the new chargé, John Appleton, to seek a commercial treaty with Bolivia and, "without interfering," to encourage Peru to cede Arica to its neighbor.[2]

The need to improve commercial contacts was an important theme of Buchanan's letter, but the bulk of its content concerned America's potential importance to Bolivia as mentor and model. Attempting to assure Appleton of the larger significance of his obscure South American posting, Buchanan stressed that "the nations on this Continent are placed in a peculiar position. Their interests and independence require that they should establish and maintain an American system of policy for their protection and security entirely distinct from that which has so long prevailed in Europe."[3] Buchanan's views echoed sentiments first clearly expressed by Thomas Paine and later repeated by Thomas Jefferson in 1820 when he described the advantages to the United States if the newly independent nations of the hemisphere were to coalesce into an American system "distinct from and unconnected to Europe."[4] The idea of two distinct spheres was most vociferously championed at the time by Henry Clay, and in moderated form it became official U.S. policy in the 1823 Monroe Doctrine. Europe, according to this view, was a continent of corrupt and tyrannical monarchs locked in an uneasy and immoral balance of power. America was both greater and better than Europe, and the new republican governments of the Americas could serve as models to Europe to the degree that they remained uncorrupted by Europe.[5]

But there was also a nagging sense among the people and leaders of the United States that Latin America might not yet be ready to join them in fulfilling this republican ideal. Fredrick Pike comments that "the notion that the United States must assume the burdens of uplifting the Latin populace so that they could join in helping to fulfill the New World's unique destiny" was implicit in the two-spheres concept.[6] In the spirit of uplift, Buchanan urged Appleton to remind the Bolivians that "the enemies of free Government throughout the world point with satisfaction to the perpetual revolutions and changes in the Spanish American Republics." "Liberty," Buchanan continued, "cannot be preserved without order: and this can only spring from a sacred observance of law."

Buchanan felt secure in his American virtues. In 1848, James K. Polk was completing his term as the eleventh president of the United States. Elections were scheduled for later that year, and, despite Polk's many enemies, few doubted that they would go smoothly and according to constitutional form. Bolivia, on the other hand, was somewhere between its thirteenth and fourteenth presidents in a history scarcely a third as long as that of the United States, and none of its presidents had yet filled a constitutionally mandated term. "In your intercourse with the Bolivian authorities," Buchanan instructed Appleton, "you will omit no opportunity of . . . presenting to them the example of our own country where all controversies are decided at the ballot box."[7]

Buchanan's commission letter to Appleton was dated 1 June 1848, less than two months after the signing of the Treaty of Guadalupe Hidalgo. The regional controversies within the United States that were stirred by the war with Mexico remained muted. It would be twelve years before those controversies—exacerbated in part by Buchanan's own blunders—would become so sharp that they proved, in this case, unresolvable at the ballot box. In 1848, however, the conflicts between the expansionist interests of the commercial North and those of the agrarian slave-holding South were not yet irreconcilable; nor were the contradictions between professions of hemispheric community and the seizure of half the territory of a sister republic within that community. The year 1848 marked the crest of what historian John Higham calls an era of "boundlessness," and in "Manifest Destiny" the apparent contradictions were temporarily resolved.[8] While Polk was president, the South got new lands where slavery could spread and the North got commercial ports on the Pacific. The United States got new territories, and the inhabitants of those territories got the benefits of North American institutions and virtues. Manifest Destiny temporarily seemed to deliver it all: union through expansion and tutelage through conquest. Buchanan's letter reflects the boundlessness of the era. Appleton was to understand that the United States was interested in Bolivia not only as a potential commercial partner but also as a struggling hemispheric neighbor in need of North American guidance.

Manifest Destiny and Bolivian Defenses

If North American confidence was high in 1848, it did not remain at that level. Appleton quickly discovered the limits of his ability to influence this distant neighbor of the United States. His first problems were basic and personal. He reported back to Washington soon after arriving in Bolivia that the country had only two North American residents, no cart roads, and a climate so "unfriendly" to his health that he wished to be recalled at the earliest convenience. More crucial to his diplomatic mission, he could find no government to whom he could present his credentials.[9]

Bolivia was in the midst of the intermittent civil wars that had plagued the country since the ouster of Santa Cruz. Finally, in December 1848, Manuel Belzú, an irascible and charismatic mestizo tyrant with an outsider's hatred of the aristocracy that had dominated Bolivia since independence, emerged as de facto president. The first president since Sucre not to have begun his military career as a royalist, *tata* Belzú (the title that of an Aymara chieftain) rhetorically championed the country's submerged classes.

> Comrades, an insensitive throng of aristocrats has become arbiter of your wealth and your destiny; they exploit you ceaselessly and you do not observe it; they cheat you constantly and you don't sense it; they accumulate huge fortunes with your labor and blood and you are unaware of it. They divide the land, honors, jobs and privileges among themselves, leaving you only misery, disgrace, and work, and you keep quiet. How long will you sleep? Wake up once and for all![10]

Bolivian historians point out that Belzú provided little beyond inflammatory rhetoric to Bolivia's lower classes, but he did introduce the masses as potent political actors who could be mobilized to march the streets and strike fear in the hearts of the elite.[11] In this sense, Belzú's presidency marked an important realignment of political power in Bolivia. The new president drew crucial support from artisans and shopkeepers, and in their name he temporarily closed British-owned warehouses and proclaimed that internal trade henceforth should become the exclusive domain of Bolivians. When the British chargé d'affaires protested this and other perceived mistreatment of British subjects in 1853, Belzú issued him his passport and ordered him to leave the country. Incensed, the British Foreign Office broke off diplomatic relations, which were not officially reopened until late in the century.[12]

José María Dalence, one of Bolivia's most astute contemporary observers, supported Belzú's protectionist measures. Dalence finished the first detailed Bolivian census in 1846 and five years later published a report that linked the country's continuing economic depression to the rising tide of foreign goods that overwhelmed small Bolivian producers and drained the country of its bullion reserves. Noting that the trade of domestic textiles, particularly *tocuyo* (a coarse cotton fabric used by the lower classes), was only a fraction of what it had been at independence, Dalence argued that Bolivia must begin its development process by protecting domestic industry and placing strict controls on imports, as the British had done during their mercantilist phase, and not pursue the free trade doctrines the British now preached.[13]

Belzú initially considered the new North American mission a useful counter to the British, but he suspected the motives of the United States and feared that U.S. competition might further undercut domestic producers of tocuyo, and thus had little interest in the trade agreement Buchanan sought. Between 1848 and 1854, four different envoys passed through Bolivia, each of the first three staying less than a year. The third, Horace Miller, detested Belzú and after witnessing a popular uprising in support of the president, offered his opinion that Belzú was a military despot of the most odious sort, "an ignorant soldier wholly destitute of either talent or education and only remarkable for courage and cruelty." "The better classes are almost unanimously opposed to the existing government," Miller added.[14] Miller's predecessor, Alexander McClung, was equally outspoken on Bolivia's commercial uselessness to the United States. "Even should the government become stable," McClung argued, "there is probably no country in the world of similar extent, which in a commercial point of view is so entirely unimportant either to the United [sic] or to other nations."[15]

Where Miller and McClung saw disorder and tyranny, the fourth and most competent of the early U.S. chargés to Bolivia, John Dana, saw potential. Dana finally brought continuity to U.S.-Bolivian relations by serving as chargé for six years. Soon after arriving in 1854, Dana sent an assessment of Bolivia's importance back to Washington that differed markedly from McClung's: "I cannot too strongly impress, upon my Government, the importance of this apparently isolated point—Bolivia, in recovering our long lost political, and commercial influence in South America." Dana believed South America's true potential lay in its interior, and "of this rich interior, Bolivia is the center and holds the navigable head waters of the two great systems of rivers, which drain the whole."[16]

Dana's ideas were influenced by Matthew Fontaine Maury, a scientist, explorer, and naval officer who supervised the National (Naval) Observatory in Washington, D.C. Maury first became fascinated with the commercial potential of the Amazon and La Plata basins during an 1827 naval mission to South America. In 1850, at his urging, the U.S. Navy undertook a series of major scientific and exploratory expeditions to the heart of South America. Access to the Plata fortuitously opened in 1852 when Argentine dictator Juan Manuel de Rosas was overthrown; however, Emperor Pedro II of Brazil denied access to the Amazon. To thwart the emperor's ban, Washington authorized two U.S. naval officers, William Lewis Herndon and Lardner Gibbon, to enter the Amazon basin surreptitiously via the backdoor. Herndon, Maury's son-in-law, rafted down tributaries from Peru, and Gibbon came to Bolivia, where he visited for more than a year before floating down the Chapare, Mamoré, and Madeira Rivers to the Amazon. While the two men descended the Amazon, Maury sent a series of articles to a Washington newspaper under the pen name "Inca" that described the commercial, mineral, and agricultural potentials of the South American interior. When the explorers returned to the United States in 1853 and issued their report, Maury disseminated their findings through southern journals and lobbied in Washington for action to force open the Amazon just as Matthew Perry was, at that very time, forcing the opening of Japan.[17]

While in Bolivia, Lieutenant Gibbon explained this vision to President Belzú in a friendly meeting. Affirmations of Bolivia's potential importance struck a resonant chord with even so xenophobic a Bolivian as Belzú. The president offered Gibbon his full support and issued a decree that opened free ports and trade on the tributaries of the Amazon and La Plata to all nations.[18] But the free ports and the trade were on paper only, and rumors began to circulate that dampened Belzú's interest. One well-educated woman in La Paz challenged Lieutenant Gibbon directly, asking him to explain stories circulating in the press that the United States wished to gain control of Cuba. "What are you doing here, Señor Gibbon?" she asked. "Do you want Bolivia also?" The Brazilian minister fed the rumors, warning Belzú that North Americans had already annexed a large territory from Mexico and that Gibbon was an agent of expansionist interests.[19]

When Dana arrived in Bolivia in 1854 to take up his post as chargé, he found Belzú's mistrust of U.S. motives growing. He heard that the Bolivian foreign minister had remarked in private that "if the North Americans could gain admission to Bolivian territory through the Amazon, they would find it as desirable as Cuba, and become as restless to acquire it." Neither the foreign minister nor President Belzú would have been reassured to know that Maury and Herndon were describing the Amazon basin to southern U.S. readers as "a continuation of the Mississippi Valley" that required only slaves on southern-style estates under the industrious management of southern planters in order to prosper.[20]

As it was, when news of William Walker's adventures in Central America reached Bolivia, negotiations for a trade treaty were scuttled yet again. Just as Manifest Destiny no longer served to bind North to South, so the contradictions in U.S. concepts of imperial tutelage now made Dana's task in Bolivia impossible. As a former governor of Maine, Dana was no champion of slavery expansionists. He soon became so frustrated at his deteriorating negotiating position that he sent a lengthy letter to Secretary of State Lewis Cass suggesting that the United States issue a new hemispheric doctrine to complement the Monroe Doctrine that clearly disavowed any intention to extend U.S. territory southward.[21]

Despite more than forty subversive movements against him during his seven-year presidency, Belzú was the first Bolivian president to oversee the election of his successor. He and Dana brought more stability to U.S.-Bolivian relations than was to be the case again until late in the century, yet the factors that kept the two nations distant were readily apparent. Little bound the United States and Bolivia to each other at this juncture except grandiose visions. But the visions of the United States were rooted in a Manifest Destiny full of contradictions and in a limited understanding of Bolivia. Bolivian visions mixed opportunism with fear, and only after both Dana and Belzú were gone did the United States finally get the "Treaty of Peace, Friendship, Commerce, and Navigation" that Dana and Buchanan had so fervently sought. The Bolivian national assembly ratified the treaty in mid-1861, and although Bolivian modernizers were now in power after overthrowing Belzú's hand-picked successor, the mounting internal crisis in the United States meant that the treaty had no immediate impact.[22]

Enthusiasm Restored . . . and Dashed

Not until the Civil War ended could the United States again turn its attention southward with renewed enthusiasm. The U.S. envoy to Bolivia, Allen Hall, urged his compatriots not to ignore Bolivia as they turned their gaze outward after the war. "Unquestionably there is a time coming," Hall wrote Secretary of State William Henry Seward, "when the trade of Bolivia will become very valuable."[23] In 1865, a U.S. company opened Bolivia's first stage line and Hall reported an overwhelming enthusiasm by "the great body of intelligent men in this quarter" toward enterprising Americans. According to Hall, such Bolivians hoped that the stagecoach line would be followed by many other such Yankee enterprises "until results of unspeakable importance to the country should be achieved."[24] A reinvigorated relationship between a newly energetic and now truly *United* States and an eagerly modernizing Bolivia seemed about to begin.

Conditions in Bolivia seemed propitious. In late 1864, General Mariano Melgarejo seized power. Although Bolivian historians generally describe him as a villainous tyrant, even his critics note that his regime (1864–70) brought an economic revolution to Bolivia. Melgarejo was a general without popular or elite backing whose influence was based on military prowess alone. With an arbitrary cruelty and self-aggrandizing disdain for legality, Melgarejo granted favorable concessions to foreign investors, decreed the privatization of Indian communal lands to benefit his own coterie of supporters, and sold immense portions of Bolivian territory at give-away prices to fill state coffers and his own pockets. But even though he was most often motivated by greed and self-interest, Melgarejo did open Bolivia to trade and investment. He no longer required that mine owners sell their silver to the government-owned Banco de Rescate—an atavistic colonial institution—and by allowing them unrestricted export of silver, stimulated the slow recovery of Bolivia's silver mines.

With the war in the United States over and Melgarejo in a cooperative mood, a flurry of North American investments followed. By the early 1870s, U.S. interests included not only the stagecoach line but also a bank, a mint in Potosí, and several generous railroad concessions. Civil War veteran and Massachusetts railroad builder Colonel George Earl Church presented the most ambitious plan: a railroad around the series of falls on the Madeira-Mamoré Rivers that Lieutenant Gibbon's expedition clearly revealed would hamper Bolivia's commercial access to the Atlantic. Melgarejo granted Church exclusive rights to build the railway and to navigate Bolivia's rivers, then ceded territory the size of Guatemala to Emperor Dom Pedro as an inducement to Brazil to grant navigation rights on the lower Amazon. In 1872, bonds for Church's company went on sale in London and were snapped up within three days.[25]

The enthusiasm soon vanished, however. The British company contracted to do the survey and actual construction of the railroad found its efforts hampered by disease, lack of manpower, and bad planning. After a year it had produced only three and a half miles of badly done survey, and in 1875 two visitors stated that there was nothing to show for the project but "a slight scratch in the ground," a bit of wreckage, a heap of rusting tins, and a pile of broken glass. Two miles of permanent track, another two miles of temporary track, and a welter of suits and countersuits were the sum product of the scheme. In fact, they turned out to be the only concrete results of any of Melgarejo's generous railroad concessions.[26]

A second phase of American interest in distant Bolivia ended in the mid-1870s, victim of world recession and overblown expectations. There were still no more than fifty U.S. citizens in Bolivia, and investments again diminished. U.S. spokesmen had tempered their postwar enthusiasm. An 1872 report on commercial relations commissioned by the U.S. Congress observed that Bolivians consumed little and wanted little, their habits scarcely changed since the days of Spanish rule. Furthermore, the report noted, Bolivia had little to export except silver bullion and cinchona bark for producing quinine. As for its other attractions, a visiting British diplomat observed in 1876 that Bolivia presented so few of them that every foreigner he met "appeared anxious to leave."[27]

Adding to the growing distance in U.S.-Bolivian relations were the efforts of Hinton Rowan Helper, a southerner and the author of the anti-slavery broadside *The Impending Crisis of the South*, to close the diplomatic mission. In 1871, Helper made the first of several trips to Bolivia as the representative of a New York mapmaker owed payment for ten thousand maps by the government of Bolivia. His biographer fittingly notes that while Helper was often rash, "no one can ever accuse him of failing to be thorough nor of lacking perseverance."[28] Over the next five years, Helper browbeat Bolivian officials, made a general nuisance of himself to U.S. ministers in Bolivia, and lobbied the U.S. Congress with the zeal he had earlier directed against the southern slavocracy. In 1876 he finally convinced the Bolivians to make a first payment on the debt, yet, ironically, through his zealotry simultaneously convinced Congress to close the Bolivian legation as a cost-cutting measure. In retaliation, the government of new Bolivian president Hilarión Daza not only suspended payments on the map debt, but also withdrew support from remaining North American projects. When the U.S. legation finally reopened in 1879, the new envoy could find no remaining signs of Yankee enterprise. Even the stage line had closed. Whether the presence of North American envoys might have helped Bolivia avoid the debacle that was to follow is doubtful, but certainly with its legation closed, the United States could provide no council or cautionary advice as Daza blundered into war with Chile.[29]

The Lessons of War

It is difficult to decide which were more spectacular, Bolivia's mistakes in precipitating the War of the Pacific or the mistakes made by the United States in trying to resolve it. Certainly the long-term costs to Bolivia were much higher: it permanently lost a seacoast while the United States only temporarily lost diplomatic credibility in the region.

The most pernicious of President Melgarejo's many controversial acts was his decision to open Bolivia's coastal region to Chilean and British investors. Until the 1880s, the Atacama Desert had been negative territory separating and isolating the three countries that shared it: Bolivia, Chile, and Peru. Then, discoveries of guano and nitrates brought a flood of Chileans into Bolivian territory and called attention to the uncertain boundaries. In 1866, Melgarejo granted a ten-year concession of all mineral rights in the Bolivian Atacama to an Anglo-Chilean company fronted by two Bolivians but with four Chilean cabinet ministers among its stockholders. Melgarejo was so taken by the qualities of the Chilean official who negotiated the treaty that he offered him a job as Bolivia's finance minister. The offer was magnanimously declined, but the official wrote back to Santiago that Bolivians seemed to consider their seacoast with as much disinterest "as if it were in Russian Siberia."[30]

As Chileans rushed to take advantage of first nitrates and then copper discoveries, Melgarejo's successors belatedly understood what they were about to lose. In the mid-1870s, Bolivia signed a secret defense pact with Peru and tried, but failed, to bring Argentina into the alliance. Argentina leaked information about the pact to the Chilean government in Santiago, and officials there responded by pressing the Bolivians to sign a new agreement to protect Chilean interests in the Atacama. Among the provisions of the resulting treaty was Bolivia's promise that it would not increase taxes on Chilean persons or industries operating in Bolivian territory for a period of twenty-five years.

Meanwhile, economic conditions in Bolivia deteriorated after Daza came to power in 1876. Local famines and epidemics exacerbated a world economic crisis, and Daza raised the tax on each quintal (hundred-pound weight) of nitrates exported from Bolivian territory by ten centavos. Chile immediately protested that the action violated the treaty and charged (probably with justice) that Daza was harassing Chilean companies in order to set the stage for confiscations similar to Peru's recent seizure of British and Chilean nitrate properties. Chile suggested that the matter be submitted to arbitration, but Daza insisted that the tax be paid. When Chile refused, Daza canceled railroad concessions and ordered the public auction of Anglo-Chilean properties. Chile issued an ultimatum and, when it was ignored, seized the Bolivian port of Antofagasta in February 1879. As an ironic postscript, six months after the seizure of Antofagasta, the Chileans levied a forty-centavo tax per quintal of nitrates to help defray the costs of the conflict caused by the ten-centavo tax, but such is the logic of war.[31]

Daza, whose actions had largely provoked the war, had no apparent plan to fight it, and by the end of March, Bolivia's entire coastal province was in Chilean hands. Peru tried to mediate, but advocates of war in Chile charged the Peruvians with stalling in order to buy time to prepare their own forces. On 5 April 1879, Chile declared war on both its northern neighbors. Chile's domination of the seas proved crucial because the early phases of the war were fought on desert terrain where logistical support by sea was essential. In control of the coast, Chile won a decisive battle with Peruvian forces in November 1879 in southern Peru. Bolivian forces never arrived to aid their allies, and for this failure Daza was removed in disgrace from command of both the army and the nation. Narciso Campero now held both positions, but his forces were decimated by the Chileans near Tacna on 26 May 1880. Five thousand Bolivians died at Tacna, and Campero was forced to retreat to the highlands. He survived that debacle and insisted on continuing the war, but never again brought Bolivian troops into active engagement with the Chileans. For all practical purposes, Bolivia became a nonfactor in the war and the subsequent peace negotiations.

Diplomats were as active as the armies through the first year of the war. After seizing the Bolivian coastal province in early 1879, Chile pursued a policy designed to entice Bolivia from its alliance with Peru by promising to help it replace its lost coastal territories with the Peruvian provinces Chile had already seized, Tacna and Arica. Not only would such an outcome guarantee Chile the mineral-rich former Bolivian province, but it would also place a Bolivian buffer between Chile and a vengeful Peru. Several approaches were made to President Daza along these lines in mid-1879, including one feeler sent through Bolivian writer, historian, and diplomat Gabriel René Moreno, who lived in

Chile. Daza supposedly responded to the proposals in a series of letters written under the pseudonym Eustaquio Sierra, offering to comply in return for a payment of one-half million pesos, but the existence of the correspondence has never been proven. In any case, when the affair became public knowledge, Daza was condemned and a Bolivian newspaper vilified Moreno with a string of invective that began with "Machiavellian" and went on to "despicable, base, and abject." Moreno, the paper concluded, was "an undignified reptile, a vile mercenary, and a bastardized Chilean."[32]

As news from the front grew increasingly hopeless, there was little Bolivians could do but inveigh against suspected acts of treason. When Tacna and Arica fell to Chile, Peru proposed a Peruvian-Bolivian federation in order to forestall pragmatic considerations of Chile's "Bolivia policy." A preliminary protocol was signed between the two countries, but the proposal never advanced beyond that stage. The two allies increasingly depended on outside intervention as their last hope, and this is where the United States entered the picture. In line with the "two-spheres" concept, U.S. diplomats were worried that European powers might be tempted to intervene in the Pacific. In mid-1880, with Chilean forces threatening Lima itself, Secretary of State William Maxwell Evarts instructed the U.S. envoys in the three belligerent states to extend their good offices. Bolivia, Peru, and Chile thus sent representatives in October 1880 to meet with the U.S. ministers on board the USS *Lackawanna* in the Bay of Arica.[33]

At the time, the British minister to Peru presciently ventured to the Foreign Office that "the interference of the United States will retard, rather than advance the negotiations for peace."[34] With its army sitting at the outskirts of Lima, Chile was in no mood to make concessions, and on board the *Lackawanna* the Chilean minister demanded direct control or joint occupation of virtually all the territories his country had already seized, plus an indemnity of twenty million pesos from Peru and Bolivia for the trouble it had been put through to seize them. The allies, for their part, insisted that Chile evacuate all occupied territory, although they hinted that they might agree to an indemnity payment.[35]

The U.S. ministers did little to advance discussions or help the belligerents find common ground. Thomas Osborne, the U.S. representative to Chile, sympathized completely with that progressive country and quickly informed the dignitaries aboard the *Lackawanna* that the role of the United States was to facilitate discussion and no more. Isaac P. Christiancy, the minister to Peru, did not even pretend to objectivity. Earlier, when the Peruvian president approached Christiancy about the possibility of U.S. mediation, the minister wrote Washington that Peru should be annexed for a period of ten years during which its people could be educated so as to become "wholly North American" in their ideas. If things went well, Christiancy added, Peru could then be admitted to the Union to provide the United States with access to the rich markets of South America.[36] The Peruvians later blamed their intransigence on Christiancy, claiming that he led them to believe that the United States would not allow the territorial integrity of Peru to be altered.

Charles Adams, the recently arrived envoy to Bolivia, also contributed to the impasse on the *Lackawanna* by intimating to the Bolivian negotiators that if talks failed, the United States would insist on arbitration.[37] Bolivia's foreign minister, who lost his job over the *Lackawanna* fiasco, complained bitterly that the United States had done nothing except issue "a polite invitation to meet and preside over our discussions without giving their presence any other character than that of the most simple and initiatory good offices."[38]

But if Bolivians complained of North American inaction, their own armies did equally little as Lima fell to Chile in early 1881. Instead, the Campero government made a desperate attempt to draw the United States into playing a more active role. The Bolivian minister to the United States, Ladislao Cabrera, presented Secretary Evarts a proposal to turn over all guano and nitrate concessions in the territories seized by Chile to a North American company. The United States would occupy the disputed zone to guarantee peace while the company provided tax revenues to the Bolivian and Peruvian governments so as to pay war indemnities to Chile.[39] Evarts apparently expressed interest in the plan but told Cabrera that he could not pursue it because of the imminent change of administrations in the United States. Soon after the inauguration of James Garfield, Cabrera met with the new secretary of state, James G. Blaine, and argued that if the United States did not intervene more actively, European nations would be tempted to do so. Only the United States, Cabrera said, had the energy, the proximity, and the similarity of institutions to make such a scheme work.[40]

Blaine was a proponent of an assertive role for the United States in the Western Hemisphere, and Cabrera's arguments meshed neatly with his views. However, there is no evidence that the secretary of state seriously entertained the Bolivian offer, and Blaine's answer to Cabrera was polite but noncommittal. The secretary clearly recognized that the Bolivians had nothing to offer and that Bolivia figured only peripherally in his diplomatic calculations—calculations that, in the end, were no more successful than those of his predecessor.

By now Peru was in near-total shambles, although many there continued to hope that the United States would somehow manage to ride to their rescue, if only to defend their territorial integrity. Attempting to salvage a deteriorating situation, Blaine sent William H. Trescott to South America as head of a special peace mission. Trescott, generally considered one of the Department of State's most able troubleshooters, was instructed to encourage peace on the basis of a paid indemnity rather than territorial cession, and to invite all belligerents to a hemispheric conference set for November 1882. Blaine hoped the conference would establish a new role for the United States as overseer of a system in which problems would be resolved through arbitration, and acts of war would not justify territorial seizures. Instead, the diplomatic efforts of the United States fell into even greater disarray.

President Garfield was shot in July 1881 and died two months later. His successor, Chester Arthur, replaced Blaine with Frederick Freylinghuysen while Trescott was en route to Chile. Freylinghuysen believed that the United States was in no position to back Blaine's policy and countermanded the former secretary's instructions to Trescott. Instead Freylinghuysen ordered Trescott to take no direct stand on boundaries or indemnity and to withdraw the invitation to a regional conference. His new orders went out by steamer to Trescott on 9 January 1882. Partisan bickering among Republicans further complicated matters. Republican "Stalwarts" launched an inquiry into the Peruvian financial interests of Blaine, the leader of the "Half-Breed" faction of the party. While Trescott's new instructions were en route to Santiago, the Senate investigating committee issued a copy of the instructions to the Washington press. The Chilean minister in Washington then telegraphed a summary to Santiago, where the Chilean foreign minister informed Trescott that his orders had changed. Thrown off balance, his mission and his diplomatic credibility undermined, Trescott accepted and signed a Chilean protocol stating that peace would require territorial transfer on 11 February, only to have Washington again change course and repudiate the protocol a few days later.[41]

All through the embarrassment of the Trescott mission, Bolivia was largely lost in the shuffle. Word of the Chilean protocol with Trescott's signature destroyed any remaining hopes of U.S. intervention. In a circular to Bolivia's diplomatic agents abroad, the foreign minister charged that while the United States had presented itself as a "missionary of peace and continental harmony," it had failed utterly to protect Bolivia from a predatory neighbor. Of Trescott's mission the minister's verdict was scathing. Instead of facilitating a satisfactory peace, it had worsened the position of the defeated, added to Chile's arrogance the pride of having diplomatically outmaneuvered the United States, and driven off other nations that might have worked more effectively than the United States to facilitate a just peace. Minister Adams wrote to his superiors in Washington that he had done his best to allay public fury and avoid possible bloodshed after news of the protocol was made public, but now found his position untenable and wished to be recalled at the earliest convenience. It was time for the United States to cut its losses, Adams wrote: "Better, much better that Chili [sic] make conquest of these Republics and reduce them herself entirely to dependencies, than that the United States should by word and deed, help to bring this about."[42]

As for the Bolivians, a newspaper phrased the sense of disillusionment succinctly: "What can we hope for or expect from the United States? Nothing, absolutely nothing."[43] British diplomats had predicted at the outset that the war would not end until Peru arrived at this same conclusion. Finally, in mid-1883, Peru too was convinced of the hopelessness of its cause and the futility of relying on the United States. After direct negotiations that involved neither the United States nor Bolivia, Peru and Chile signed the Treaty of Ancón in October—a treaty that by implication established permanent Chilean control of Bolivia's former maritime province because it lay south of territories Peru ceded to Chile in the treaty.

The first major involvement of the United States in South American affairs had been, to put it mildly, a learning experience. Washington had interjected itself into the middle of the controversy without developing a realistic position: the moralizing of the United States had an air of hypocrisy in light of its own history, and veiled threats carried no weight. Certainly Chileans saw the close parallels between their war and the one the United States fought with Mexico some forty-five years earlier: an expansive and assertive nation had been tempted by nearby empty and underutilized lands possessed by weaker neighbors, had found reason to take those lands, and took them. Freylinghuysen was right that the United States had no credible commitment to back the policies Blaine had chosen, but his own blunders added to the embarrassment.[44] Meanwhile, U.S. efforts prolonged rather than shortened the war and accomplished little beyond creating ill will all around. In the War of the Pacific, American pretensions outran the actual interests of the United States and the result was a diplomatic fiasco. For Bolivia, the consequences were more serious and permanent, although not, it turned out, entirely negative.

Years of Transition

The War of the Pacific made Bolivia all the more peripheral to the United States, and both diplomatic and commercial contacts between the two nations decreased during the decade that followed. Nonetheless, this was a significant decade of internal political and economic change in Bolivia, and it owed little or nothing to North American initiative and guidance. Helped in part by Melgarejo, Bolivia's moribund mining sector began to stir after mid-century. A small core of Bolivian entrepreneurs, financed by Chilean merchant houses, began to refurbish the nation's silver mines, and the war sparked a vigorous political debate on proper relations with Chile that stimulated the development of the first true political parties in Bolivia.[45]

The parties took labels then common in other Latin American nations—"Conservative" and "Liberal"—although in Bolivia, the content of both parties' programs was unique. Both were actually "liberal" in the late nineteenth-century, social Darwinist, entrepreneurial, modernizationist sense of that word. Both parties sought order and progress through free trade and trickle-down development. Neither was strongly pro- or anticlerical, because the Bolivian church was already weak; the initial distinction between the two parties had to do with the war itself. Conservatives favored a quick settlement with Chile that would include an indemnity for lost territories that could be applied to railroad investments. Liberals favored strengthening ties with the United States and waiting for the North Americans to help them recoup losses to Chile.[46] When disillusionment with the United States was finally complete, the Conservatives restored peace with Chile.

Ironically, just as Bolivia gave up its coast, new railroad lines significantly reduced the country's isolation and altered its relationship with the outside world. The highlands had been indirectly connected by rail to the Peruvian port of Mollendo since the mid-1870s, but all goods had to be transferred from railroad car to steamer to cross Lake Titicaca, and then to mules for the final passage to La Paz. During the presidencies of Conservative silver baron Gregorio Pacheco Leyes and his successor, Bolivian mining entrepreneur Aniceto Arce Ruíz, British capitalists built a direct rail line to the now Chilean port of Antofagasta. The Huanchaca Mining Company, which Arce administered, leased and operated the new British-built line, and the government, over which Arce presided, paid much of the rent. The new rail line reduced freight costs to less than one-half of what they had been when everything came to Bolivia by mule, and a trip that once had taken weeks now took two days.[47]

Bolivia was beginning to change in ways the silver oligarchs could not completely control. Railroads altered economic networks, increasing the influence of new rail centers like Oruro and La Paz while isolating old commercial centers like Cochabamba, Sucre, and Santa Cruz. Railroads brought a flood of new goods—Chilean wheat, Brazilian and Peruvian sugar, U.S. lumber and textiles—that destroyed the local producers of those goods as well as the Indian entrepreneurs who had carried almost everything by mule and llama. Land policies, designed to privatize and liberalize land tenure, increased the size of land holdings and antagonized not only the Indian communities but also a swelling population of mestizo squatters. Furthermore, "silver constitutionalism" rested on an insecure economic as well as social base. Major silver strikes in the western United States sent silver prices into steady decline after the War of the Pacific, a decline that turned precipitous in the 1890s when virtually every nation in the world switched to the gold standard. At the end of the century, a series of coinciding tensions spilled into open civil war.[48]

In 1898, political "outs," headed by the still frustrated Liberals, forged a diverse and ephemeral alliance of dissatisfied regional elites and mestizo and Indian peasants to oust the silver oligarchs. Once safely ensconced in power, however, the newly triumphant Liberals discarded their banner of federalism and resolved class tensions in their alliance through bloody reprisals against the peasants. They then reaffirmed the essence of the silver oligarchs' program with three fundamental changes: political "outs" became "ins," La Paz replaced Sucre as Bolivia's de facto capital, and tin replaced silver as the economic base of the new Liberal order.[49]

During the 1890s a transition was under way in the United States as well. With its frontier officially declared closed by the 1890 census and with the panic of 1893 apparently illustrating the saturation of the North American market, U.S. economic and cultural insecurities turned North American eyes inevitably southward. As Fredrick Pike puts it, ever-expanding America went forth, not in quest of God, glory, and gold, but rather for conversion, competition, and commerce.[50] In 1895, Richard Olney made his famous assertion of U.S. hegemony in the Venezuelan border affair: "Today the United States is practically sovereign on this continent [hemisphere] and its fiat is law upon the subjects to which it confines its interposition." Both the success of the United States and its proximity to Latin America made it so.[51] In the years that followed Olney's declaration, the United States intervened in Cuba, took a colony in Puerto Rico, fomented a revolution in Panama, began work on an isthmian canal, and unilaterally declared its right to intervene in the affairs of its neighbors for their own good. A new chapter in U.S. relations with Latin America began, and the interests of the United States as an emerging world power and the continuing claims of America to be model and mentor to the hemisphere created no great dissonance in the minds of most North Americans.

North America's new attention to its southern neighbors was directed, at least peripherally, even to those as distant as Bolivia. The 1889 Inter-American Conference in Washington proposed an intercontinental railroad that again roused American dreamers to suppose that Bolivia was the geopolitical key to the untapped commercial potential of South America's interior. The idea of an intercontinental railroad network was the brainchild of none other than Hinton Helper, Bolivia's old nemesis. Helper's travels in South America as an advocate for the New York–based mapmaker opened his eyes to the need for a railroad connection to the United States that would expand a natural and mutually beneficial trade network. From 1878 on, Helper devoted a good portion of his remaining years to promoting what he called the Three Americas Railway.[52]

Helper's goal was more than just commercial success. A railroad would open the way not only to American goods, but also to American values and to Americans themselves: an influx of upright, North American white men into Latin America would "supplant entirely the cumbersome and worthlessly base . . . black and brown elements," he wrote. With an alliterative flourish, Helper claimed that both Americas would be "rendered richer," Latin America in "mind and morals," the United States in "money and manners."[53] The intense Helper pushed his vision passionately and tirelessly, through literary contests and lobbying, and convinced James Blaine, who was again secretary of state from 1889 to 1893, to support his general idea, if not all his wild flights of fancy.

In 1895 Helper sent a lengthy epistle to Thomas Moonlight, minister to Bolivia, with a copy to be sent to Bolivia's president. The gist of Helper's argument was that the railroad could be Bolivia's salvation. "There is now in Bolivia," he wrote, "too much sameness and tameness and supineness; too much apathy and languor and inertia; too much aimless repose and contentment with inauspicious and unwholesome stations." In all of South America, Bolivia was precisely the country that would be most invigorated by a railroad that would end the isolation of South America's interior and reduce "the concentration of its baser ingredients." Helper was willing to advise Bolivia on how best to take advantage of the opportunities the Three Americas Railway would provide; all he asked for tendering his services was that Bolivia finally pay its map debt in full.[54]

There was a certain monomaniacal quality to Helper's entreaty, and as his biographer notes: "One should never forget that, to Helper, [the railway] was the means to an end—the one way to destroy the inferior, non-Caucasian, Catholic civilization of Latin America." The *New York Times* wondered if "the half-breeds of the Aleutian Islands and the nomads of Patagonia" would be thrilled at the news that Helper's railway brought "the blessings of a civilization which has produced the genius of a Mr. Helper."[55] But other voices, more sober than Helper's, confirmed the essence of his vision. An 1895 commercial report commissioned by the U.S. House of Representatives described how current railroad-building plans could make Bolivia a major thoroughfare for trade to and from the Atlantic and Pacific as well as from the Amazon to the prosperous southern cone. A slick promotional pamphlet published in 1919 called Bolivia pivotal in that "much of the traffic developing in contiguous territories seems destined to pass outward over Bolivian railroads and rivers." The pamphlet, quoting British statesman Viscount Bryce, added that the Bolivian railway crossroads at Viacha "may someday be an important railroad center, like Crewe, Chicago, or Cologne."[56]

In the 1890s, a rubber boom made the talk of potential riches in the interior of South America more than mere fantasy. Since the discovery of the vulcanization process by Charles Goodyear in 1839, both the price and the demand for rubber had risen steadily. In 1839 the Amazon basin exported 388 tons of natural rubber at fifteen cents a pound, but by the end of the first decade of the twentieth century, rubber exports had risen to 42,000 tons at a price pushing two dollars a pound.[57] Bolivia's northern province of Acre, with a climate less humid and hot than most of the Amazonian basin, was particularly rich in rubber. But Acre lay some six hundred miles from the nearest telegraph station in Bolivia and was defended by a force of only 350 men, months distant from re-inforcements in the highlands. Drought and famine in northeast Brazil in the 1880s sent thousands of Brazilian squatters streaming into Acre, where they set up rubber collection routes in the unclaimed wilderness. A Bolivian military officer named José Manuel Pando led a military and scientific expedition into the area in the early 1890s in order to establish a Bolivian presence, but by the end of the decade it was becoming ap-parent that the seacoast saga was about to repeat itself.[58]

In 1899, Pando, now president, built a customs station on the Acre River at the Brazilian border and placed a 30 percent export duty on all rubber transported downstream. The tax was designed to assert Boli-vian control over Acre and stanch the hemorrhaging of its natural wealth, but it satisfied neither the largely Brazilian population of Acre nor the Brazilian territorial government in Manaus, which had been charging duties on Bolivian rubber in transit as if it were Brazilian. Spurred by the discontent, Spanish adventurer Luis Gálvez Rodríguez led an uprising against Bolivian authorities in July 1899 and declared Acre independent. Pando sent a military expedition to defeat Gálvez, a move that Brazil formally recognized although it refused to allow a Bo-livian relief expedition to use Brazilian rivers in the operation.[59]

In the aftermath of Gálvez's failed attempt, Bolivia made a desperate bid, similar to the one made earlier during the War of the Pacific, to re-tain control of the endangered territory and its wealth: it offered North American and British investors exclusive rights to Acre rubber. In 1901 an Anglo-American company called the Bolivian Syndicate registered in New York; its shareholders included J. Pierpont Morgan, the Vander-bilt family, and a cousin of President Theodore Roosevelt. The Bolivian government granted the Bolivian Syndicate rights to all mineral and rubber in Acre, a navigation monopoly on Bolivia's rivers, tax-free status for sixty years, and full powers as fiscal trustee in the region with the right to retain up to 40 percent of all tax revenues it collected for its services. Finally, the company was given full policing powers within the jurisdiction of its concession as well as an option, for five years, to purchase any unclaimed land in the district at ten centavos a hectare.[60]

The Bolivian Syndicate concession drew immediate and fervent protests from Brazil. Charging that Bolivia had effectively delivered disputed territory in the heart of South America to imperial powers, Brazil rallied support from other South American states and took steps to display its unhappiness. In mid-1902, Brazil closed the upper Amazon to Bolivian commerce, a pointed reminder to Syndicate investors that profits from the Bolivian concession depended on transit through Brazil. Brazil also gave indirect assistance to a second secessionist movement in Acre that broke out soon after the river was closed. Bolivia protested vehemently and called for support from the United States and England. In response, the U.S. consul general in Brazil issued a strongly worded message to the Brazilian foreign minister informing him that the United States had interests in the upper Amazon and considered navigation of that river through Brazil a right of all nations. If Brazil did not end its obstruction of Bolivia's outlet to the Amazon, the consul general wrote, it "would be a death blow to our vast interests in eastern Bolivia." But the United States was unwilling to go beyond mere protests, even when Brazil refused to allow a visiting team from the Syndicate to travel upriver from Manaus to visit its concession.[61]

In January 1903 Bolivia put together a military expedition to put down the second secessionist movement. Brazil tried to convince the Pando government that Acre was already lost and that armed confrontation would be fruitless, and hinted instead at territorial exchange and other concessions. The military expedition left Cochabamba and arrived in Acre two months later too depleted to engage Brazilian troops. Bolivian diplomats and Syndicate officials by then recognized the fait accompli. The Syndicate threatened suit but settled quietly when Brazil offered a cash indemnity of £110,000 sterling. Late in 1903 Brazil and Bolivia reached agreement in the Treaty of Petropolis. Brazil received Acre from Bolivia in exchange for a small piece of Brazilian territory on the Paraguay River, promises to build a railroad around the Madeira-Mamoré rapids, pledges of free transit on Brazilian rivers, and a two million pound indemnity.[62]

Bolivia lost not only any benefits it might have received from its contract with the Bolivian Syndicate, but Acre itself. Once again, turning to the United States for protection had proved fruitless. U.S. interests were too small, Bolivia's own influence over Acre too tenuous, and the parallels between the Acre story and the Texas story too close for the United States to take a strong moral stand. As for Brazil, Barbara Weinstein notes that "once it became apparent that the Bolivian government intended to turn most of the territory into a Yankee colony, Brazil had the moral and political grounds it needed to annex a region that indisputably belonged to Bolivia."[63]

The loss of the valuable Acre province was a bitter pill for Bolivians to swallow, but one to which they now were becoming accustomed. In 1895, the resurgence of perennial conflicts between Chile and Argentina had led the former to seek ways to improve relations with its northern neighbors, and Chile suggested a final settlement in which Bolivia would officially cede its former coastline in exchange for a corridor to the Pacific. After the Liberal revolt in 1900, the new government attempted to reopen talks with Chile. Calm had again returned to the southern cone, however, and Chile no longer needed Bolivia's friendship. The Bolivians were bluntly informed by the Chilean minister to La Paz, Abraham Koenig, that the altiplano country needed no seaport. "In wartime," the minister wrote, "Chilean forces will take hold of the only Bolivian port with the same facility with which they occupied all the Bolivian seaports in 1879." Chile's rights to it, he added, were "by the same title with which the United States of North America has taken Puerto Rico. Our rights rise from victory, the supreme law of the nations." Then, with logic that reflected the social Darwinism of the age, Koenig continued: "That the Bolivian seacoast is rich and worth many millions, we have always known. We keep it because of its worth; if it had no value there would be no interest in keeping it."[64]

The tone of Koenig's letter was duly and properly protested by the Bolivians and formally disavowed by Santiago; nevertheless, the central point got through to the Liberal pragmatists who now ran Bolivia. Schooled as they were in positivism and its social Darwinist derivatives, they ceded their country's seacoast permanently to Chile in 1904 in exchange for an indemnity, Chile's pledge to build a railroad connection between Arica and the altiplano, and a promise that food could be freely imported duty-free through Arica and Antofagasta.[65] In Chile as in Acre, Bolivia had essentially traded territory it could not hold for improved access to world markets.

The pills were indeed hard to swallow—Bolivia would henceforth be landlocked, and Acre was the largest single cession of territory in Bolivia's history. But there were trade-offs, and in the early decades of the new century Bolivia was finally finding its niche in an expanding world economy. It had become a producer of tin.

Tin had been mined in Bolivia since colonial days, but had primarily been viewed as a low-value by-product of silver production. Pentland, writing just after independence, noted that in the late colonial period, as much as five hundred tons of tin was produced annually from silver mine tailings near Oruro. Some of Bolivia's tin then went to the United States, but tin production declined precipitously during and after the war of independence. As late as the 1880s, when silver entrepreneur José Avelino Aramayo sent an ore sample from one of his mines to Great Britain, he was informed that it contained mostly tin, "a mineral with little application or demand." But over the next two decades, improved tin-plate processing and new applications for tin in the food preservation, armaments, and fledgling auto industries fostered a growing industrial appetite for the metal. Because tin was a by-product of many of its existing silver mines, Bolivia moved easily into tin production. In 1895, silver exports were seventeen times greater than tin exports, but by 1908 tin produced 66 percent of Bolivia's export revenue versus only 17 percent for silver.[66]

The Liberal government of Ismael Montes began a rapid program of rail expansion in 1904. Combining moneys from the Brazilian and Chilean territorial indemnities with credits from New York banks, Bolivia in 1906 contracted with a U.S.-based company to construct a network of rail lines connecting its major cities and mining centers. Bolivia's annual

obligation on its first major foreign loan since independence was estimated at £187,000 sterling. Sixty thousand pounds was to be raised by
increasing duties on coca and alcohol, the rest was to be drawn from the
national budget or the indemnity fund.[67] The tin-mining companies, the
primary beneficiaries of the improved rail links, were asked to contrib-
ute nothing directly to the railroad-building program. A line connecting La Paz with the lake port of Guaqui, thence by steamer to Puno and
by train to Mollendo, was completed in 1908, and the line from Arica
was finished five years later. By World War I, Bolivia had three direct
rail routes to the Pacific.

This bonanza of railroad construction had decidedly mixed results.
Only a fraction of the network of lines contracted by U.S.-owned Speyer
and Company were completed, and all suffered substantial cost over-
runs. The completed lines were then leased for ninety-nine years to the
British-owned Antofagasta and Bolivia Railway Company, thus giving
that line a monopoly on the feeder routes. The company used differen-
tial rates to channel a significant portion of mineral exports to Antofagasta even after the much shorter line to Arica was completed.[68] Meanwhile, trains, by whichever route, trundled over the Andes and down
to the coast loaded with bags of tin ore and brought back not only foreign manufactures but also Chilean and North American wheat, California timber, and Peruvian sugar, all replacing domestic suppliers.
With transport from Bolivian territory east of the Andes still by mule,
Peruvian sugar sold for less than half the price of Santa Cruz sugar, and
much the same could be said of Cochabamba wheat. Compounding this
effect was the fact that railroads subsidized inbound freight to Bolivia
so that the cars that carried out ore would not return empty.[69]

After the loss of Acre, Bolivia's lowlands again became a backwater.
As promised by Brazil, construction of the rail line around the Madeira-
Mamoré rapids began in 1908, also under contract to a North American
company. It was a mammoth operation, employing nearly five thousand men from around the world, but costs were high, casualties among
the workers were even higher, and work on the 210-mile line went
slowly. The first stretch of track was completed and dedicated in late
1910. Fifer quotes a press release describing the event: the short cere-

monial train, decorated in the colors of Brazil and Bolivia, flew the Stars and Stripes, "its silken folds fluttering proudly as though the far-away Republic was rejoicing that in the building of the Madeira-Mamoré Railway she had been given the privilege of thus helping to draw closer together her two sister Republics of the south."[70]

The story was not to end so gloriously. The year those words were written, the price of rubber stood at a record high of three dollars per pound, but by 1913, when the line was finally completed, the price stood at seventy-three cents a pound. The cause of the sudden collapse: Far Eastern plantation rubber. In 1876 Henry A. Wickham had brought seventy thousand seeds of *Hevea brasiliensis* (the Amazonian rubber tree) to England, and successfully germinated three thousand. Wickham did not technically "snatch" the seeds, as has often been charged, since Brazil had no law against exporting the plant, but his little project had a disastrous impact on rubber producers in the Amazon basin. By the late 1890s, plantations in Asia had begun to produce rubber for export. Total exports in 1899 were only 4 tons, but by 1900 exports had grown to 50 tons; in 1914 Asian production matched that of the Amazon for the first time. By 1930 the Far East produced 800,000 tons of rubber versus only 14,000 for the Amazon.[71] The Madeira-Mamoré Railroad was completed just as the rubber boom ended. A visitor in 1936 commented that "only one train every two weeks runs over those rails figuratively laid on human bones."[72]

Illusions of Proximity

By World War I, much of Buchanan's 1848 vision remained unfulfilled. Not only had Bolivia failed to obtain Arica, it had lost its entire coastline; its interior still lay largely untapped by either Bolivians or North Americans; and several large pieces of valuable territory were lost to Brazil. But if the United States and Bolivia remained distant neighbors, there appeared to be an increasing proximity in their views about development. Between 1898 and 1906, Bolivia's export earnings doubled, with tin exports alone rising from 9,739 tons in 1900 to more

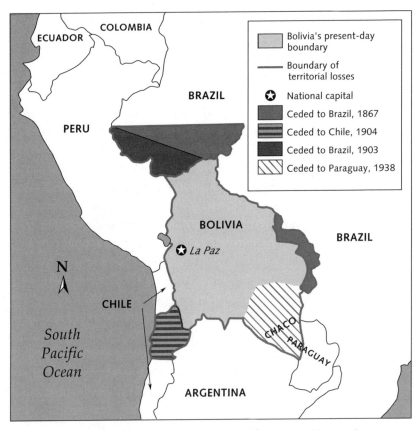

Original Claims and Major Bolivian Territorial Losses, 1867–1938
Based on a map from *Bolivia: A Country Study,* ed. Rex A. Hudson and Dennis M. Hanratty
(Washington, D.C.: 1991), 24.

than 20,000 tons by 1909. Taxes were low—as little as 4 percent on exported tin—yet government revenues also rose due to the overall expansion of the export economy. Adding to these signs of growth was the first significant influx of U.S. investments in railroads and mining.[73]

But perhaps it was at less easily quantifiable levels that contemporary observers believed they saw progress and a growing affinity between the United States and distant Bolivia. If all political disputes there were not yet settled at the ballot box, as Buchanan had hoped, at least there was satisfying political peace. From 1900 to 1920 Liberals ruled without a single serious extraconstitutional threat from their opponents. Elections were still marked by fraud, and politics remained the province of a tiny minority, but this did not overly concern U.S. observers, who were themselves generally members of an elite that distrusted the lower classes, the source of disorderly pressures that had clouded the political scene in their own country during the 1890s. In any case, movement in Bolivia seemed in the right direction.

Psychologically and philosophically, the Bolivian elite also seemed to be evolving toward a wholesome pragmatism and faith in progress that reminded North American observers of themselves. North American and Latin American elites shared a new consensus on the notion of orderly progress. In the social Darwinist concepts of the day, Bolivia was usually seen as being on the same evolutionary continuum as the United States, but behind it. Americans saw Bolivia as a promising place for tutors and profit takers, and those roles were seldom viewed as contradictory.[74]

But beneath the appearance of evolving similarities were great differences that separated early twentieth-century liberalism in the United States from its Bolivian variant. Despite continuing and even growing inequities in the North American system during the Gilded Age, the Progressive movement of the first decades of the twentieth century marginally improved access to expanding wealth in postfrontier America. Progressivism was a course correction carried through by a coalition of politically potent groups who wished to save American capitalism by reforming it and more broadly distributing its benefits. Progressivism balanced what Fredrick Pike calls the "unsublimated search for mammon" that characterized the Gilded Age and was an aspect of the North American system that Bolivian elites did not particularly feel the need to emulate. Bolivia's tiny middle class was in no position to demand or direct such a course correction, and the popular masses were still too divided and powerless to suggest an alternative to trickle-down capitalist development. Bolivia instead evolved toward an increasingly dualistic society with enclaves of modernity in a few key cities and mining centers, separated by a stagnating countryside that continued to lay outside the modernizing influence of railroads and tin, and conveniently provided a pool of cheap labor to mine owners and landlords.

Adding to the dualistic features of laissez-faire development in Bolivia were the mutually reinforcing cleavages of race and ethnicity. In 1909 Alcides Arguedas argued in *Pueblo Enfermo* that Bolivia's progress was stymied by those cleavages. Next to Bolivia's isolation, he wrote, the predominance of the Indian had most hampered the country's development. More a social Darwinist than a blatant racist, Arguedas directed much of his fire at a social environment that, he believed, reinforced the worst traits in the Indian character. Nevertheless, his aristocratic views and pathological analysis led Arguedas to misdiagnose the disease and in the process to lay much of the blame for Bolivia's malaise on those most victimized by it.[75]

At the time, many in the United States shared Arguedas's views of Bolivia's "Indian problem." Bolivia's "Indianness" had negatively impressed North Americans from the outset. Accustomed to the way their own nation had handled its "Indian problem," they saw Bolivia as an untamed land where only a thin veneer of civilization kept savagery in check. In his initial letter of instructions to John Appleton in 1848, Secretary of State James Buchanan observed that Bolivians had an "enemy within their own bosom . . . ever ready, when a favorable opportunity may offer, to expel or exterminate the descendants of their conquerors." The secretary went on to observe that in a country where "three fourths of the inhabitants belong to the Indian race," it was unfortunate that "the Spanish race there should be weakening themselves by warring with each other" so constantly.[76]

Now, at the close of the nineteenth century, the United States was flirting with direct imperialism and North Americans exhibited some of the ugliest aspects of their endemic racism. Pike states that "at home [in the United States] and in imperial domains, racist prejudice both demanded and justified the repression of groups allegedly refractory to civilization"; and in Bolivia that attitude included the Indian majority.[77] When Bolivia's Liberal-Conservative civil wars at the turn of the century weakened the elite and threatened to involve the native peasantry, official U.S. observers sent dispatches to Washington filled with accounts of "wild Indians" and rampaging "savages." The U.S. minister, George Bridgman described one particularly offensive case: the "murder outside of Cochabamba of inoffensive soldiers" by "savage Indians" at the instigation of "a wicked priest." Later Bridgman reported "the gratifying news" that more than three hundred of the Indians involved in the incident had been executed. It was, he said, "a most decided and encouraging symptom of liberal government."[78]

This was liberalism late nineteenth-century style: open to foreign and domestic entrepreneurs, closed to the indigenous population—in fact, still rooted in a neocolonial, parasitic exploitation of Indians and Indian communities. Meanwhile, Bolivia moved closer to the North American model in only the most superficial and unfortunate of senses. Development based on tin exports did not require the transformation of Bolivian peasants and laborers into consumers. The tin entrepreneurs had no incentive to destroy the existing aristocracy or to tamper with traditional mechanisms that maintained social peace in the countryside. The Indian uprisings in the aftermath of the Liberal revolt were further proof to Bolivia's tin-based elite of the need to maintain those mechanisms. An immense pool of impoverished workers kept wages low and profits high, and the railroads that facilitated the import of foreign goods for elite consumers only further depressed the non-tin sector. Bolivia's tin entrepreneurs, their foreign collaborators, and their political and managerial attendants were citizens of the world, not of Bolivia, and participants in a world economy, not a national one.[79]

But Bolivia lay at the periphery of the world system, whereas the United States was ready to challenge for its center. By 1910 the United States was developing an appetite for the economic fruits of world power, even if it was not yet ready for all the attendant headaches and responsibilities that accompanied that role. For the time being the United States was content to limit its hegemonic pretensions to the Western Hemisphere. For Bolivia, the results of taking its place in the world and hemispheric systems were elitist political and social structures, islands of modernity amidst great backwaters of colonialism, and growing dependency on the world's capitalist centers. At the end of the first decade of the twentieth century, the most optimistic North American observers saw Bolivia as merely behind the United States in its development. In fact, the two nations were almost as different and distant as ever.

3　Center, Periphery, and the Tin Nexus

In 1896, American businessman William Grauert wrote the U.S. minister in Bolivia:

> I have persistently worked to draw the attention of America's capitalists, enterprising men and manufacturers to the abundant riches of Bolivia, and also to the fact that it is, as yet, the only remaining country in South America not in the hands of England. . . . [I have worked] to retain the development of her immense territory and her almost boundless riches for North American enterprise, instead of delivering the last remaining spot [in South America] worth having through Chile into the hands of England.[1]

Mr. Grauert—enterprising, energetic, and more than a little unscrupulous—was a representative American of the Gilded Age, and his views were the conventional wisdom of the time. Yet his assessment had several inaccuracies. Only a year before, Secretary of State Richard Olney had declared U.S. hegemony in Venezuela, and the British backed off. In Bolivia as in several other Latin American countries, it was Germany, not Great Britain, that now provided the greatest commercial challenge to North American businessmen like Grauert. An official U.S. trade report admitted that German agents spoke Spanish and worked harder to cultivate the local market than did their U.S. counterparts.[2]

Most important, perhaps, Grauert's fervent views ignored a reality that Americans are only now, late in the twentieth century, coming to fully recognize: capitalism is an international system with a logic that often conflicts with the logic of nationalism. Soon after Grauert wrote the lines quoted above, a consortium of British and U.S. capitalists was given a generous concession to develop rubber in Bolivia's Acre district. Not long after that, Bolivians borrowed money from U.S. banks and contracted with the U.S.-owned Speyer and Company to build a railroad network that was subsequently leased to a British line. In both cases Anglo-American competition was less a concern than was profit taking by capitalists within a global system.[3]

The most significant arena of U.S.-British collaboration after the turn of the century was tin mining and exportation. A closer look at the exact nature of U.S.-British tin relations and the relative position and role of Bolivia as a major tin producer reveals dynamics more complex than Grauert understood. England had been the nineteenth-century overseer of the global economic system, and London the financial and peace-keeping epicenter. Both the United States and Great Britain were bene-ficiaries of this economic system, however adversarial their political relations in the late nineteenth century may have been. By the early twentieth century, the role of system hegemon began gradually to shift from Great Britain to the United States, but with relatively little fric-tion. For Britain, the benefits gained from an orderly world system out-weighed the blows to national pride that accompanied the surrender of preeminence; for the United States, the benefits of maintaining the system eventually outweighed the costs of being overseer and chief policeman.[4]

This is not to say that the transition was without friction. World War II, for example, was a time of close U.S-British collaboration against the Axis, but beneath the surface of their alliance, the two countries struggled for economic influence in the postwar world. The tin story both reveals that struggle and illustrates how the nationalist feuds that accompanied the passage of organizing and policing power from one nation to the other overlay the logic of collusion between U.S. and Brit-ish capitalists and opened space for a peripheral actor, Bolivia, to nego-tiate better terms for itself.

The United States largely prevailed in the struggle for economic dom-inance and became the central actor in the postwar tin market. Thus, during and after the war, tin provided a new nexus binding the United States and Bolivia more closely to each other than ever before. It was an asymmetric bond between a central power and a peripheral one, with all of the tensions inherent in such a relationship. An examination of the tin nexus from a world systems perspective illustrates those tensions.

The world systems approach also reveals why Bolivian tin capitalists took steps that made them objects of the animus of their countrymen. Systems of economic and political power overlapped and complicated relations between these historically distant nations and culturally different peoples.

The Devil's Metal

The tin drama had a number of significant actors, and providing a bit of background on each will better illustrate the dynamics of the tin market. Modern consumers in the United States, accustomed to aluminum and plastic packaging, forget tin's former importance. Despite its pejorative connotations (*tinny, tinhorn, tin ear, tinsel, tinker,* etc.) tin is the most scarce and valuable of the base metals. At the close of the nineteenth century, its qualities—malleability, easy fusion to steel, resistance to corrosion, and nontoxicity—as well as improved tin-plating technologies fostered a growing industrial appetite for the metal. By one estimate there were 1,250 different uses for tin by the 1920s, and even the Lincoln penny was 2.5 percent tin. North Americans "literally wallow[ed] in tin," according to that same account. Each year the United States alone consumed 160 billion tin cans and 75,000 tons of tin metal—approximately 45 percent of the world's annual consumption.[5]

Although the United States was the world's leading tin consumer, it was heavily dependent on foreign supplies; domestic production of tin ore averaged well below 100 tons annually. From the turn of the century until 1940, the United States spent more to import tin than to import any other nonferrous base metal, with 83 percent of its tin imports coming from smelters in Great Britain or its colonial possessions. Meanwhile, until 1940, Bolivia was the second largest tin-producer in the world and the only major producer not directly controlled by a European colonial power. Bolivia's tin industry was also the only commercially viable one in the Western Hemisphere, and tin made up 72.9 percent of its aggregate export earnings.[6]

In light of U.S. industrial capacity, its role in the hemisphere, and its voracious appetite for tin, one would logically assume that the United States would buy directly from Bolivian producers. The reasons why this did not happen illustrate both the workings of the international market and the political factors that inevitably distorted the market. Bolivian tin was the most expensive in the world to mine because the ores ran in seams deep in the earth and could be exploited only by underground shafts. Because existing tin-smelting technology required energy sources unavailable in Bolivia and was in any case difficult in the rarefied atmosphere of the altiplano, Bolivian producers exported ore and tin concentrates, not refined metal. The smelting problems were compounded by the fact that Bolivia's ores contained a mixture of metals and a relatively low tin content; they were most efficiently refined when mixed with mineral-rich ores.[7] Thus the British supplied the enormous U.S. market from its Malayan smelters while meeting its own domestic needs with metal produced from Bolivian concentrates "sweetened" by rich alluvial ores from Nigeria. The British, who had no desire to see either Bolivia or the United States develop a smelting capacity, protected this arrangement by tacking a 40 percent ad valorem tax on ores produced in British colonies that were shipped to any but commonwealth ports.[8] Thus, Bolivia's tin concentrates went to England, the United States bought tin metal from the British, and the British played a key role in ordering the volatile international tin market.[9]

Initially, international investment capital flowed into Bolivia's mining operations. In 1922 the largest Bolivian tin venture was owned jointly by Chilean and British capitalists; the Guggenheim family of New York controlled the second largest mine. But after a consolidating shakedown in the mid-1920s and another during the 1930s, virtually all production was eventually concentrated in the hands of the "Big Three"—all of whom technically were Bolivians. The Aramayo family was one of the few silver-mining families to successfully transfer its operations to tin, and by the 1930s was Bolivia's third leading producer. Mauricio Hochschild, a naturalized Bolivian born in Austria, entered the tin market late as a buyer. During the shakedown phases he took control of many of his suppliers and by the 1930s produced some 20–25 percent of Bolivia's tin. The third and most interesting of the Big Three was Simón Patiño, a mestizo of humble origins from Cochabamba, who began as an apprentice and eventually built the world's largest tin empire by dint of hard work, luck, access to local knowledge, proper attention to political connections, and ties to foreign capital. At its height, the Patiño enterprise produced almost 50 percent of Bolivia's tin concentrates and had extensive interests outside the country.[10]

The last significant players in the tin drama were the workers, many of them descendants of the colonial mitayos. To them, tin was the "devil's metal," luring them from more virtuous pursuits as tillers of the soil, tempting them to strip the mother earth—Pachamama—of her treasures in order to satisfy the greed of foreign and domestic capitalists and the demands of far-off consumers. No longer compelled against their will by colonial fiat, the tin miners were seduced by wages that were always too low and by dreams that the devil's metal would somehow help them escape their poverty. Tin miners were exploited workers in an exploited and peripheral nation; yet, as June Nash has argued, because of their continuing ethnic identity and the solidarity fostered by their isolated mining camps, they were neither alienated nor politically powerless. Because Bolivia was so dependent on tin, because the United States was so dependent on foreign tin supplies, and because the tin miners were to become so politically potent, they too were important participants in the international drama of tin.[11]

Consolidation and Crisis: Tin in the 1920s and 1930s

The first two decades of the twentieth century were a period of rapid tin expansion, rising tin prices, and relative social and political peace in Bolivia. Then World War I began to relocate the center of the global economic system and redefine relations between the United States and Bolivia. Related changes brought significant unrest to Bolivian politics. Until the 1920s, tin capitalists such as Patiño paid attention to business and cultivated important international connections but, unlike the silver oligarchs who preceded them, did not play a direct political role in their own country. They stood both above and outside the political system and worked indirectly through a circle of associates—white-collar employees, lawyers, and Liberal party politicians who were known collectively and derogatorily as the *rosca*. The term *rosca* can be translated in a variety of ways, including "screw," "small kernel," and "coterie of sycophants"; but perhaps the most descriptive translation is the one used by the U.S. State Department: "a small, tightly woven ring"—that is, a circle of professional *políticos* closely knit to the interests of the great tin barons.[12]

World War I marked the zenith of the mining capitalists' indirect political control just as it also began to alter U.S.-Bolivian relations. As the Kaiser's armies stormed Belgium and France, Patiño quickly understood both the threat and the opportunity that war in Europe presented. Severing his previous ties with the Germans, Patiño joined with the British smelting firm Williams Harvey and the North American Guggenheim interests to finance the first tin smelters in the United States. During the war a substantial portion of Bolivia's tin trade shifted from Great Britain to the United States, and the value of Bolivian exports to North America grew from $200,000 in 1913 to more than $35 million by 1918. When peace returned, the North American tin-plate industry again sought cheaper and higher-quality processed Straits tin from British Malaya, and in 1923 the U.S. smelters closed.[13]

Other wartime changes were more permanent, however. World War I weakened even the victorious European powers and made the United States a creditor nation for the first time in its history. North Americans were still wary of accepting the broader international responsibilities that came along with their new status, but generally they supported efforts to consolidate U.S. influence in the hemisphere. With the direct threat from Europe reduced, U.S. policies in the 1920s relied heavily on the nation's new economic muscle to carry out strategic goals. In Bolivia, traditional European neglect and the elite's eagerness for foreign investments facilitated U.S. economic penetration.[14] After the war, President José Gutiérrez Guerra abandoned earlier attempts to protect Bolivia's petroleum reserves and in ten days granted more than 2 million hectares in oil concessions to foreign investors. Standard Oil of New Jersey consolidated 3,708,295 hectares of the most promising concessions in 1921 and set up a Bolivian subsidiary.[15]

That same year a severe economic recession sent tin prices and government revenues plummeting, and Bolivia turned to U.S. banks for funds. In exchange for a $33 million loan, Bolivia pledged its customs receipts as security and, to guarantee payment, agreed to create a three-member Permanent Fiscal Commission (two of its members to be chosen by the U.S. banks) to collect taxes over the twenty-five-year life of the loan. The Permanent Fiscal Commission reformed the tax code to raise government revenues, but tin industry resistance, increased capital flight, and rising state expenditures led Bolivia back for more loans in 1927.

Afraid now that the heavily mortgaged Bolivian government could not meet its obligations, the banks demanded that a mixed commission of U.S. experts and Bolivian bankers be formed to reorganize the nation's finances. Princeton University economics professor Walter Kemmerer headed the commission, which recommended further tax reforms, a return to convertible paper currency backed by gold, and the creation of a central bank modeled on the U.S. Federal Reserve Bank to regulate gold-backed currency. With Bolivia duly certified by Kemmerer, the original "money doctor," more loans followed.[16]

By 1927 U.S. companies controlled Bolivia's international communications network and monopolized petroleum exploitation. U.S. investments exceeded those of any other country by some $40 or $50 million, and U.S. banks collected Bolivia's taxes, oversaw customs receipts, and played a direct role in setting government fiscal policies. North American construction companies built Bolivia's railways, sewers, and roadways with U.S.-made materials and were paid with proceeds from the Bolivian bonds. The U.S. economic advisers were, in the words of Paul Drake, "missionaries" easing Bolivia's entry "into an international system wherein the United States appeared to guarantee stability and a chance at prosperity."[17] But Margaret Marsh, who studied U.S. economic penetration in the 1920s, sensed an illusory quality to the boom. The slightest economic reversal, she warned in 1928, could send the value of Bolivian bonds tumbling like a house of cards, and then the U.S. banks would exert pressure on the State Department to intervene to help them recoup speculative loans.[18]

The reversal that Marsh feared was imminent, but the result was not the direct U.S. intervention she expected. World depression combined with changes in both Bolivian and U.S. domestic politics to reduce U.S. influence and involvement in Bolivian affairs over the next decade. The Great Depression dealt the tin industry a series of cruel blows. Prices that had exceeded forty-five cents a pound in 1927 plummeted to less than twenty cents a pound by 1932, but because tin was a minor component of finished consumer products and the depression was so profound, the drop in price did little to stimulate demand. By 1930 world tin production outstripped demand by 21,000 tons; Bolivian production fell from an all-time high of 46,000 tons in 1929 to 14,700 tons in 1932. Bolivia was particularly vulnerable to economic disaster because the depression followed a period when rising prices and declining ore quality had stimulated large investments in Bolivia's mines.[19]

But if the depression dealt a series of blows to the tin industry, it devastated the Bolivian state and exacerbated tensions between the tin barons and Bolivia's government that had been escalating through the 1920s. The Bolivian government kept taxes low on tin through World War I, but after the war, a penurious Bolivian state, saddled with debts contracted to pay for a railroad system that primarily benefited the tin mine owners, began to vie with the tin barons for control of the foreign exchange generated by the mines.[20]

New factors further complicated relations between the government and the tin barons. In 1920, two decades of political peace and Liberal rule came to an end when political "outs," employing new antiliberal and antipositivist currents of thought, galvanized groups hurt by the war and the subsequent economic readjustments into a coalition capable of seizing power—one that was less subservient to the tin barons. The new president, Bautista Saavedra, was an astute and wily politician who had become adept through his long and convoluted political career at channeling new ideologies and political sectors to his personal political benefit. His Republican party incorporated the urban middle class that emerged from the genuine if superficial modernization of the Liberal era, and Saavedra employed a new political language invoking Hispanicist and nationalist ideological attacks on the moral vacuity and materialist values accompanying the Spencerian brand of laissez-faire liberalism that had guided Bolivia's ruling elite since the War of the Pacific.[21]

When the new government turned to U.S. bankers to solve its fiscal problems in 1921, another complication arose. The North American banks demanded tax increases and collection of back taxes from the mine owners. Their unwelcome intrusions irritated mining capitalists, who fought back with such success that government tax revenues actually decreased.[22] Patiño responded to the new pressures by internationalizing his holdings; in 1924 he moved his corporate headquarters to Delaware. The move solidified a growing public perception that, however humble and authentically national his origin, Patiño was now a foreigner. Pike notes that to Bolivians, Patiño was no Horatio Alger hero. Instead he represented the "bad aristocracy"—characterized "by their individualism, their refusal to be burdened by paternalistic ties to clients, and, in consequence of all of this, by their heedless upsetting of the delicate balance in the distribution of the limited good."[23]

But there was more to the growing Bolivian resentment of Patiño than culturally based norms. In the United States, a Horatio Alger hero, no matter how international his investments, contributed to the health of the center by strengthening the overall world economy. The contradictions between the logic of international capitalism and the logic of nationalism are muted close to the center, but at the periphery the contradictions are acute. Each of the so-called tin barons was technically Bolivian: Patiño by birth, Hochschild by naturalization, and Aramayo by citizenship even though the family patriarch, Felix Avelino Aramayo, was born and lived most of his life in Paris. But each, in fact, had chosen to become a citizen—if that word is appropriate—of the larger world capitalist system. The logic of that system drove each to affiliate ever more closely to the system center and to use his international connections to advance and protect his wealth from an impoverished

Bolivian state with few weapons to fight back. Of the three, only Hochschild spent much time in Bolivia after 1920. Following Patiño's lead, Aramayo incorporated in Switzerland, and Hochschild in Chile and Argentina. Patiño, the Bolivian mestizo from humble roots, spent the rest of his life in Europe and the United States, for the most part residing in a deluxe suite at the Waldorf-Astoria in New York City. He worked closely with British and North American interests and amassed a diversified fortune that briefly made him one of the world's ten richest men. Official tax records reveal that at the height of his wealth, Patiño and his family paid only $415 dollars in taxes to the Bolivian state.[24]

The Bolivian state was much less adept than the tin barons at weathering the depression, and the limited options open to the state contributed to the last and most important source of rising national trauma—war. As the depression dragged on, government tax revenues continued to fall and by 1932 stood at 18 percent of their 1925 levels. Bolivia became the first Latin American nation to default on its international bond obligations. Under mounting pressures from layoffs, food shortages, import restrictions, strikes, and civil disorder, President Daniel Salamanca experimented desperately, first with a classic free-market approach, then by going off the gold standard to spur inflation, and then by manipulating exchange rates. Under heavy political fire, Salamanca finally turned to foreign policy, where the issues seemed clearer and his actions less inhibited, and picked a war with a neighbor that Bolivia mistakenly believed it could defeat.[25]

The frontier with Paraguay was another border left uncertain under the principle of *uti possidetis.* The earliest Bolivian claims, based on the jurisdiction of the colonial Audiencia of Charcas, reached south and east to a point south of Asunción. Paraguay's claims, on the other hand, reached almost to Santa Cruz. The area in contention, an area of scrub land the size of Wyoming, was known as the Chaco. By the principle of *uti possidetis de facto,* Paraguay had better claim to the disputed area. The few residents of the Chaco were Paraguayans who raised cattle or gathered the iron-hard, rot-resistant *quebracho* wood. In 1926, the Paraguayan government authorized nearly two thousand Canadian Men-

nonites to form a colony in the disputed territory; a few years later immigrants from Germany and the Soviet Union joined the Mennonite
colony.

Bolivia largely ignored the Chaco until the turn of the century, when
it began to fortify the north bank of the Pilcomayo River. The first serious border incident occurred in 1928 when Paraguay attacked one of
the forts, perhaps to call world attention to the disputed area. For the
next decade a great deal of world attention would be devoted to this obscure border conflict.[26]

The Chaco had by then taken on new importance to Bolivia as the
result of a series of developments. In 1928 Chile and Peru ended their
Tacna-Arica dispute, with Peru receiving Tacna and Chile, Arica. Once
again Bolivia was left out, despite a suggestion by U.S. mediators in
1926 that Bolivia be given the two territories in exchange for a cash
settlement. Peru vetoed that proposal, but in the final settlement it was
Chile that suggested a complementary protocol in which each of the sig-
natories agreed not to cede any territory in the two provinces to a third
party without the approval of the other. That agreement effectively
scuttled all hopes for a corridor to the Pacific, and Bolivia now turned
toward the Paraguay River as its most feasible outlet to the sea. The
value of such an outlet was further enhanced by the discovery of oil in
the Standard Oil concession east of the Andes.[27]

As noted above, the final factors raising the stakes in the Chaco for
Bolivia were the depression and the domestic economic and political
crisis it caused. In mid-1932 the tin market collapsed. All through July
and August Bolivian mines closed and thousands of miners were laid
off. On 18 July, President Salamanca announced that Paraguay had
seized a Bolivian fort (neglecting to add that it was one the Bolivians
had earlier taken from Paraguay), then deliberately fanned this border
spark into a conflagration that would continue to smolder at the heart
of Bolivian politics long afterward. Despite initial opposition from the
army general staff, Salamanca mobilized Bolivian forces, cracked down
on domestic dissenters, and seized three Paraguayan forts in the Chaco
as retaliation.[28]

The initial response from the depression-battered Bolivian populace was a surge of jingoistic pride. Bolivia entered the war confident in the superiority of its military forces. In 1911, the Bolivian government had engaged the services of an eighteen-man German military mission headed by Major Hans Kundt of the Berlin General Staff. Kundt not only organized and trained Bolivian soldiers, but also provided them the rudiments of literacy and began the slow process of institutionalizing a military that, to this point, had been highly personalistic and patronistic. During World War I Kundt returned to Germany, but when the war ended, he came back to Bolivia, became a naturalized citizen, and again advised the Bolivian military. As tensions in the Chaco increased in the 1920s, Bolivia used some of the funds borrowed from U.S. banks to buy modern arms and solidified its claim to being the "best high altitude army in the world." A U.S. official who heard the Bolivian foreign minister expound on Bolivia's military preparedness supposedly remarked with certain sarcasm, "I tremble for the United States."[29]

But the war in the Chaco was not fought at high altitude. Supply lines were long and tenuous, and control of the Chaco was far easier for—and more essential to—Paraguay than Bolivia. As stories of Bolivian defeats began arriving back in La Paz in late 1932, the press and public clamored to place Kundt in charge. But while the German was an excellent organizer and trainer, he knew nothing about the Chaco or about fighting under its wilderness conditions. By mid-1933 Kundt's original seventy-seven-thousand-man army was down to seven thousand effectives still in the field and Kundt was replaced. A year later, Paraguay possessed the entire Chaco and threatened Bolivia's oil fields.

Diplomats were active, attempting first to avert a war that seemed unnecessary and yet somehow inevitable, then trying to restore peace. The story of the maneuvering by the United States, Argentina, Brazil, Chile, and the League of Nations during the war and the subsequent peace conference is more convoluted than that of the military campaigns—and hardly less important in explaining the results of the war. It is a story too complicated to tell in full here except to say that the United States did not wish the League of Nations to play a major role in settling a hemispheric conflict, but locked horns with Argentina on a regional solution. Political scientist William R. Garner calls the intense and often acrimonious conflict between the United States and Argentina a contest for "prestige dominance." Economic interests competed with intangibles like prestige and pretensions of regional hegemony to help delay a final treaty until 1938—almost three years after the fighting ended.[30]

Bolivia meanwhile improved its negotiating position by fighting more effectively when its armies were backed against the Andes, and in July 1935 the two sides agreed to a truce. The subsequent peace settlement gave Paraguay nine-tenths of the disputed land and kept Bolivia blocked from access to the Paraguay River except for several small and relatively useless windows along the Brazilian border.[31] But the treaty also provided a substantial buffer around Bolivia's oil lands. By the time the fighting ended, the Chaco War had become the most deadly armed struggle in the hemisphere since the U.S. Civil War: 100,000 died on both sides, and 21,000 Bolivians were taken prisoner. The war cost Bolivia more than $200 million, and President Salamanca was a political casualty of it. As losses mounted, the president and his military command feuded, their struggle culminating in Salamanca's forced resignation on 27 November 1934. Although not a reputed wit, Salamanca supposedly remarked of the generals who forced him to resign, "This is the only maneuver in which they have been successful."[32]

The army did, in fact, fare better in politics than on the battlefield, and after a brief interlude under Salamanca's vice president, nearly half a century of civilian rule ended. Seizing direct control of the government in 1936, the army provided an antiliberal and corporatist solution—influenced by Italian fascism—to the political and social chaos its military blunders had helped to create. David Toro, a man responsible for his share of the Chaco disaster, and then Germán Busch, one of the few military officers to distinguish themselves in the war, instituted state-sponsored reform from above. Busch brought military reform to its zenith with a constitution modeled on the 1917 Mexican charter, the nation's first labor code, and decrees requiring the mining industry to surrender all foreign exchange earnings to the Central Bank.[33] But if Busch's reforms were the most far-reaching and significant, a specific act by his predecessor, Colonel Toro, best epitomized "military socialism" in the popular imagination. On 13 March 1937 Toro confiscated

Standard Oil properties in Bolivia, the audacious move anticipating the more famous Mexican action by more than a year and taking both Standard and the U.S. State Department by surprise.[34]

Toro's action likely resulted from a series of coinciding calculations. It was a political move designed to win public acclaim, display military decisiveness, and undercut opponents to military rule. It was also an economic move by a penurious state seeking revenues for social and economic development under state control and afraid to tackle the tin barons directly. Finally, it was a nationalist move resulting, as Bolivia's foreign minister, Enrique Finot, told the North American ambassador, from the "natural aspiration of a country to control its petroleum resources." Finot later added that the nationalization had been designed "to dispel the impression current throughout the world that weak and impoverished Bolivia had been merely an instrument of the all-powerful, imperialistic world monster, the Standard Oil Company, [and] that the Chaco war had been fought merely to protect the Standard Oil properties."[35]

The seizure of Standard properties drew broad popular support in Bolivia because it demonstrated strength from a nation whose weakness had just been reconfirmed in the Chaco. But it was also popular because it was aimed at the United States, a nation increasingly linked in the public mind to exorbitant loans, unwelcome meddling, and new threats to national sovereignty; and at Standard Oil, a company believed to share responsibility for the Chaco debacle. Many Bolivians continue to believe that Standard Oil not only provoked the war but— in something of a contradiction—then obstructed the war effort by refusing requested loans, declining to refine aviation fuel for Bolivia's air force, and transferring petroleum illegally to its Argentine holdings for transshipment to Paraguay. Many Bolivians also continue to believe that the United States served as mere agent for Standard Oil interests at the Chaco peace conference. Toro's move against the company thus met near-unanimous and enthusiastic public approval from Bolivians and demonstrated the degree to which North American influence and popularity had declined since 1929.[36]

Toro's moves against a nation as powerful as the United States and a company as well connected as Standard Oil also indicate that this was a particularly ill-defined and thus creative juncture in the history of the global economic system. Capitalism was reeling from the depression, and both the United States and Great Britain were in retreat—both nations lacking the will or the resources to play the role of hegemon for a system out of kilter. In Europe, Great Britain practiced appeasement as it attempted to hold together its world empire with diminishing economic and military resources. The United States drifted back toward isolationism as the collapse of prosperity provoked a loss of confidence and stanched the flow of dollars that had been the primary instrument of U.S. policy in the 1920s.

During the 1930s, the United States became more circumspect in Latin America and pledged itself to nonintervention. Its efforts to avert the Chaco War had proven ineffective, and in the midst of the peace talks, the Bolivian foreign minister told the North American ambassador that "since the neighboring powers cannot, and the United States will not, do anything to expedite the talks, Bolivia simply had to play up to Argentine imperialism in order to obtain an acceptable settlement." It was the U.S. ambassador's opinion that the seizure of Standard Oil properties and the subsequent reorganization of those properties into a state-run oil company like Argentina's was designed to "guarantee Bolivia a powerful neighbor, who would never again let Paraguay menace its territory," and thus revealed Bolivia's lack of faith in the United States to do the same.[37]

Bolivia in its weakness was searching for a patron. The European authoritarian states were first to recover from the depression, making them and their policies of economic nationalism attractive models to depression-ravaged states in Latin America. Convinced of the decadence of traditional liberalism, Latin American elites and militaries turned toward fascism with its promises of orderly, authoritarian modernization and strengthened national states. Germán Busch, himself of German ancestry, consulted regularly with the German minister to Bolivia and discussed barter agreements and credits for the new Bolivian oil company, Yacimientos Petrolíferos Fiscales Bolivianos (YPFB). Rumors circulated at the time that Busch's foreign exchange surrender decree was a first step toward nationalizing the Big Three and diverting Bolivian tin to a new smelter in Germany. By 1939 it appeared that the United States and Bolivia were as distant as ever and that a potent challenger to U.S. hemispheric hegemony was on the horizon.[38]

Unequal Partners

But several events in 1939 and 1940 had the effect of bringing the United States and Bolivia into closer contact than ever before in their histories. The first was world war and its impact on the global tin market. During 1939 the growing threat and then reality of another world conflagration endangered traditional U.S. tin supplies and drove up prices. In June, the U.S. Congress approved acquisition of strategic raw materials. A year later Congress authorized the Reconstruction Finance Corporation (RFC) to establish a tin smelter at Texas City, Texas, that was specifically designed for Bolivian ores. Then, in November 1940, the United States signed a five-year tin contract with Bolivian producers to buy 18,000 tons annually at a base price of 48.5 cents per pound. From the time of that contract until the mid-1950s, the United States would buy about one-half of all Bolivia's tin concentrates.[39]

The war also brought into focus another issue related to tin and the crisis of world capitalism. As early as 1929, when the results of overproduction and overinvestment first became apparent, Simón Patiño purchased a controlling interest in the British smelting firm Williams Harvey and then, as the depression deepened, joined a British consortium to absorb smaller smelters in England and Malaya into Consolidated Tin Smelters.[40] Now in control of nearly half the world's total smelting capacity, Patiño and his associates sought to restore order to the collapsing tin market. To that end, they turned to direct government regulation of tin production—a measure made feasible by the concentration of smelters in a few locations and the fact that an effective cartel need include only Bolivia, Great Britain, and the Netherlands. After secret negotiations, the three nations, who between them and their colonies produced nearly 90 percent of the world's tin, formed the International Tin Control Scheme in March 1931 and assigned each member a quota. By 1934 the tin cartel, now called the International Tin Committee (ITC), had successfully restricted production, reduced stockpiles, and raised tin prices. That year a second agreement extended the ITC until 1937 and added an important new feature—a buffer stock.[41]

Tin prices now were rising more rapidly than those for other base metals, and the United States led other consuming nations opposed to the ITC and the buffer stock. U.S. officials seeking ways to break the hold of the British-based cartel naturally looked to Bolivia, a nation in their own hemisphere that was not a European colony. Feelers from U.S. officials in the mid-1930s about a direct tin contract sparked enthusiastic responses from Aramayo and Hochschild. Under the ITC, the Bolivian government set quotas among the Big Three, exacerbating political struggles among the tin barons. Patiño, with international smelting connections and sheer domination of Bolivian production, held the high cards. Now his Bolivian competitors saw a new U.S. market as a way to reduce Patiño's influence both domestically and inside the ITC. Washington understood these dynamics, and a State Department memo warned that if the United States established smelters for Bolivian tin, it "would involve that industry, and the American Government, in the internal economic and political situation in Bolivia." At that juncture, this was not something the United States sought, and so, with supplies from the Far East still strong and the ITC making certain concessions to consumers, the matter was set aside.[42]

But with the threat of war building in 1939, Congress changed course. Through that year, Secretary of State Cordell Hull pressed a reluctant ITC to raise its quotas and make more tin available. In September, after Germany's invasion of Poland, Hull's fears of a tin shortage were realized: the tin buffer stock was quickly exhausted and the London Metals Market closed with no ready supply to meet the sudden increase in demand. This was the final proof Secretary Hull and many North American congressmen needed to convince them that the United States must build a smelter and control its own tin stocks. Legislation to those ends quickly followed, and in December 1940 the United States and Bolivia signed their tin contract.[43]

With the threat of war looming, the United States now devoted un-precedented attention to the Western Hemisphere in an effort to rein-force inter-American solidarity, reduce Axis inroads, and increase sup-plies of essential raw materials. Through 1938 and 1939, the United States searched for new instruments to increase hemispheric security. The Roosevelt administration expanded Export-Import Bank (ExIm Bank) operations in Latin America, and in 1938 the bank issued Haiti the hemisphere's first development loan. Quickly, other nations, includ-ing Bolivia, scrambled to receive the assistance that could stimulate their depression-ravaged economies. After the 1939 Panama Confer-ence, Bolivians proposed an aid-for-tin deal but were informed that no loans would be forthcoming without prior compensation to Standard Oil. Standard, which had no desire to regain its Bolivian properties, de-manded compensation because larger issues of precedent were in-volved for the company—particularly after the Mexican seizure in 1938. The State Department also worried about precedent, but did not wish to see the unresolved issue drive Bolivia still closer to Germany.⁴⁴

A month before the Panama Conference, in August 1939, President Busch cleared a major hurdle in the way of an agreement with Standard Oil by committing suicide—a final gesture of despair at his inability to reconcile forces that were ultimately irreconcilable. The new govern-ment was friendlier to the tin barons and the Allied cause and watched in concern as the unresolved Standard Oil issue blocked access to the development and military assistance Bolivia's neighbors were receiv-ing. The new government had no desire to allow the Standard issue to fester, but it also understood that a compensation agreement would cre-ate a storm of protest from nationalist and pro-Axis opponents.⁴⁵

The key to unlock the dilemma came with the so-called Nazi putsch of July 1941. Ambassador Douglas Jenkins delivered a letter to the Bo-livian government detailing a supposed pro-Axis plot that had received direct German encouragement. In response, the Bolivians declared the German ambassador persona non grata, decreed a state of siege, im-prisoned key antigovernment figures, and censored the press. The let-ter was likely a forgery produced by British agents, but despite its dubious authenticity, the letter and the affair benefited three of the governments involved. For Britain, it linked the United States and Bolivia ever more tightly to the Allied cause; for the Bolivians, it provided both an excuse to crack down on a vocal and effective nationalist opposition and an opening to finally resolve the Standard Oil issue; and for the United States, it further guaranteed tin supplies and reduced German influence in South America.[46]

The various issues separating Bolivia and the United States moved quickly toward resolution. Already in May, under heavy pressure from the United States, the Bolivians nationalized their German-run airline and turned the management contract over to Panamerican Grace (Panagra). On 1 August, the State Department proposed long-term assistance to improve communication and transportation facilities (particularly primary roads), expand and diversify agricultural production, stimulate mining, and stabilize the currency. As a first step the United States sent a technical mission headed by Merwin Bohan to Bolivia in December.[47] Meanwhile, on 4 September the two nations signed their first military assistance pact and on 6 December agreed to a lend-lease agreement allocating Bolivia $11 million in armaments. The attack on Pearl Harbor the next day finally ended the U.S. government's indecision over whether to enter the spreading war, and at a subsequent hemispheric conference in Rio de Janeiro in January 1942 the United States and Bolivia signed agreements settling the Standard Oil case. Bolivia agreed to purchase Standard Oil maps, surveys, studies, and properties for $1.5 million, and in a separate agreement the next day, the United States allocated ExIm Bank loans to Bolivia for development projects cleared by Bohan's study mission.[48]

The Standard Oil conflict was finally over, although the evaluation of winners and losers would continue. Neither a total Bolivian victory nor an illustration of good neighborliness, the tin contract, the Standard Oil settlement, and the accompanying agreements marked a fundamental shift in the nature and intimacy of U.S.-Bolivian relations. North American dollars began to flow into Bolivia for highway projects, and Nelson Rockefeller's Office of Inter-American Affairs inaugurated a public health program in the rubber and quinine zones. A new era in the relationship had begun, and both Bolivian and U.S. policy makers worked to seize the moment.[49]

The new closeness was epitomized by the first visits in history between leaders of the two countries. In April 1943, Vice President Henry Wallace visited Bolivia. While he was in La Paz, his hosts officially declared war on the Axis. In Washington a month later, President Enrique Peñaranda of Bolivia signed the Declaration of the United Nations and met with President Franklin Roosevelt. An expansive Roosevelt suggested that the United States would help Bolivia build its own smelter after the war. As to postwar tin prices, Roosevelt told his Bolivian counterpart that he had no objection to cartels as long as they were organized on a governmental as opposed to a private basis. He suggested a postwar cartel that would buy from producers at a price directly related to the cost of production, a suggestion received enthusiastically by the Bolivians. Meanwhile, on trade matters, Roosevelt counseled Bolivia to "follow a strongly nationalistic policy avoiding so far as possible dependence upon other countries and particularly upon capitalistic interests in other countries."[50] As was often the case, Roosevelt was adept at saying what his listeners wished to hear, and his words undoubtedly raised false hopes.

In previous European wars, the United States had championed neutral trade rights. Now a belligerent itself, the United States quickly moved to monopolize the hemisphere's essential resources—in Bolivia's case, tin, cinchona bark for quinine, tungsten, zinc, lead, and rubber. Of these, tin was the most important. Between December 1941 and the spring of 1942, all the major tin-producing areas in Asia came under Japanese control, and Bolivia became the only secure source of ores for the Allies. The United States wanted as much of Bolivia's tin as it could obtain at as low a price as possible; Bolivians wished to take advantage of the favorable market conditions to drive up the price. In a market with few buyers and sellers, noneconomic factors of power and leverage accompanied on both sides by emotional appeals to wartime solidarity and hemispheric unity determined the price. In that emotional power struggle, the United States held the high cards. In a dispatch sent to Washington in early 1942, a U.S. official in Bolivia laid out Bolivia's dependency on a monopsonist market quite explicitly: "Arguments [by Bolivians] that Bolivia should sell on the open market [thus] taking advantage of rising prices ignore the fact that there are no rising prices, the market being controlled by the United States and Great Britain."[51]

Recent research by John Hillman suggests that actually an underlying competition between the United States and Britain to control the postwar market gave Bolivia and Bolivian producers more leverage than they would have had if immediate military requirements had led to closer Anglo-American collusion. Several times during the war, despite strong British objections, the United States raised the price it paid for Bolivian tin, driving up the price the British were forced to pay as well. The United States was hoping to build its tin stocks by providing incentives to Bolivian producers to increase production; and indeed, as the price rose from $0.485 per pound in 1940 to $0.635 per pound in 1945, Bolivian production rose even faster—from 25,484 tons in 1938 to its second highest level ever, 42,487 tons, in 1945.[52] Bolivian nationalists, then and since, have argued that real prices would have risen even higher in a truly competitive market. By comparing the price paid by the United States with the prices offered at the same time by Argentina, historian Mariano Baptista Gumucio calculates Bolivia's losses at $670,315,000—far more than the total of all U.S. aid to Bolivia through the 1960s.[53]

Since the tin market has always been notoriously influenced by political factors, there is no satisfactory way to resolve this debate. Suffice it to say that while Bolivia perhaps benefited marginally from U.S. wartime jockeying to replace Great Britain as the major player in the tin market, several key facts cannot be disputed: buyers controlled the wartime market, and when the war ended, the United States (a consumer only) had largely superseded Great Britain (a nation with both consumer and producer interests) as the key player in the world tin market. Because the United States played a prominent role in curbing tin price increases after the war, it is perhaps inevitable that Bolivia vented its frustration and ire on the United States as the postwar market went through a prolonged period of readjustment.

The changing political realities of the tin market led to new political dynamics in Bolivia itself. Bolivian nationalists vociferously opposed the 1940 tin contract with the United States, and in 1941 coalesced into a new political party, the Movimiento Nacionalista Revolucionario (MNR). The MNR led vocal and damaging attacks on the tin contract and the increasingly ineffectual Peñaranda government, attacks seconded by tin miners. Under wartime conditions, Bolivian tin producers worked to maximize both production and profits in a suddenly secure market by continuing the depression-era policy of decapitalizing their mines. As the mineral content of Bolivia's ores continued to drop, mining became increasingly labor intensive. Employment and wages both rose, but inflation rose even faster, creating near ideal conditions for labor militancy. In late 1942, labor tensions exploded at Patiño's Catavi mine, where at least thirty-five miners were killed in a clash with the army on 21 December.[54]

Patiño had argued that he could not raise wages without endangering supplies for the war effort, and Secretary Hull went for the bait by instructing U.S. officials to discourage concessions to workers "which would inhibit the full performance of contracts with the United States."[55] When labor militancy subsequently threatened tin supplies, Hull sent a U.S. commission to Bolivia to evaluate conditions in the mines. In a cautiously worded but damning report, the commission roundly criticized working conditions not only in the mines but also on surrounding haciendas and emphasized the need for bilateral collaboration in the areas of agriculture, health, sanitation, worker housing, and education.

In separate statements, two commission members revealed a basic dichotomy concerning the role of the United States in Bolivia. Robert J. Watt of the American Federation of Labor (AFL) believed that the only remedy for Bolivia's "rotten" economy was for the United States to take "a mandate for 25 years" and rule it "autocratically in the interests of revamping economic conditions completely." On the other hand, Martin Kyne of the Congress of Industrial Organizations (CIO) issued a widely circulated minority report that stated in part: "In Bolivia the inference is as plain as it can be: the workers of Catavi were massacred because, as they were told, the government had international commitments which left no other course of action open to it." Did the United States offer solutions to Bolivia's problems, or was it a source of the problems? That nagging question was to dog U.S.-Bolivian relations from World War II onward.[56]

Back in North American Laps

Secretary Hull ordered the study commission that he sent to Bolivia after the Catavi massacre not to discuss tin prices. Nonetheless, the commission head, Judge Calvert Magruder, commented privately to the State Department that Bolivians would be interested to know how they could finance the programs the commission recommended without assurance that the United States would assist them or continue to buy their tin for a reasonable period after the war. "In one way or another," Magruder added, "the question will be back in our laps."[57] He was prescient. Until the mid-1950s, the issue of fair tin prices returned stubbornly to North American laps and revealed another face of the dilemma. How deep was U.S. commitment to Bolivia's development, and would this commitment continue once the war ended and the United States no longer needed Bolivia's tin, rubber, and quinine?

In late 1943, the domestic political fallout that accompanied the Catavi massacre led the MNR to join a dissident faction of military officers headed by Gualberto Villarroel to overthrow President Peñaranda. The State Department had been suspicious of the MNR since it formed, and several MNR leaders had been implicated in the "Nazi putsch." Immediately Secretary Hull sent a memorandum to other South American nations stating that the United States would withhold recognition of Villarroel on grounds that the MNR was profascist, anti-Semitic, and linked to the German embassy. The evidence to support these charges was mostly circumstantial, but to Hull it was evidence enough that the new regime included several vocal critics of existing minerals contracts with the United States.[58] Bolivians had been calling for another upward revision of tin prices since early 1943, but negotiations were at an impasse when Villarroel seized power in December. Thanks to wartime rationing, increased recovery of secondary tin, and new electroplating technologies, the United States had greatly reduced its tin consumption during the war. U.S. strategic tin stocks now stood at a seventy-five-week supply, and the State Department concluded that it could afford to pressure the new government.[59]

The market for other Bolivian products was changing even more rapidly. In January 1944 a U.S. official reported that Bolivia was the only remaining source of cinchona bark, but in April of that same year the development of the synthetic drug Atabrine made Bolivia's quinine no longer critical. The United States demanded that Bolivia comply with the existing contract only to keep quinine out of Argentine (and presumably Axis) hands.[60] Through late 1944 and early 1945 the United States continued to insist that Bolivia adhere to the terms of prior rubber contracts, even though the Argentines offered better prices. Eight days after Hiroshima, however, four days after Japan surrendered, the State Department informed Bolivia that the United States had no interest in a new rubber contract.[61]

These precedents frightened Bolivians, for if they were repeated in the case of tin, the nation's economy would be devastated. The signs from the north were not reassuring. When the United States finally restored relations with Villarroel, in June 1944, U.S. procurement officials made it clear that tin talks would begin from scratch. Bolivian negotiators responded by proposing a bilateral agreement that shrewdly linked a price increase to measures increasing worker benefits.[62] The proposal challenged the North Americans to back the Magruder Commission's recommendations and confront the social implications of falling prices, but would also increase the Bolivian government's leverage against the tin producers (a key objective of the Villarroel regime), augment funds for social programs (of obvious political and economic value to the populist Villarroel government), and ensure a predominant role for the Bolivian state in subsequent tin negotiations. Hull, then in his final days as secretary of state, rejected the proposal. He claimed that the State Department gave the proposal careful consideration, but that the United States now sought to direct foreign procurement programs back into private trade channels as soon as possible. Hull claimed that "no political considerations" colored this refusal, but his protestations seem either disingenuous or uninformed in light of subsequent U.S. policy, which frustrated the Bolivian initiative at every turn and contributed to the increasing instability of the Villarroel regime.[63]

In mid-1945, with Roosevelt dead and the war in Europe over, the Bolivians quickly felt the impact of philosophical, personnel, and priority shifts in Washington. In July, U.S. officials presented Bolivian negotiators with "take it or leave it" terms: a one-year contract, with the price dropping 1.5 cents each quarter from the current level of 63.5 cents a pound. The chief North American negotiator informed his three Bolivian counterparts that "the honeymoon [is] over and if one of you wishes to dispute these decisions, I have arranged for three chairs to be placed out there under a tree. I can assure you, however, that I will not occupy one of those chairs."[64]

Ambassador Víctor Andrade, who headed the Bolivian negotiating team, was genuinely livid at this high-handed ultimatum and complained bitterly to State Department and congressional leaders. The ambassador explained at length why the new contract was unjust from Bolivia's point of view and unwise from that of the United States. Current tin prices remained controlled, Andrade charged, and experts agreed that if controls were lifted, the price might rise above a dollar a pound. The United States was gambling on the questionable assumption that more ample supplies soon would be available from British Malaya, and was using the leverage its accumulated stockpiles afforded to arbitrarily drive down prices.[65]

Andrade's charges were justified. Postwar turmoil in Southeast Asia meant that the United States continued to control tin prices until 1948, when prices finally conformed to North American predictions that they would fall. Its immense stockpiles gave the U.S. government significant leverage over the postwar tin market, but also opened new lines of argument for a shrewd negotiator like Andrade. Bolivia's wartime loyalty to the United States had costs, Andrade argued. Falling tin prices would devastate his country unless the United States helped cushion Bolivia by paying a price for tin that reflected production costs, or, alternatively, assisted Bolivia to diversify its economy and reduce its dependency on tin revenues. If the United States did not accept its responsibility, the ambassador warned, Bolivia would have to be written off as a wartime casualty. On the other hand, if tin prices stayed high, Bolivia could complete the development plans laid out by the Bohan mission and gradually alter its tax system to assist the mining industry. It would emerge with a diversified economy able to meet its own basic needs and therefore no longer depend on high levels of foreign exchange to survive. The alternative, Andrade warned, would be for the Bolivian government to meet the pending economic crisis by nationalizing the mining industry.[66]

The issue, as Magruder had warned, was back in North American laps. Although Andrade's government fell in mid-1946, his argument remained at the heart of Bolivia's negotiating position for the next seven years. Ironically, Andrade was back in Washington as ambassador in 1953 when the matter was finally resolved. As men like Sumner Welles and Franklin Roosevelt disappeared from the scene—men who had promised U.S. assistance to help Bolivia make the transition to peacetime market conditions—North American policy makers increasingly countered arguments like Andrade's with claims that Bolivia had reaped a wartime bonanza. The tin barons' profits had risen, and the government's foreign exchange reserves topped $34 million by 1946. Such claims ignored the fact that these reserves resulted from an unusual wartime market when demand for Bolivian tin was high and manufactured consumer goods from the developed world were unavailable. When the world market returned to more normal conditions, Bolivia's foreign exchange reserves were rapidly depleted.[67]

As Bolivia's reserves dwindled, its growing fiscal problems confirmed a counterposition that had existed among North American policy makers all along. This position cautioned against lavish U.S. commitments to Bolivia and argued for increased oversight and a shorter leash. Even as details of the North American aid were being hammered out prior to the 1942 Rio Conference, U.S. embassy official Allen Dawson urgently waved caution flags. All through late 1941 and early 1942, Dawson kept Washington apprised of perceived political errors, two-facedness, and outright perfidy by the Bolivians. In November 1941, just before the arrival of the Bohan Commission, Dawson wrote the State Department that Bolivia probably needed financial assistance "less than . . . almost any other country in Latin America." While reluctantly recognizing that Bolivia could not be excluded from the general program of continental economic cooperation "for obvious international political reasons," Dawson counseled it would be wise to "make haste slowly" and keep a tight grasp on the purse strings.[68]

In 1945, with the war over and Bolivian raw materials no longer crucial, voices like Dawson's became louder at both the embassy in La Paz and the State Department in Washington. Increasingly, U.S. officials blamed Bolivians for their own dilemma. In 1946 the new assistant secretary of state for Latin American affairs, Spruille Braden, asked department lawyers whether it might not be possible to renege on earlier development aid commitments made at the 1942 Rio Conference and instead press the Bolivians to allow private U.S. companies to come in and "do a real job."[69] It was time, Braden believed, to get the issues of tin prices and Bolivian development definitively out of the laps of the U.S. government and the State Department.

Implications of an Unequal Partnership

Relations between the United States and Bolivia changed fundamentally after the two countries signed their first tin agreement in 1940. In 1946 the United States purchased more than half of Bolivia's tin and dominated the tin market on which Bolivia depended for its economic livelihood. Over the previous six years the United States had intervened directly in Bolivia's internal affairs on several occasions and in a variety of ways, but it had also promised long-term commitments to Bolivia's development: President Roosevelt implied that Bolivians could expect postwar market conditions for tin in which prices would be adjusted to production costs; Merwin Bohan laid out a development plan to diversify Bolivia's economy with U.S. assistance; Sumner Welles promised that aid agreements signed in Rio were "but the prelude to a long-term, mutually beneficial program of economic cooperation"; and the Magruder Commission's report indicated a continuing U.S. interest in Bo-livia's deep-seated economic and social problems.[70]

These commitments were products of a particular historical moment when the discourse between two distant neighbors was as focused as it might ever be. Special historical conditions came together in the 1930s and early 1940s to create a sense of genuine, if limited good neighborli-ness. The depression increased the importance of hemispheric trade for the United States, and by the mid-1930s, with war again brewing in Eu-rope, hemispheric solidarity was a form of internationalism acceptable even to Fortress America isolationists. For Americans, there was an ad-ditional cultural convergence that served as a vital backdrop. For the first time, North Americans and Bolivians shared a culture of poverty—the standards relative, of course—and Americans turned less judgmen-tal eyes southward. Fredrick Pike notes that "people who make a habit of intervening in the affairs of foreign countries, in order to improve and develop and uplift those countries, must have supreme confidence in their own political, social, and economic wisdom and virtue."[71] The Great Depression undermined such confidence in America.

Early in the 1930s, historian Herbert Eugene Bolton suggested that the nations of the hemisphere shared a common history and destiny. Throughout that decade, a fascination with things Latin grew in the United States: Diego Rivera was commissioned to paint a mural for Rockefeller Center; at the Copacabana and Latin Quarter clubs in New York City, Americans danced the rumba, the tango, and the cha-cha; Carmen Miranda and Dolores del Río graced North American movie screens; and a 1940 public opinion survey suggested that 84 percent of the American people wanted to know more about Latin America, 75 percent wanted more news from Latin America, and 50 percent ad-vocated more assistance to Latin America. Helping Americans discover their neighbors to the South, John Gunther published the first edition of his influential *Inside Latin America* in 1941; that same year Walt Disney launched the first of a trilogy of animated features on the region.[72]

Bolivia, both as a nation and as a cultural entity, also reconsidered the United States. For a time in the 1930s the United States did not seem a worthy patron, and with resentment high and a sense of national powerlessness intensified by the Chaco War, Bolivia flirted with others. But the new tin relationship and U.S. wartime commitments restored and deepened the relationship between the two nations. Aware of the special conjunction of historical factors and the unprecedented focus to the discourse, the Bolivian ambassador to Brazil wrote the foreign minister after the 1942 agreements at the Rio Conference:

> The moment is exceptional and necessarily brief. . . . For that very reason, we must hasten to take advantage of it since, when the war ends, the economic conditions of the world will be very different from those of today. The policy of the U.S., especially in its relations with our country, will change fundamentally and never again will there be present to us the opportunity for organizing the development of our basic wealth with the conditions that are presented to us now.[73]

Bolivia had found a patron, and as the quotation above makes clear, a conjunction of factors made it possible to see that patron not only as an antidote for Bolivia's ongoing weakness, but as a source of support in efforts to build future strength.

As Bolivians reconsidered the United States during this period, one of the things they saw and appreciated was a U.S. president who blended patrician refinement with a populist touch, a gentle Machiavellian pragmatism with an expansive tendency to say what people most wanted to hear, and a patron's confident power with an understanding of the principles of reciprocity—all very Latin American attributes. As Pike comments, too often in the past, Latin Americans had been convinced that U.S. leaders cared nothing about them. With Franklin Roosevelt, they could not be quite so sure.[74] The interests of the United States as a great power and of America as a cultural and ideological entity converged, as did the Bolivia needing a patron and the Bolivia wishing desperately to become sovereign and economically developed. That brief convergence is what gave the Good Neighbor policy substance.

To be sure, ambivalence ran beneath all the neighborliness. The Disney films reinforced a host of American stereotypes and, according to one critic, were a metaphor for North American conquest as well as a

repackaging of Latin America "for enhanced North American consumption."[75] Historian Stephen Rabe doubts that the Roosevelt team
would have redeemed its pledges of long-term support and high tin
prices even if it had remained intact. In any case, Bolivians soon came
to resent the swarm of North American experts and diplomatic attachés
who descended on their country during the war. U.S. journalist Carlton
Beales wrote in 1945 that North American propaganda material from
Nelson Rockefeller's office was "far too slick" and reeked of "power,
wealth and arrogance." After experiencing the U.S. wartime invasion of
Bolivia, Fernando Diez de Medina observed that "the United States,
idealistic in thought, is commercial in action. They demand and receive
everything. They give back only what they don't need."[76]

By the mid-1940s, the special moment was past. Successful in war,
their economy again booming, Americans looked south with returning
scorn for the lingering social, economic, and political malaise they
thought they saw there. The declining need for tin and other raw materials and the reduced threat from spreading Peronism after the fall of
Villarroel in 1946 added to the growing U.S. and American disinterest.
Then, in April 1945, a man Pike calls "the archetypal gringo" replaced
Roosevelt as president. The convergence of factors that briefly made the
Good Neighbor policy more than mere slogan no longer existed.[77]

The essence of the new mood is best caught in Henry Luce's famous
essay "The American Century." From regional hegemon to apparent
good neighbor, the United States now had pretensions, perhaps even
responsibilities, as global hegemon in a dangerous postwar world. Arrogance, idealism, self-interest, and a sense of responsibility came together to shift the North American focus far beyond the Western Hemisphere. The dominant theme in U.S. policy toward Bolivia for the next
several years was disengagement. Ultimately committed neither to but-
tressing the existing Bolivian system nor to financing its transformation, the State Department tried to back away from previous promises
and to shove Bolivia's problems out of its lap.

Much had changed since the beginning of the war, and the United
States and Bolivia were no longer distant neighbors with only a tenuous
relationship. However, the catchphrase "Good Neighbors" does not ac-

curately convey either the new U.S. prominence or Bolivia's increased dependency. In Bolivia, the sum of prewar and wartime policies ultimately created something quite different from "good neighborliness." The new relationship was, at best, a patron-client bond, but as North American interest in Bolivia receded, the United States became a reluctant patron. If the need had arisen, there is little doubt the United States would have exerted its new influence in Bolivia, but for the next six years no such need appeared. Thus U.S. policy makers attempted to disengage, and it was the Bolivians who constantly tried to reconfirm the special wartime relationship between the two nations and remind Washington of its unfulfilled obligations. Finally, the political upheaval of April 1952 and changing market conditions for tin at the close of the Korean War combined to force State Department officials to abandon their policy of disengagement. A long history as distant neighbors, followed by an intense six-year wartime relationship, followed by yet another six years of U.S. withdrawal and Bolivian appeals for renewed commitment, set the stage for the unexpected U.S. response to the revolution of April 1952.

4   Bolivian Dilemma and a Pragmatic Experiment

Early on the Wednesday morning of Holy Week 1952, the Movimiento Nacionalista Revolucionario made yet another of its periodic bids to return to power. The day before, on 8 April, the ruling military junta had tried to revitalize its floundering, strife-ridden government by asking several cabinet ministers to resign. Minister of Interior Antonio Seleme, one of those asked to leave, immediately offered his services and those of the police under his command (the *carabineros*) to the MNR. Seleme asked only the presidency in exchange. By 8:00 A.M. on 9 April the revolutionaries had seized an army arsenal and controlled central La Paz. Carabineros and party faithful armed with rifles circulated through the city shouting their support for Villarroel, the party, and exiled leader Víctor Paz Estenssoro, but the fighting was far from over. Despite early rumors that army commander General Humberto Torres Ortiz would join the revolt, he instead sealed off the city and attacked the rebels. Through the afternoon, fighting was heavy and casualties were high on both sides.[1]

During the night that followed, both the rebellion and the course of Bolivian history took a distinct turn. Seleme, fearing the tide had turned against the revolt, took asylum in the Chilean embassy and his carabineros no longer played a crucial role. Armed power passed into the hands of party faithful and union militias. Now facing strong resistance in the popular quarters of La Paz, Torres's forces began to lose the initiative. Early Good Friday morning, 11 April, miner militias took over an army garrison in Oruro and intercepted a train near La Paz that was bringing arms and ammunition to resupply Torres's forces. In the subsequent assessment by the U.S. military attaché, the capture of the train was "the crowning blow" to the military's hopes. Soon after, Torres and other officers fled to Peru, leaving a decapitated army; by afternoon only sporadic resistance remained.[2]

Although it had begun as just another of Bolivia's many palace coups, the Holy Week Rebellion of 1952 ended as a popular insurrection that left the military in disarray, the carabineros leaderless, the armed worker and party militias triumphant, and the MNR at the forefront of a potential social revolution. But with the leverage afforded by tin and with rising concern about communist infiltration in the hemisphere, the United States would play an important role in shaping the final outcome of this revolutionary moment.

The Making of a Bolivian Dilemma

Most students of Bolivian history maintain that the MNR leaders were reluctant revolutionaries who neither planned nor anticipated the sudden and complete collapse of the existing order.[3] But neither was this turn of events mere historical accident. Both the collapse and the MNR's ascendancy had been in preparation for some time. The MNR had its origins in the Chaco War. In his memoirs, Víctor Andrade, a Chaco veteran, participant in the growing postwar challenge to the old political order, and future MNR ambassador to the United States, succinctly summarizes the psychological and political impact of the war on his own generation:

> The Chaco War presented violent, Dantesque contrasts between the most holy examples of self-renunciation and the most abominable acts of cowardice. . . . The war was the culmination of an epoch of total falsity, one in which a defective social order had devalued and neglected an entire nation. . . . The seed of the revolution germinated from the common experience of the civilian and military youth in the war: a national consciousness was formed.[4]

A period of political ferment followed the war, and writers began pouring out torrents of words to challenge traditional verities, raise the social content of politics, and provide a new slogan to animate the disillusioned: "*Tierras al indio, y minas al estado*" (Land to the Indians, mines to the state). By the early 1940s, two formal political parties had coalesced, each reflecting the leading ideological currents of the day. Marxists formed the Partido de la Izquierda Revolucionaria (PIR), which took as its model the Soviet Union and strove for a workers' revolution. In early 1941 a small group of vociferous nationalist deputies formed the MNR, a party heavily influenced by spiritualized nationalism and European fascism but which also looked inward and backward to Bolivia's Hispanic and indigenous roots. Most *MNRistas* were at the margins of Bolivia's tiny political elite. They considered the Chaco War their baptism by fire and berated *PIRistas* who went into exile rather than fight an "imperialist" war.[5]

The MNR and PIR initially allied to oppose the tin contract with the United States and a settlement with Standard Oil, but parted company after Hitler's invasion of the Soviet Union in June 1941. Thereafter the PIR took a pro-Allied stance while the MNR bore the brunt of U.S. displeasure and was the chief victim of the purge that followed the "Nazi putsch" in July. As a political "out-group," the MNR joined Villarroel and his junior military officers in the December 1943 coup. U.S. opposition to Villarroel fastened on the MNRistas, however, and Villarroel was forced to rid his government of MNR support as the price for U.S. recognition. Nonetheless, the MNR reemerged in the 1944 elections as the major party in congress, forcing the U.S. embassy to concede that whether because of Villarroel's "ineptitude" or his "connivance," the MNR was once again in the driver's seat. As Andrade later put it: "The MNR representatives left through the windows, thus providing an excuse for the reconsideration of the previous nonrecognition policy. They then returned through the door after the elections as a part of the constitutional government."[6]

Villarroel never completely clarified his program, and his government was constantly hampered by internal contradictions. Nevertheless he broke new ground by forming the first government in the twentieth century to rule without the direct collaboration of at least a faction of the tin industry. Villarroel also took the first tentative steps toward incorporating Bolivia's large indigenous population into national life.

His tolerance of the first industry-wide mine workers union, the Federación Sindical de Trabajadores Mineros de Bolivia (FSTMB), organized in 1944, was equally significant. Over the next six years the union became a major political force, and it played a decisive role in the revolution of 1952. Villarroel was more interested in co-opting the peasants' and mine workers' movements than in supporting their agendas, yet peasants and workers liked him because of his relative openness, and after his violent death formed a strong symbolic bond with the fallen president that the MNR was able to exploit.[7]

Because of his innovations, Villarroel was constantly under attack. The tin barons fashioned a strange coalition of traditional right-wing parties and orthodox pro-Stalinist leftists to undermine his regime. Militarists within the Villarroel government responded brutally, and policy slipped from the control of the quiet, scholarly president. The United States contributed to Villarroel's problems by accepting opposition charges of human rights abuses at face value and by assuming a tough negotiating stance during tin contract talks.[8] Finally, on 21 July 1946, with the army divided and confined to barracks, antigovernment mobs ransacked the buildings around the central plaza in La Paz, then seized Villarroel and hanged him from a lamppost across from the government palace. Recently arrived U.S. ambassador Joseph Flack telegraphed Washington that "a popular revolution in every sense of the word" had just occurred. "Democracy's first steps are apt to be faltering," Flack commented, "and in Bolivia they should be supported in every reasonable and decent way by our country. The last days of Villarroel's tyranny were so frightful that no opportunity should be lost to avoid a repetition."[9]

The first phase of the relationship between the United States and the MNR ended when the party the United States detested was ousted along with Villarroel, but over the *sexenio* that followed—the six years between Villarroel's death and the MNR's return—a number of factors changed. As noted previously, the United States lost interest in Bolivia, reduced its commitments, and withdrew its funds. In 1948, soon after the Bogotá Conference, Secretary of State George C. Marshall spoke with Bolivian special ambassador Javier Paz Cámpero about the turmoil in the streets of Bogotá that surrounded the conference. Marshall reminded his guest that "conservative and responsible people of this Hemisphere" could not sit back and allow bad conditions to play into the hands of Communists, but instead should themselves confront the problems facing their countries. Paz Cámpero retorted that lack of U.S. support now endangered measures begun in Bolivia during the war that could perhaps cure the "bad conditions" that so worried the secretary.[10] The exchange summarizes the impasse U.S.-Bolivian relations had reached by the end of Truman's first term. U.S. officials fulminated on the importance of self-help and the rising international threat of communism while Bolivians called for recommitment to past obligations and fulfillment of unrealized promises. Relations between the United States and sexenio governments steadily deteriorated.

In light of changing U.S. priorities, perceptions of the MNR in Washington also began to shift. Throughout the sexenio, the State Department closely monitored communist activity in Bolivia, but was not overly concerned. A 1950 embassy study identified no more than 150 fully indoctrinated Communists in the entire country and stated that the MNR and the army were the key domestic forces limiting "the chances for full development of a Communist movement." The survey went on to speculate that even if, as the Bolivian government was charging, the MNR had formed a tactical alliance with Communists, it would only be a matter of time before the party turned on its leftist allies and "liquidated them."[11] Under the new cold war conditions, the right-wing nationalism and fascist brutality imputed to the MNR were no longer such liabilities.

Ironically, these putative qualities kept U.S. officials from fully understanding the changes the MNR itself underwent during the sexenio. Since the insurrection of July 1946 that left Villarroel swinging from a lamppost on Plaza Murillo, the MNR had steadily plotted its return to power. In 1947 the party elite purged members who recommended collaboration with sexenio governments and instead followed the line of exiled party leader Víctor Paz Estenssoro, who held up fallen nationalist martyrs Busch and Villarroel and called for intransigent opposition and armed revolution. It was a wise decision. As in the early 1940s, the

MNR proved an adept and formidable party of opposition. It avoided the ideological and programmatic orthodoxies that limited the Marxist parties and worked its nationalist agenda to draw every dissatisfied group into its coalition.

General public dissatisfaction rose during the sexenio. Among those attracted to the MNR were urban voters hurt by rising inflation and workers angry at repression under sexenio governments. The PIR lost legitimacy among workers for participating in Villarroel's ouster, and early in 1950 remnants of that disintegrating party formed the Partido Comunista de Bolivia (PCB). With the PIR self-destructing and the MNR proscribed, leftist opposition during the early sexenio centered in the mine workers' union, the FSTMB. The MNR had few direct grassroots contacts with miners, but rather forged links to FSTMB leaders such as the charismatic Juan Lechín. The tendency of sexenio governments to blame MNR agitators for labor conflicts, the party's identification with Villarroel, and the growing identification of labor leaders with the MNR made that party increasingly the political vehicle of worker aspirations. When a revolt instigated by the MNR failed in August 1949 due to lack of military support, the party took another step toward truly challenging the existing system by deciding to involve mobilized workers and peasants in future attempts.[12]

The party worked within the system as well. Although MNR candidate Víctor Paz was not allowed to return to Bolivia to campaign in the 1951 presidential elections, he received more than twice the votes garnered by the official government candidate in the capital—a sign of the growing political appeal of the MNR to alienated urban middle and working classes. With Paz winning a clear plurality nationwide, President Mamerto Urriolagoitia voluntarily surrendered control of the government to the army to keep the MNR out of power. His reason, Urriolagoitia said, was that the MNR was now in league with Communists.[13] The State Department put little stock in these charges and did not wish, openly, to support the military takeover. Neither, however, did it oppose military intervention, and the department's "Bolivia Policy Statement" issued that year succinctly states why:

An experiment in democracy has failed in Bolivia due to the lack of developed natural resources on which to base a sound and diversified economy, the poverty and ignorance of the masses, the weaknesses of Bolivian administrators and traditions of political violence. The Bolivian experience should prove to us that we cannot export the U.S. type of democracy to be superimposed on a backward country.[14]

But Bolivia's stability and development remained low priorities in Washington, and U.S. tin policies immediately undercut the new military regime. From the end of the war until mid-1949, Washington kept tin purchases under government control and used its new influence in the tin market to keep a lid on price increases and to stymie attempts to revitalize the International Tin Committee. When, in the fall of 1949, world prices finally began to decline, the United States relaxed the controls, only to restore them a year later when the outbreak of the Korean War and insurgencies in British Malaya and Indonesia drove tin prices to an unprecedented high of almost $2.00 per pound.[15]

Just before the Bolivian junta took power, Truman named Stuart Symington as head of the tin-purchasing agency—the Reconstruction Finance Corporation (RFC)—and Congress authorized Symington to use existing commercial tin stocks to force down the world price. Backed by Lyndon Johnson's Senate Preparedness Subcommittee, Symington refused to budge from a $1.03 per pound offer, and he and the Bolivians remained locked in mutually acrimonious debate until October 1951 when the military junta angrily broke off negotiations. An official Bolivian press release charged that "it makes no sense for the U.S. to spend millions fortifying nations in distant parts of the world and then to dispute Bolivia a few cents for its life-blood."[16]

Press organs controlled by the Big Three added their voices to the clamor, blaming Wall Street and economic imperialism for policies that damaged inter-American relations. Symington and the U.S. press responded in kind, referring to greedy tin barons who expatriated huge profits from an impoverished country. Communist leader and writer Sergio Almaraz noted with sardonic glee that suddenly the North American press, which always before had considered the Big

Three to be "examples of entrepreneurial skill and irrefutable evidence of the creative force of private initiative," now joined Bolivian critics to call the Bolivian barons "greedy, stingy, and exploitative."[17] And although the MNR remained officially banned, it gained strength as the barrage of charges and countercharges repeated what the party had asserted all along—the United States was imperialist and the tin barons selfish. Meanwhile the impasse highlighted the growing weakness of the tin oligarchy and the ineffectiveness of the military government that it continued to dominate.

Belatedly aware of the political ramifications inside Bolivia of a continuing stalemate, the State Department facilitated the reopening of formal tin contract talks in early 1952. But the talks remained stalled until the April revolution, hampered by falling world prices and by the most-favored-nation clauses in U.S. tin contracts with Great Britain, Indonesia, and Belgium that assured that any price concession to the Bolivians would require similar concessions to other producers as well.[18]

By then, in the words of political scientist Christopher Mitchell, the MNR virtually monopolized all claims to political legitimacy. During the sexenio, events transpired so that the MNR consolidated support from its own urban middle-class cadres, added labor and peasant support, and even drew the endorsement of the newly formed Bolivian communist party. The 1951 elections gave the MNR political legitimacy. The PIR had disintegrated, and the parties on the right that controlled the sexenio governments revealed their own bankruptcy and incompetence each time they capitulated to the mine owners. The military became implicated in the failing system by stepping in after the 1951 elections without a clear program of its own, and once in power proved just as divided and subservient to the tin barons as the civilian parties of the right. Meanwhile, the barons were in the midst of bailing out of a system that no longer effectively protected their interests.

Under such conditions, putting together an opposition coalition around a unifying core of vaguely defined nationalism was easy. But the MNR's ascendancy would have been far different if this essentially moderate, nationalist, middle-class party had been allowed to assume power legitimately or with strong military backing. Instead, as a result of the dynamics of both the sexenio and the April rebellion, moderate politicians led a heterogeneous coalition under volatile conditions in which armed labor militias held a crucial balance of coercive power. The contradictions were to present formidable challenges to the MNR and opened space for the United States to play a crucial role in tilting the revolution in a direction with which it felt comfortable.[19]

A Cautious Appraisal of Cautious Revolutionaries

In light of the history of hostility between the United States and the MNR, it is not surprising that initial reactions to the April revolution in the United States were negative. *Time* magazine headlined its story of the revolution "Bolivia: Blood-Drenched Comeback" and stated that "fanatical members of the totalitarian MNR clawed their way back" to power. But *Time* also revealed confusion in the United States about the party and its leaders, noting that the new president, Víctor Paz, had been called everything from "the number one Nazi of the Americas" to "a Communist of the right."[20] Such imprecision demanded definition. In an era of bipolar simplicity when Communists were being uncovered everywhere from the State Department to Hollywood, to be suspected a Communist, even if "of the right," was a damning charge. With armed worker militias patrolling the streets; with the newly organized central workers' union, the Central Obrero Boliviana (COB), having prominent Marxist leaders and a direct voice in government policy making; and with known Communists in important government posts, the MNR government roused U.S. concern. By the simple syllogism of the times, to act like a Communist was to be a Communist, and to be a Communist was to be an instrument of international Soviet aggression.

Nonetheless, U.S. officials approached the party with a caution that avoided simplistic syllogism. Progressively over the six years since Truman officials celebrated the fall of Villarroel and his MNR collaborators, Washington had lost faith in the "democratic" parties of the right and then the army, while tin negotiations distanced it from the Big Three as well. U.S. officials looked with more favor on the MNR than they had in

1946, aware of the party's popular support. They believed it to be an effective counter to communist influence in the mine workers' union and hoped it might have the strength, will, and popularity to resolve what U.S. officials had come to call the "Bolivian dilemma."

Only days before the revolution, the embassy sent a lengthy document under that title to Washington. Several fundamental contradictions convinced even U.S. officials of the need for basic structural reform. First, although Bolivia had a population roughly the present size of Alabama spread over a territory the size of Texas and California combined, it could not feed itself. Land was badly distributed, and even though food consumption stood at only two-thirds of the standard requirements, inefficient production forced Bolivia to import 40 percent of the nation's food supplies according to embassy estimates. Second, as the "Bolivian Dilemma" document recognized, the tin industry was sick. Mines employed 3.2 percent of the labor force to produce 25 percent of the GNP and 95 percent of Bolivia's foreign exchange, but the average mineral content of ores was still falling—down to 1.11 percent in 1952—and Bolivia was the highest-cost producer in a volatile world market. Mine owners, with their larger international interests, found it easier to pull out than to invest and had laid little foundation for diversified growth of the national economy.[21]

Largely as a result of the problems in its two leading economic sectors, Bolivia was poor. At the time of the revolution, the per capita GDP stood at $118.60, ahead of only Haiti in the hemisphere. Such poverty had social consequences: 70 percent of the population was illiterate and 75 percent did not participate in the political process. Health services were deficient nationwide and virtually nonexistent in rural areas, where life expectancy was the lowest in Latin America. The debilitating effects of poverty were further compounded by deep social and ethnic divisions. In rural Bolivia, Indians lived in near-feudal conditions, working the *hacendado*'s lands three or four days a week and performing personal service, or *pongueaje*, several times a year for a week or more. Indians not obligated to the haciendas (about 18 percent of Bolivia's rural population) continued to be effectively exploited through discriminatory taxes and corvée labor obligations that differed in form and degree but not in substance from colonial patterns of exploitation. In the cities, Indians were expected to stay off the main streets and out of sight. A U.S. citizen visiting Bolivia before the revolution recorded watching a man struggle to carry a two-hundred-pound wooden box up hotel stairs because Indians were not allowed to use the elevator. Force and brutality ultimately reinforced such discrimination.[22]

At mid-century several documents brought these conditions to international attention as well as to the attention of literate Bolivians. The government census commissioned in 1950 underscored Bolivia's poverty and the skewed access to land. A year later, the United Nations Keenleyside Report built on those findings to outline the structural roots of Bolivia's problems as well as to criticize existing government policies.[23] In light of these reports, U.S. embassy officials now cautiously accepted a central MNR thesis: the tin barons, the landlords, and the traditional parties of the right stood in the way of solving the dilemma. The "Bolivian Dilemma" document stopped far short of endorsing the MNR, but its underlying tone was so relentlessly pessimistic, except when favorably noting how Víctor Paz had handled finances under Villarroel, that the implication was clear: Washington did not fear the return of the MNR as it once did. A few in the embassy even saw the MNR as Bolivia's last remaining hope—particularly when the revolution itself left no immediately acceptable alternatives.[24]

Coming to power had been relatively simple for the MNR, and the tasks facing the new government were easy to define. But the methods by which those tasks might be addressed brought the weaknesses of the MNR and its multiclass, multigroup nationalist coalition into focus and roused U.S. fears. The United States did not recognize the MNR government until June. In the interim, U.S. officials determined that neither communist nor Peronist influence was decisive and that a central core of party leaders such as President Paz provided the best alternative to either chaos or communism. One embassy source provided an analogy that greatly influenced thinking in Washington. The new government "is similar to the Karensky [*sic*] government of Russia," he observed, "in that if it fails, now that the army is defeated and discredited, there seems to be no alternative for Bolivia but Communism."[25] If Paz was Bolivia's Kerensky, then FSTMB leader Juan Lechín was its Lenin. As Carlos Navia has observed, U.S. views of these two men tended toward Manichaean simplification. Paz personified the revolution that the United States could support, and Lechín that which it feared and opposed.[26]

Truman administration officials believed their task was to help Paz consolidate his position, and to that end they applied the leverage provided by the still uncompleted tin contract. Tin remained at the center of U.S.-Bolivian relations in the postwar years, although now the key issue was that the United States no longer *needed* Bolivia's tin. Because few U.S. investors held stocks in Bolivian tin companies and because Washington was aware that intransigent opposition to reforms might play into the hands of the most radical faction within the MNR, the U.S. government was flexible and applied pressure only sporadically.

Much of the Truman State Department's initial views of the Bolivian situation hinged on the belief that Paz preferred not to nationalize—a questionable assumption in light of Paz's own pronouncements. As both an economist and a political realist Paz understood that marketing and management problems would accompany nationalization of the tin mines, but nationalization was crucial to the unionists and so popular among virtually all party factions that his economic instincts clashed with his political calculations. As was nearly always the case during the first four years of the revolution, Paz's political calculations triumphed. Six months after the revolution, on 31 October 1952, Paz and Lechín signed a decree that nationalized the mines. As a concession to U.S. pressure, the decree affected only the Big Three, promised compensation, and reconfirmed the government's acceptance of the principles of private ownership.[27]

As for land reform, North American officials were ultimately reassured by the limited nature of MNR reforms and the Paz government's reaffirmation of capitalist principles of private ownership. In the months immediately preceding reform, rural violence spread—justifiably likened by Herbert Klein to the "Great Fear" in revolutionary France. But with no direct U.S. interests at stake, North American observers could allow themselves to understand that reforms were a necessary blow to feudalism and the legacy of Spanish colonialism. The most sympathetic North Americans went further. Ambassador Edward Sparks attended the signing ceremony at a little town outside Cochabamba and considered the event an affirmation of human dignity. "I remember vividly an enormous crowd of Indians silently listening to the proclamation in Spanish of the Agrarian Reform decree," he later recalled. "Then the Foreign Minister, Wálter Guevara Arze, stood up and extemporaneously summarized the decree in Quechua. What a sensation to see that silent mass come to life!"[28] The division of large estates into private plots resonated with the American myth of a Jeffersonian yeomanry and prompted Milton Eisenhower to later write, "feudalism is far closer to Communism than the system of owner-operated farms installed by the Paz Estenssoro Government."[29]

Leading the political and unionist factions of the MNR, Paz and Lechín together bargained and negotiated their way through the most radical, promising, and dangerous phase of the revolution—a phase culminating in August 1953 with agrarian reform. Balancing the imperative to reform with the demands of survival, and the unifying appeal of nationalism with the lingering reality of dependency, Paz and Lechín each played an important role in maintaining the pragmatic equilibrium that political stability and revolutionary reforms required. Meanwhile, U.S. officials watched closely and were, in the main, reassured by the course Bolivia's revolutionaries were navigating.

The Decision for Aid

As it turned out, the reforms shaped by Paz and Lechín's intense political bargaining tended to worsen the economic problems facing the regime, and in turn to disrupt the complex political balance they had already achieved. At the end of 1952, 70 percent of Bolivia's normal mineral export trade was suspended, fueling rumors that the newly nationalized mines faced an international boycott. Dwindling foreign exchange hampered the flow of food imports and severely exacerbated a chronic inflation dating back to the Chaco War. Rising economic problems led to complaints from all groups in the MNR's diverse coalition and to rumors of new plots.

The tin contract with the United States was still unsigned, and the MNR was more than ready to see Truman leave office. An editorial published after Dwight Eisenhower's election in the semiofficial newspaper, *La Nación,* observed that while the Republican party by tradition and background could be considered "conservative and imperialist," it was also more "realistic and thus sincere." "It is better," the editorial concluded, "to seek understandings with those who present their position frankly, rather than with those who pretend to be good neighbors."[30] In this context, MNR leaders compared Truman's "good neighborly" interference with the straightforward commercial stance assumed by British negotiators who in January 1953 agreed to buy tin at world prices from the new national mining company, the Corporación Minera de Bolivia (COMIBOL). The agreement with British smelters assured a market for more than 50 percent of Bolivia's ores and ended rumors of a boycott.[31]

But hopes in La Paz that the new Republican administration in the United States would quickly see the commercial value of a long-term tin contract proved a miscalculation. As Eisenhower moved to end the war in Korea and U.S. stockpiles filled, tin prices began a long and drastic decline. The Texas City smelter was losing money, and Republican businessmen in Washington decided that for both economic and philosophical reasons it was time the United States government got out of the tin-smelting business. In early March, State Department officials told Víctor Andrade, who was again ambassador to the United States, that current contracts would fill both strategic and commercial stockpiles by the end of the year, and that the RFC had no further interest in either long-term or spot contracts for Bolivian tin.[32]

The announcement fell on the MNR government like a bombshell. Foreign Minister Wálter Guevara Arze asked Ambassador Sparks if the United States had decided to force Paz out of office.[33] The Paz government used the festivities marking the first anniversary of the revolution in April to express its anger at the U.S. position and increase Bolivian solidarity with other Latin American countries. In pointed protest to official U.S. policy, the list of those invited from the United States consisted almost entirely of labor officials. Gardner Jackson of the CIO and Ernesto Galarza of the AFL were among those who attended.[34] Galarza got into the mood of the event by discussing the exploitation of Mexican migrant workers in the United States and calling for the cooperation of all Western Hemisphere workers. He frankly told peasant and labor leaders to keep their guns "since there had been too many cases of popular revolutions which had been on the verge of final success but had been ruthlessly suppressed once the people had been beguiled by their former masters into laying down their weapons." Embassy officials commented ruefully that Galarza had chosen "an unfortunate focus for his remarks," but took comfort in the fact that at this difficult time he had "unquestionably convinced Bolivians that there was at least one American worth listening to."[35]

The State Department was more concerned about President Paz's remarks. At the anniversary celebrations Paz stressed the anti-imperialist and antifeudal nature of the revolution and warned celebrants of the dangers that imperialist interests posed to true revolutions. Despite its difficulties, Bolivia would not relinquish its sovereign rights, he warned.[36] The angry rhetoric intensified in mid-April as the price of tin slid below $1.00 per pound for the first time since June 1950—a drop that cost Bolivia $18 million in lost foreign exchange. As domestic prices rose and tin prices fell, the Paz government tried to deflect the workers' anger in the direction of the United States. Labor protests took a strong anti-American tone, charging the United States with economic aggression and calling for a spirit of continental solidarity in a "backs-to-the-wall struggle against imperialist machinations." Paz followed on May Day by telling a gathering of miners that he planned to establish relations with Czechoslovakia and was prepared to sell tin wherever he could, "whether to the United States or the popular democracies" of the Eastern bloc.[37]

Eisenhower did not respond well to such rhetorical challenges. The new president was a fervent "cold warrior" with anticommunist beliefs nurtured by the McCarthyite mood of the times as well as by his perception that the Truman administration had failed to maintain sufficient vigilance against the red menace. In a famous passage from his diary, written just before his inauguration, Eisenhower delineated his views of the connections between communism and rising nationalism of the type that led the MNR to nationalize Bolivia's mines and flirt with Eastern bloc nations.

> Nationalism is on the march and world Communism is taking advantage of that spirit of nationalism to cause dissension in the free world. Moscow leads many misguided people to believe that they can count on Communist help to achieve and sustain nationalistic ambitions. Actually what is going on is that the Communists are hoping to take advantage of the confusion . . . to further the aims of world revolution and the Kremlin's domination of all people.[38]

Secretary of State John Foster Dulles's views of the communist threat were well known. He revealed his concerns about Bolivia soon after taking office. In late January, an MNR opponent sent the U.S. embassy in La Paz a document detailing deep communist infiltration of the MNR government. The embassy forwarded the memo to Washington along with a note indicating that the allegations were not new and could not be confirmed. In response, Dulles himself cabled back that there remained "a substantial number of allegations that, if corroborated, would be cause for serious concern as to the present orientation and probable future development of Bolivian government policy."[39]

Coincidentally, the same day the State Department received the document detailing communist infiltration of the MNR regime it also learned about the visit to La Paz by Vice President Julio Estrada de la Hoz of Guatemala, who commented publicly on the similarities and the solidarity existing between his government and Bolivia's.[40] In Guatemala, as in Bolivia, the Truman administration had handed Eisenhower and Dulles unfinished business. Over the next nine months the new administration resolved the two cases with definitive yet sharply contrasting policies by committing funds to help prop up a nationalist revolutionary government backed by Communists in Bolivia and by organizing to covertly overthrow a similar government in Guatemala.[41]

There are a number of reasons why Dulles's concerns about possible communist infiltration of the MNR government did not escalate, as they did in Guatemala, into open U.S. hostility and eventual covert action. Bolivia remained low on priority lists in Washington, partly because it was so distant and different, and more immediately because the United States was awash in tin. Basic U.S. policies in Bolivia emanated from the lower reaches of the State Department and thus perhaps reflected the bureaucratic tendency of diplomats to seek diplomatic solutions in problem areas.[42]

It certainly helped that there was no United Fruit Company in Bolivia to plaster news of radical MNR reforms across the front pages of U.S. newspapers, and that the Bolivian tin companies did not have the same connections at the highest levels of the U.S. government as United Fruit did. Lack of deep economic interests certainly allowed a more dispassionate analysis of events in Bolivia than Guatemala received. Milton Eisenhower, an important advocate of aid to Bolivia, later wrote:

> Sometimes men with selfish interests knowingly make false statements which poison the American mind and enrage the Latin Americans. When Víctor Paz Estenssoro nationalized the tin mines and started a modest program of land reform, many American business leaders promptly called him a Communist. Their statements were widely published. Their view was upheld, in strong language, by the previous mine owners who lived sumptuously abroad.[43]

There is no indication that Eisenhower saw parallels to Guatemala, despite United Fruit's active campaign against the Arbenz government. As Richard Immerman has noted, there was "a fine line [in Washington] separating nationalist reformers from Communist agitators, so fine a line that the distinguishing factor was often the effect of reform on United States interests."[44] Fortunately for the MNR, few U.S. businesses had direct investments in Bolivian tin.

Perhaps more significant in explaining why the U.S. government did not directly intervene to remove the MNR government was the lack of an acceptable alternative to the MNR once the military was decimated, the traditional political parties discredited, and the conservative classes defeated and in retreat. This reality also affected perceptions in

Washington of the threat communism posed. Guatemalan Communists provided a small but well-organized core of support for Arbenz in his struggle against powerful right-wing forces. But in Bolivia, Paz's key initial struggle was with a powerful left. Although Communists likely had as much influence during the early years of the MNR regime as they did in the final years of Arbenz, Washington perceived their influence to be declining in Bolivia while the reverse was true in Guatemala. The MNR's earlier "fascist" label also helped protect it from charges of communism and contributed to the view that the party might, in fact, be the best bulwark against communism in Bolivia.

The way these factors came together to affect U.S. views is illustrated by the embassy's role in the troubled days between the RFC's announcement in early March and Paz's May Day speech. Ambassador Sparks kept the State Department apprised of anti-American developments in Bolivia during the days following the RFC announcement, but he and his staff also took pains to stress the MNR's plight, the political logic behind Bolivian complaints, and the Paz government's attempts to maintain a moderate position. A dispatch to Washington on 30 April contained a thick packet of press clippings on anti-U.S. statements by labor and government leaders. The embassy's commentary merits quoting at length:

> While the present Government retains a high measure of popularity, it lacks a strong military or police force with which to preserve order in the face of a deteriorating economic situation. Consequently as the demagoguery against the United States increases, it will become increasingly difficult for the Bolivian Government to engage in acts of conciliation vis-à-vis the United States. The corollary is that the longer the tin problem remains unsolved, the Government will be less able to resist the Communist attempts to undermine it. Accordingly, it appears urgent that the United States firm up its policy toward Bolivia and, if this policy is to be one of assistance in this difficult period, that it seize the initiative in offering the financial and other aids that may be necessary to keep this tinder box, which might set off a chain reaction in Latin America, from striking fire.[45]

The very same day this message went out to Washington, a memo titled "A Suggested Approach to the Bolivian Problem" circulated in the State Department. The memo began with four premises: the alternatives to the MNR government were chaos or communism; the Bolivian government had managed to win international sympathy and support, meaning that its collapse would seriously damage U.S. relations with hemispheric neighbors; for all its faults, the MNR government came closer than any other entity in Bolivia to "combining the *will,* the *ability,* and the *popular support"* (emphasis in the original) necessary to successfully attack fundamental Bolivian problems; and the MNR was "still somewhat plastic," and thus afforded an opportunity to positively influence a popular government and counter charges that the United States preferred to deal with regional dictators.[46]

The memo went on to outline the gist of what would become U.S. policy toward Bolivia for the next eleven years: a tin contract and food assistance for short-term relief combined with development assistance to reduce Bolivia's long-term dependency on tin. Both types of assistance would encourage the MNR to make Bolivia's economy more market responsive and would further reduce the role of Communists in the Bolivian regime. In July, President Eisenhower himself approved the essence of the plan, and his brother Milton visited Bolivia to discuss it with Paz and other Bolivian leaders. The formal aid package was introduced in October: $9 million in surplus food, $2 million in emergency technical assistance, and an additional $2.4 million for road construction.[47]

Pragmatic Experiments

The flexible U.S. response in Bolivia avoided the hardening hostilities that were to doom President Arbenz in Guatemala. In October 1953, the same month the Eisenhower administration signed the formal aid package with Bolivia, it set in motion Project PBSUCCESS to undermine and overthrow Arbenz. The crucial distinction, according to John Moors Cabot (one of the few U.S. policy makers who provided a public explanation), had to do with the attitude of the Bolivian and Guatemalan regimes toward communism; but since Communists supported both regimes and controlled neither, another difference was likely more important. Bolivia had just reaffirmed its dependency and accepted its place in the hemispheric system dominated by the United States while Guatemala had done neither. These fundamental facts made Guatemala's nationalism less acceptable to U.S. policy makers and caused them to attribute the motives for Guatemala's challenge to U.S. hegemony to unfriendliness, communist infiltration, and "playing the Communist game."[48]

During March and April 1953, the MNR, in frustration, had joined Guatemala in challenging both its dependency on the United States and its subordinate place in the hemispheric system, but on 11 May the State Department informed Ambassador Andrade that a plan of assistance was under discussion. The department made it clear at the same time that neither Congress nor the highest levels of the Eisenhower administration would support the proposal unless the Bolivians worked out compensation agreements with the Big Three—particularly Patiño's North American investors—and returned to a moderate course. Within a month the Bolivians and Patiño had struck a deal.[49] Just as quickly, the MNR dropped initiatives toward the Eastern bloc nations and adopted a politically explosive economic stabilization package in mid-May.[50] Although tin prices continued their slide through May and June, MNR officials scrupulously avoided suggesting U.S. economic aggression, despite the still unfinished tin contract. When in mid-June the Paz government uncovered new rightist plots, MNR and labor union speeches carefully avoided references to *yanqui* imperialism and instead blamed the rosca, Peru's reactionary government, and the Catholic church hierarchy for trying to sabotage pending agreements with the United States.[51]

The MNR's sudden shift from overt anti-Americanism in April and early May 1953 to careful concern not to antagonize the United States by late May and June is striking—so striking, in fact, that some analysts have claimed that this ostensibly nationalist regime was composed of "master-moochers" whose threats and nationalistic posturing were primarily designed to wheedle support from nervous diplomats in Washington.[52] Fredrick Pike claims that because Paz and his close collaborators feared real change emanating from below, intimate relations with the United States were imperative from the outset. To the twin panaceas (land to the Indians, mines to the state) "they added a third: dependency on the United States."[53] But MNR leaders did not command the situation to the degree Pike's statements imply. Both the overt anti-Americanism of April and the compliant acceptance of U.S. dictates in June were products of the same logic of dependency. If anti-Americanism was a genuine and deep-seated reaction of nationalist frustration to Bolivia's weakness, coming to terms with the United States was the product of the regime's acute sense that it needed outside support to survive.

The MNR took Bolivia's development seriously. The country's poverty, dependency, and continuing feudal features were the raison d'être of the revolution, and development was central to the MNR's self-defined task of gaining greater freedom and sovereignty for a weak and dependent nation. Development was also crucial to the party's populist governing strategy of "unite and distribute."[54] Domestic legitimation came from co-optive reform, and satisfying the demands of the party's various constituents required economic growth. Nationalization unequivocally had been the regime's most popular act—a bold assertion of national sovereignty.[55] But nationalization also revealed the depth of Bolivia's historic weaknesses. Bolivia's mines were no longer profitable, tin prices continued in sharp decline, and while tin still provided the bulk of Bolivia's foreign exchange, nearly all its ores went either to the United States or to smelters controlled by the men whose property had just been seized.

Compounding these old problems were new ones. The temptations to overtax the mines, deny them needed investments, and use their resources to grant co-optive concessions to miners or to pay off political supporters became overpowering. Nationalizing the mines had been a popular act of defiant independence that paradoxically revealed the depth of Bolivia's dependency, worsened the regime's development dilemma, and intensified an awareness that Bolivia must diversify its productive base by turning outside for help. In short, nationalist revolutionaries paradoxically needed a powerful patron to carry through their program. These were the bases of the decision by nationalist anti-imperialists to seek outside assistance.

The decision of the United States to provide that aid was equally pragmatic, although the sources of U.S. pragmatism were profoundly different. Many in the Eisenhower administration believed aid to Bolivia was a bad idea; certainly it was a break from normal policy. But for a few in the administration, including Milton Eisenhower and, through him, the president himself, the aid was a quiet experiment in regional cold war hegemony.[56] Convinced that Latin America's deep social and economic ills increased the threat of communism, the Eisenhowers saw Bolivia as a place to experiment. If in Guatemala, as in Iran, they backed covert operations to hold the lines of containment, they were also willing to support fiscally questionable policies to buy tin and send aid to Bolivia if such policies reduced instability in an area where communism threatened to take root. Bolivia caught their attention and drew their sympathetic support because it seemed at once authentically reformist and authentically noncommunist.

The strategic interests of the United States and a larger vision of America and its role in the hemisphere came together to pique the Eisenhowers' interest in this small, impoverished, and faraway place. But perhaps because Bolivia was small, impoverished, and isolated, President Eisenhower failed to sustain his interest. Instead of inaugurating a fundamental change in cold war policy toward Latin America, Eisenhower's action in Bolivia was essentially a crisis-managing contingency plan—at best a pragmatic experiment under special conditions when normal policies no longer worked. The decision to cancel tin discussions in March made economic sense to a fiscally conservative administration, but without prospects of a tin contract there was no leverage on Bolivia's nationalist regime, and without tin revenues, Bolivia descended rapidly toward chaos. As Judge Magruder had warned a decade earlier, the issues of tin and tin prices were back in North American laps. U.S. policies during World War II had done little to decrease Bolivian dependency on tin, and the increased U.S. leverage over the tin market did nothing to solve the problem. Now that prices were falling and its tin stocks were rising, the United States was forced to confront the legitimacy of Bolivia's postwar negotiating position. Bolivia either needed special treatment or it must be written off as a wartime casualty—a casualty that U.S. officials now feared Communists could exploit.

Even fiscal hard-liners in the Eisenhower administration such as Secretary of the Treasury George Humphrey preferred giving direct assistance to help Bolivia diversify away from tin rather than to subsidize the nationalized mines by paying above-market prices. Economic aid theoretically avoided propping up a sick industry, but it also gave the United States maximum leverage over the nationalist regime and, by reducing the importance of the tin industry, undercut the power of Lechín and the labor-left. The objectives of aid were to provide enough support to keep moderates in power and to nudge Bolivia in what was considered a proper direction. The goal was to withdraw aid as soon as feasible and to maintain a low profile to discourage other Latin American countries from seeking similar assistance. As a contingency plan, Eisenhower's decision to provide aid was rooted in a cold war frugality that encouraged minimal efforts and expenditures to accomplish essential strategic goals in a less than strategically crucial place. Meanwhile, Bolivia's willingness to accept U.S. aid was a measure of that country's weakness, dependency, and rising desperation. A relationship fashioned under such conditions must inevitably be riven by conflict.

5   The Limits of Pragmatism and the Disintegration of a Special Partnership

In early March 1959, Bolivia erupted in several days of violent anti-American protests. The triggering incident was a story in *Time* magazine that quoted an unnamed U.S. embassy source to the effect that Bolivia and its problems should perhaps be divided among its neighbors. Bolivians' response to the alleged comment was immediate and furious. In La Paz, protestors seized copies of *Time* from newsstands and burned them, along with flags and other U.S. symbols, in front of the U.S. embassy. Over the next several days, public protest spread to other cities and escalated into attacks on U.S. property and denunciations of U.S. imperialism. When calm finally returned on 5 March, two Bolivians had died, scores had been injured, and damage to U.S. property topped $70,000.[1]

The explosive resentment unnerved U.S. citizens residing in the lower reaches of La Paz. Only a single access road wound up through the heart of the workers' district to possible rescue at the airport on the altiplano, and evacuation procedures were useless. A visiting administrator from the University of Tennessee described the city as "a giant trap." "Bolivians," he added, had acquired "a sudden taste of hate-America and were not prepared to do more than destroy accessible property." The next time, he predicted, would be worse.[2]

What motivated such anti-Americanism in a country that had received more U.S. assistance per capita over the previous six years than any other country in the Western Hemisphere? Víctor Andrade, Bolivia's foreign minister at the time of the riot, later wrote that "morbid anti-Americanism . . . has no historical justification" in a country without a history of direct U.S. exploitation.[3] Yet Andrade, a major advocate and architect of the special aid partnership between the United States and Bolivia's revolutionary nationalist regime, complained bitterly to *Time* that North America was tight-fisted and controlling, and during the riots he exacerbated tensions with fiery anti-U.S. rhetoric.[4]

Andrade's role reveals the irony of the situation: it was the special partnership itself that was primary source of this "sudden taste of hate-America." Over the previous six years the reality of U.S. power, the assumptions underlying U.S. policy, and the fact of Bolivian dependency made it all too easy for conflict to escalate. U.S. assistance slipped easily into a series of impositions, and Bolivia's need for assistance moved just as easily into submission, resentment, and then bitter hostility. Adding to the irony is the fact that these conflict-filled dynamics played out not just once but twice during the decade following the initial aid decision in 1953, revealing that the cause was more than mere misunderstanding and that the conflicts were, in fact, rooted in several deeper paradoxes.

Aid and the Paradox of Bolivian Dependency

The MNR government formed its special relationship with the United States because party leaders hoped a patron could provide the development assistance necessary to reduce future dependency. The Paz government understood that demands would accompany the assistance—that is the way a patron-client bond works—and Eisenhower officials quickly made one condition abundantly clear: the Bolivian government must make a complete and open break with Communists and fellow travelers.[5]

MNR leaders were not particularly averse to such an imposition. The relationship between the Movimiento Nacionalista Revolucionario and the Marxist left had always been a marriage of convenience, and Paz was not about to jeopardize U.S. assistance to maintain a loveless bond to the Bolivian communist parties.[6] But events in Guatemala revealed the costs of cold war conformity for nationalists who based part of their multiclass appeal on anti-imperialism. MNR leaders and Bolivians in general sympathized deeply with President Arbenz of Guatemala. He had been the first Latin American leader to recognize Bolivia's revolutionary regime in 1952, and his conflicts with the United Fruit Company reminded Bolivian nationalists of their own struggles with the tin-mining "superstate." Nonetheless, at the Caracas Conference in March 1954 Bolivia reluctantly backed U.S.-sponsored anticommunist initiatives aimed transparently at Guatemala. In June, Bolivia supported U.S. calls for hemispheric consultations when Guatemala "violated" the Caracas accords by importing arms from the Soviet bloc; and later that month, when Arbenz fell, the Bolivian government was silent.[7]

None of this had been easy for nationalist revolutionaries. The U.S. call for joint hemispheric consultations was particularly unpalatable to party leaders because it reminded them of the consultations held in 1943 to sanction Villarroel. Paz's cabinet held lengthy and heated discussions before a consensus emerged that Bolivia could support the United States only if allowed to explicitly separate the issues of communism and United Fruit, and then only in exchange for more assistance. Washington, anxious to guarantee the support of at least one popular reform government for its anticommunist initiatives, quickly cleared an additional $3 million in food aid and kept the Texas City smelter open for yet another year. In turn, Bolivia fell in line.[8]

The Guatemalan situation forced the MNR to forfeit foreign policy independence, desert a sister revolutionary regime, and violate its own noninterventionist principles in order to guarantee the continuing flow of assistance deemed necessary to survival and development. Much later, Wálter Guevara Arze, the foreign minister at the time, described Bolivia's position as "stretching one's feet to the edges of the sheets."[9] The aphorism makes sense to anyone who has spent a frigid night in an unheated room in La Paz: there is freedom of movement, but only within circumscribed limits. Beyond those limits lies exposure, and Bolivia's patron had clearly placed Guatemala outside the sheets.

When the party newspaper, La Nación, broke its silence on Guatemala after the coup, it put a spin on the story that justified the regime's compromises and reinforced its relationship with the United States. Developments in Guatemala, the paper editorialized, showed that communist allies could not be trusted. Communists operated under international orders and were willing to expose and betray legitimate nationalist aspirations—as recent events in Guatemala, British Guiana, and Iran revealed.[10] Left unstated was the fact that Communists had directly caused none of these nationalist governments to fall. Privately, Juan Lechín put it more bluntly to a U.S. official: "Understand, I'm an anti-imperialist. Naturally, because I'm Bolivian. But when it comes to a choice between Russia and the United States, I'm with the United States. Who do we think we are—a small and impoverished country—that we can afford to disregard the fact that we are a part of the American orbit?"[11] The regime had set its course, and the core of labor and political leaders accepted Bolivia's place as a satellite in North American orbit. It was often an uncomfortable place for nationalists, but because the Paz government accepted it, Bolivia received some rewards and expected others. The key reward the MNR continued to seek was assistance to diversify the country's economy, for only by doing so could MNR leaders perhaps resolve their nationalist paradox and escape the humiliations implicit in their weakness.

The MNR accepted the recommendations of the 1942 Bohan report that Bolivia steer investments away from tin and toward petroleum and agricultural development in the eastern lowlands.[12] This emphasis on developing Bolivia's frontier east has come under retrospective criticism, but in the context of 1953–54, with tin prices falling, world surpluses mounting, and Bolivia's production costs rising, the economic wisdom of diversifying away from tin and the political logic of pursuing a plan to which the United States was already ostensibly committed seemed self-evident. During the year and a half after the first aid agreement was signed, the Paz government poured its own limited resources into exploring for petroleum and constructing an all-weather road to Santa Cruz. Sympathetic officials in Washington dangled the carrot of development assistance before them, conditional on meeting cold war requirements. The Paz government responded dutifully by attacking Communists and fellow travelers and following the U.S. line in international affairs.

Unfortunately, in many ways the carrot was an illusion. Eisenhower was in an economizing mood, as was Congress, and together they trimmed commitments to foreign aid except in high-priority cold war areas. U.S. development loans to Latin America shrank from $275 million in 1952 to $40 million in 1953, and ExIm Bank credits went from $147 million to $7.6 million in the same period. The Eisenhower administration instead pushed Latin American governments to attract private investors, even though direct private U.S. investments in Latin America between 1952 and 1955 also fell.[13]

Bolivia offered few attractions to private U.S. investors, and, ironically, the more the Paz government cooperated on cold war issues, the less interested Washington became. After the Guatemalan coup, technical assistance to Bolivia was reduced as the State Department channeled its limited pool of discretionary funds to "higher priority" projects in that new anticommunist showcase.[14] Meanwhile, the ExIm Bank trimmed loans allocated to the Santa Cruz road project to less than one-fourth the amount requested by the State Department, even though the Paz government made more progress on the highway in two years than its predecessors had in ten. Despite promising oil discoveries, the Eisenhower administration also refused to consider loans to Yacimientos Petrolíferos Fiscales Bolivianos because of policy strictures against assisting state-run oil companies.[15]

What the United States *did* have, and for domestic reasons *could* provide, was surplus food, and of the $13.4 million in aid authorized in November 1953, $9 million came as food, with another $3 million added the following March as a reward for Bolivia's position at the Caracas Conference. The donated food was sold for local currency (counterpart funds) that was to be invested in agricultural development projects approved jointly by U.S. and Bolivian officials. This was a creative approach, considering the policy restrictions imposed in Washington, but the pitfalls of using food assistance to encourage agricultural development are obvious. Food shipments swamped Bolivia's limited port facilities in Chile and Peru; wheat imports caused domestic grain production to shrink by two-thirds by 1955; and imports of surplus flour meant that by 1960 Bolivian millers were operating at 11 percent of capacity. Sometimes the ironies were striking. A project to produce yucca flour failed because the flour competed neither in price nor in taste with the surplus U.S. wheat flour sold to finance the project.[16]

In a deeper and less humorous irony, food assistance reinforced structural economic distortions that eroded MNR legitimacy. The donated food prolonged economically foolish but politically expedient policies to subsidize food imports, policies that pleased urban consumers and miners but prolonged the stagnation of the grain-growing peasant highlands. And though donated foodstuffs were to be sold at market value, their prices were pegged at an official exchange rate that by 1955 was one-fourth the black-market rate. Access to U.S. surplus food thus became a lucrative perquisite to those well connected to the regime that allowed them to smuggle commodities into neighboring countries or resell them on the black market. It would be unfair to blame U.S. food assistance for all the distortions in Bolivia's economy or for the erosion of MNR legitimacy, but surplus food clearly contributed to both processes and did little to diversify or develop Bolivia's production.

Through 1955, with tin prices still low and foreign exchange reserves dwindling rapidly, Bolivia's inflation rate began to escalate geometrically. At a private dinner party with President Paz and his cabinet in April 1955, U.S. ambassador Gerald Drew tentatively tossed out the idea that the United States could send a team of North American experts to survey the fiscal and economic crisis. Drew cabled Washington that both Paz and Foreign Minister Guevara "jumped at the idea gleefully," adding that this was "perhaps a Bolivian conditioned response."[17]

If, indeed, there *was* such a response, it was one conditioned by deepening dependency and rising desperation. Bolivia's negotiating position had deteriorated since U.S. aid began. Two months after Drew made his offer, the United States and Bolivia agreed to a ten-point "Joint Program" that essentially linked continuing levels of assistance to deeper Bolivian concessions of autonomy. The Bolivians agreed, among other things, to invite U.S. consultants to survey COMIBOL and suggest ways to improve its productivity; to contract a fiscal mission, approved by the United States, to help them control inflation; to begin servicing their defaulted international debt from the 1920s; to promulgate a liberalized oil code that would open the country to private oil companies; to issue investment guarantees and other incentives to reassure foreign investors; and to intensify efforts to "eradicate the influences of international Communism." There was no need for quid pro quos, one State Department memo noted, because all these measures were deemed beneficial to Bolivia. Nonetheless, to make the package more politically palatable in La Paz, the United States agreed to extend the tin contract another year (Congress had already decided to keep the Texas City smelter open another year for domestic political reasons) and to provide Bolivia an additional $6 million in food grants.[18]

Certainly Paz and Guevara now understood that U.S. assistance was no panacea. Yet that realization only reduced their options. Because Bolivia had not been directly dependent on the United States in the past, new aid commitments from Washington fostered hopes in La Paz that North Americans had the answers if the regime submitted still further. But Richard Frederick observes that as such hopes faded into disillusionment, a growing number of Bolivians came to believe that the United States, not the tin barons or the rosca, was the cause of their country's continuing poverty, governmental incompetence, and dependency.[19]

Aid and the Paradoxes of North American Power

In January 1954, Milton Eisenhower sent his brother a confidential appendix to the report on his trip to South America.

> The emergency aid extended Bolivia by this government has been of fundamental importance in easing the critical situation and preventing Bolivia's rapid descent into economic chaos with consequences that could have been favorable only to the Communists. . . . Our extension of aid to Bolivia had immediate success from the viewpoint of our political interests through the strengthening of moderate members of the government and by making it possible for them to take increasingly strong steps against Communist elements in the country. We should continue our emergency efforts which are in our own national interests to help Bolivia strengthen

and diversify. . . . Now that we have begun this program, we must not abandon it in mid-stream.[20]

In forwarding this confidential supplement to Secretary of State Dulles, the president added a note: "I am struck by the fact that in a number of cases, a very small loan investment or grant on our part might reap very extensive advantages to us." This was policy as Dwight Eisenhower liked it—effective and cheap.

That same month an embassy report from La Paz sounded a more somber note. There was no immediate prospect that Bolivia could develop its internal resources sufficiently "to lift itself by its own boot straps" anytime soon; the country would remain "something of an international ward for several years to come." Nonetheless, the report continued, aid maintained relative political stability and provided leverage for "channelizing [*sic*] Bolivian emotions and energies toward a type of society broadly consistent with American objectives." "Especially," the memo added, "if the aid given continues to be contingent upon a Bolivian trend in this direction."[21]

In fact, U.S. policy makers were nowhere near the middle of a stream that would prove frustratingly difficult to "channelize." They knew that food grants and technical assistance programs would provide no quick fix, but a year and a half into the aid relationship, their answer to the problems emerging to that point was more of the same—more food, more conditions, more direct involvement in Bolivian affairs, and more emphasis on playing by the capitalist rules that had worked so well for the United States. From President Eisenhower on down, U.S. officials overestimated their ability to mold their Bolivian clients and failed to recognize the limits of North American power.

Some of the limits were self-imposed. President Eisenhower's cold war frugality placed fiscal and philosophical restrictions on his administration and limited its ability to act except where strategic stakes were high. Yet there were other, more profound limits, and Eisenhower revisionists now argue that a measure of Dwight Eisenhower's greatness as president may rest in his awareness of at least some of them. He knew that finite material resources meant that the United States had to prioritize and choose what *could* be done rather than try to do everything that *might* be done. He also understood that creating programs and throwing taxpayer resources at distant and difficult problems had no intrinsic merit. What he perhaps did not fully realize was the limits of the ideological and spiritual resources that he considered America's greatest strengths or the limited value of his own successful country as a viable model to a country like Bolivia.

Louis Hartz, in an extended discussion of Tocqueville's observation that Americans are "born free," argues that the North American dilemma "is that of a liberal nation seeking and needing to understand a world that is largely illiberal." Because Americans did not have to undergo a profound social revolution in order to become free, they tend to exaggerate the ease by which societies modernize; and because their nation was, from the beginning, decidedly and precociously independent—even when weak—they fail to give sufficient weight to the structures of exploitation and dependency that complicate the process of development and modernization in much of the world, particularly when that dependency is on the United States.[22]

The story of aid to Bolivia between 1953 and 1964 is a small part of the larger story of a progressive realization of the difficulties of remaking the Third World in the North American image and the disillusionment that accompanied that realization. The passage of the Joint Program marked the first stage. By 1955, Eisenhower officials understood that a minimal investment might *not* reap "extensive advantages to us," as Eisenhower himself had initially hoped, and that more direct pressure and guidance were required to "channelize" Bolivia's revolution.

Both the United States and the MNR moved quickly to implement the Joint Program. The degree, nature, and extent of the new North American tutelary role are perhaps best exemplified by the oil code opening Bolivia to private foreign investors, which was written by U.S. lawyers and enacted without public debate or modification by Bolivian authorities. The most immediately difficult and significant provision of the Joint Program was the one requiring fiscal stabilization. Negotiations continued through late 1955 and early 1956 against the backdrop of Bolivian elections. The MNR candidate, Hernán Siles Zuazo, won a resounding victory, although the strength in the cities of the rightist Falange Socialista Boliviana (FSB) revealed the MNR's eroding middle-class support. The irony was that after four years of populist appeal to labor and peasants, the MNR was now ready, with U.S. assistance, to reconfirm its own essentially bourgeois-capitalist vision.

The State Department contracted George Jackson Eder from International Telephone and Telegraph to lead the stabilization team. A colorful, self-assured man with a strong free-market bias and a broad definition of his mandate, Eder believed that the remedy for runaway inflation was simple: Bolivia's economy must be opened to market forces and the public sector dismantled. He pushed, probed, cajoled, and set limits; at times his profile was too high to suit the State Department. One memo called him "hard to control" and added that his public statements left the United States "unnecessarily open to imputations of 'imperialism,' 'intervention,' and 'colonialism'" (Eder's own, remarkably candid, account of his mission clearly reveals how each of those terms might apply). But whatever the department's reservations concerning Eder's methods, it gave him full discretion to use aid as a lever to push his agenda—an agenda, Eder was quick to admit, that meant "the repudiation, at least tacitly, of virtually everything that the Revolutionary Government had done over the previous four years."[23]

The stabilization plan went into effect in December 1956, creating a single fluctuating exchange rate that reflected supply and demand. Overnight a complex system of multiple exchange rates ended—a system that, in some way, subsidized every key faction in the MNR coalition except peasants. Prices jolted suddenly upward while wages remained frozen. Juan Lechín initially supported stabilization, but ever sensitive to changing political winds and to the complaints of rank-and-file miners, went instead into opposition. Labor's conflict with the Siles government escalated through the early months of 1957, and a showdown loomed on 1 July, when the Central Obrera Boliviana planned a general strike to force Siles to abandon what it now called "Plan Eder." At the last minute the crucial transport workers' union broke ranks, spurred by Eder's approval of new fuel subsidies, despite his free-market principles, and the strike collapsed.[24]

Eder, the State Department, and the Siles government each had expected immediate political conflicts but were sustained, to varying degrees, by their assumption that once the economy became responsive to the market, economic growth would soothe political tensions. Instead the market played a cruel trick. In early 1957, tin prices began another slide and tin earnings for the six months after stabilization fell almost 27 percent from the previous year. Then, in mid-year, the world economy began to slip into a sharp recession that reduced tin exports from 28,242 metric tons in 1957 to 18,013 metric tons in 1958.[25] Both the United States and Ambassador Andrade blamed Soviet dumping of Chinese tin for the sudden collapse of prices, but since other Bolivian metals showed similar export declines, the 1957–58 metals market recession cannot be attributed solely to the Soviets, even if doing so had obvious propaganda value to both MNR moderates and the United States.[26]

U.S. policies also contributed to Bolivia's problems. In 1957 Congress finally closed the Texas smelter, forcing Bolivia to find new buyers at a time when the market was particularly weak. Congress also suspended subsidies to tungsten producers that had been initiated in 1950 to encourage friendly countries to replace supplies lost to Communist China. With its tungsten reserves filled, the United States in 1957 abruptly ended the subsidy, costing Bolivia between $10 and $15 million annually in lost revenue. A year later, under strong pressure from domestic U.S. producers, President Eisenhower also approved a new tariff on lead and zinc. Bolivia's lead production fell only slightly, but its annual zinc earnings plummeted by 83 percent between 1957 and 1959. The whole matter reminded Bolivians of a lesson they already knew quite well— the invisible hand that their U.S. advisers so highly touted was often influenced by strong arms that were not their own. By the end of 1958, Bolivia's total foreign exchange earnings were at 60 percent of their 1955 levels.[27]

To stabilize the tin market, the International Tin Council cut Bolivia's quota 31 percent, thus setting in motion layoffs mandated by the International Monetary Fund (IMF). To keep costs in the state-run mines in line with earnings, and to keep stabilization on track, the IMF also pushed another sharp devaluation of the boliviano. Siles resisted, knowing that a devaluation would upset the delicate balance of prices, wages, and budgets already achieved, but with the United States backing the IMF's position and now providing 32 percent of Bolivia's total central government revenues, he had little room to maneuver.

In September 1958 the International Tin Council abandoned price supports and the London market suspended tin sales. Bolivia faced an immediate foreign exchange crisis. At an angry meeting with U.S. ambassador Philip Bonsal, MNR leaders charged that U.S. policy had failed in every way except to create ill will toward the United States. Bonsal gamely defended stabilization and the U.S. aid program, but the criticisms he heard at the meeting were similar to ones he was voicing privately to his superiors in Washington.[28]

Bonsal had more than a bureaucrat's interest in the Bolivian experiment. He had been a member of the Good Neighbor policy team assembled by Sumner Welles in the late 1930s and had been recording officer during Franklin Roosevelt's 1942 meeting with Bolivian president Enrique Peñaranda. In his memorandum describing that conversation Bonsal noted that Roosevelt "advocated that Bolivia follow a strongly nationalistic policy, avoiding so far as possible dependence upon other countries and particularly upon capitalistic interests in other countries." That position clearly clashed with Eisenhower's policies.[29] Just before being assigned to Bolivia, Bonsal had been recalled from Colombia when dictator Gustavo Rojas Pinilla complained that the ambassador maintained open contacts with Colombia's democratic opposition.[30] Bonsal came to Bolivia as a friend of democratic reform who could help steer U.S.-Bolivian relations through the turmoil that was certain to accompany stabilization. Now Bonsal warned Washington that, despite U.S. aid, Bolivia was worse off than it had been in 1956.[31]

In early 1959, on his way to a new assignment as ambassador to the government of Fidel Castro, Bonsal told his superiors in Washington that aid to Bolivia still had not moved to the promised development phase. Summing up his frustration, Bonsal stated:

> In the 6th year of U.S. aid for Bolivia and the 3rd year of stabilization, the free world system is really on trial. What we are trying to do is demonstrate that our system is good for Bolivia and can solve its problems. We are trying to do this in the face of attractive blandishments and opposition from the Communist and anti-U.S. world. Unfortunately, we have not yet demonstrated we can handle the problem. . . . What the U.S. and the free world have to offer Bolivia today is still a picture of decreasing employment . . . and the prospect of only vague compensations in return for the sacrifice which is said to be inevitable.[32]

In Cuba, Bonsal would again be reminded of the limits of U.S. power. For all its influence and despite its own success and apparent good intentions, the United States was finding it increasingly difficult to guide, much less "channelize," its neighbors to the south.

Aid and New Sources of Conflict

Unrest in the mines threatened Vice President Richard Nixon's visit to Bolivia in early May 1958, part of his grand tour of South America. Problems had already erupted in Argentina and Chile along the vice president's route, and security officials briefed Nixon and the Secret Service on the dangers his party might encounter along the narrow streets of La Paz. Nonetheless, things remained calm along the five-mile route from the airport down through the workers' district that less than a year later would remind North Americans of a giant trap. This time the route from El Alto was lined with cheering throngs who welcomed Nixon with placards, miniature American flags, and showers of confetti.[33]

But this surface cordiality hid the erosion that became apparent a year later. Stabilization and the resulting conflicts had changed Bolivia's political rules. In the new market-oriented economy, Siles and his party could no longer serve as popular brokers dispensing economic favors to satisfy the interests of competing groups. As tin and other mineral revenues declined through 1958, the MNR government faced the task of allocating losses in a negative-sum game, and Siles preserved his delicate political balance by pitting interest groups against each other in an increasingly complicated strategy of divide and dominate. He reintroduced the military as a political actor, involved peasant militias as a counter to labor, and worked to widen splits in the labor movement by encouraging the personal ambitions of anti-Lechín labor bosses. It was a highly complex and divisive political strategy, and it was not so much that the party and the president lost political support as that their support fragmented into all its component interest groups.[34]

As North Americans watched their experiment founder, they were divided on where to place the blame. A few like Bonsal questioned underlying U.S. assumptions and commitment. Others blamed Bolivians. In 1956, historian J. Fred Rippy wrote an article titled "Bolivia: An Exhibit of the Problems of Economic Development in Retarded Countries," which describes Bolivians as an "enervated people" cursed with an unfavorable physical environment and "a wretched state of mind." The article liberally quotes a piece in the *National Review* that claims that Bolivians suffer "a particular kind of madness" that makes them blame their problems on everyone but themselves. It is foolish, the *National Review* concludes (with Rippy obviously concurring), to treat madness with dollars and technology.[35]

As problems grew within the program and criticism mounted from without, those still committed to assistance were inclined to increase U.S. control and direct involvement in the daily operation of the Bolivian government. Most of the technical assistance to Bolivia was channeled through *servicios*, institutions originating in Nelson Rockefeller's wartime Office of Inter-American Affairs. The OIAA created the first servicios to attack public health problems and increase production of such vital wartime resources as rubber. Fearing that advisers might be ignored or that direct U.S. control of programs would spark nationalist resentment, the OIAA developed the servicio as a compromise solution, "endowed with special authority" by the host country and "with special personnel" by the United States.[36] President Truman expanded the basic partnership concept in his Point IV program, and by 1958 Bolivia had servicios for agriculture, education, public health, and road maintenance. Together the servicios employed 118 North Americans and 5,000 Bolivians.[37]

But this partnership, too, was weakened by patron-client dynamics. Because the United States provided almost all the funding for the servicios, it insisted on selecting the Bolivian personnel. The Bolivian government complained bitterly that U.S. administrators often filled positions with MNR opponents, thus creating a subversive "fifth column" within its own ministries.[38] A study commissioned by the International Cooperation Agency (ICA; an independent agency of the State Department that was the predecessor to USAID) admitted that U.S. advisers often promoted techniques without sufficiently understanding their applicability to the Bolivian situation and had little respect for their government "partners," who were paid a fraction of what they received. Although the servicios attempted to introduce administrative reform, they were themselves an administrative nightmare, answering to the ICA, the embassy, and the Bolivian government.[39]

As Bolivia's negative-sum game worsened through 1958, the conflicting objectives of those three bodies became obvious. Bonsal argued that the United States must back Siles more unequivocally and withdraw philosophical objections to assisting state entities such as COMIBOL and YPFB. On the other hand, the ICA, which provided the bulk of the stabilization fund, saw its role as keeping Siles's toes to the coals. Many in the ICA shared Eder's view that the MNR government was corrupt and incompetent. According to one ICA official, the problem, in a nutshell, was that "the U.S. gives advice and when the country doesn't take it, we help them anyway"—an indirect rebuke of Bonsal's advocacy in Washington.[40] Meanwhile, MNR leaders lost faith that U.S. assistance would resolve their nationalist paradox and stood at the fringes of the debate, their resentment growing.

New international conditions complicated matters. In 1953, when Bolivia first turned to the United States for assistance, the world had been a simpler place—locked in a bipolar struggle that provided few options to a small nation in the Western Hemisphere. During the interim, new nations emerged from colonialism and began to articulate a nonaligned position that appealed to many in the MNR. Sputnik added credence to the Marxist thesis that the capitalist nations were in decline and the socialist nations in ascent, especially as another recession slowed the dynamism of the capitalist world system. By 1959, Stalin and his fierce insularity were gone, replaced by a more activist and friendly Khrushchev. Soviet imports from Latin America grew from $40 million in 1953 to $180 million by 1955, and their exports showed a similar rise at a time when U.S. private investment and government assistance were declining. In mid-1958, the Soviets took advantage of simmering Bolivian resentment at continued U.S. refusals to loan money to YPFB by offering the national petroleum company a $60 million loan at 2.5 percent interest. Siles assured Washington that he was not inclined to accept the Soviet offer but was furious when the Eisenhower administration still refused to consider assisting YPFB despite Bonsal's entreaties on his behalf.[41]

Finally there was Cuba. The day after Fidel Castro took power, *La Nación* devoted its entire editorial page to the successful revolution, praising it, analyzing it, making explicit comparisons with the 1952 revolution in Bolivia, and offering advice to Cuba's new leaders. But with a showdown looming with the International Monetary Fund, the Cuban revolution also reminded many Bolivians of the degree to which they no longer controlled their own revolution. On 5 January large crowds gathered in La Paz to celebrate Castro's victory, then marched on the American embassy to chant, "¡*Bolivia libre, sí! ¡Colonia yanqui, no!*"[42]

The IMF now insisted not only on devaluation, but also that the government end its subsidies to the COMIBOL stores, or *pulperías*. Prices of staples in the *pulperías* were often set at a fraction of market prices and subsidized miners' salaries in two ways—by keeping miners' food costs low, and by providing them with a small surplus that they could resell.[43] The miners fiercely resisted losing this perquisite, and to stiffen the government's will, the United States withheld aid in early 1959, making it contingent on the government meeting IMF requirements.

In mid-1958, Siles had brought Wálter Guevara back from France to become his minister of government, and Víctor Andrade from Washington to serve as foreign minister. Guevara and Andrade were the MNR's strongest advocates of the special partnership with the United

States, and Siles placed them in those positions to consolidate the influence of those committed to stabilization before the 1960 elections. Now it was Guevara who confronted the internal disorders that accompanied each new round of IMF-mandated belt tightening; and it was Andrade who had to defend the increasingly unpopular relationship with Washington.

Both men had a host of reasons to resent the heavy U.S. hand, some of them personal. More than thirty years later, Guevara clearly recalled an incident in January 1959 that symbolized all that frustrated him. During his 1956–58 term as ambassador to France, Guevara had been impressed by a group of Chinese acrobats who came to Paris. When he invited them to La Paz in 1959, however, he was forced to withdraw the invitation after U.S. officials expressed "deep concern" about the visit by "a propaganda wing of the Chinese Communist government."[44] Andrade had his own incident that rankled. Soon after returning to La Paz from the embassy in Washington, he paid a courtesy call at the home of a departing ICA official. The American did not recognize the foreign minister, whose indigenous features did not immediately mark him as a member of Bolivia's elite, and yelled to his wife in English—which Andrade spoke perfectly—that a "savage" was at the door.[45]

It was Andrade who confronted embassy officials with the quote in *Time* on 27 February. The next day, he broke the story to Bolivians at large at a morning press conference, saying that his government recognized the "just popular reaction" that the story might evoke. It was Guevara who, in consultation with Siles, vetoed security measures outside the U.S. embassy the next day because, in Siles's words, "the people must be allowed to demonstrate." In part because of the lax security, the situation deteriorated quickly during the afternoon. By nightfall, Siles, Andrade, and Guevara realized that they had underestimated the depth of public hostility to the United States. All through that night, Siles and his cabinet met with Lechín and other labor leaders, trying to convince them to exert their influence to avoid violence at the COB demonstration scheduled for the next afternoon. Meanwhile, the president advised the U.S. embassy to evacuate, and for the first time since the revolution, called up military forces to keep peace in the capital.[46]

Amid stringent security measures, Siles himself spoke at the COB rally. Back in 1953, Bolivian leaders had argued that the country could find economic independence by turning to the United States for assistance. Now coming full circle, the president told Bolivian workers that only self-sacrifice could free Bolivia from dependency on aid and lead to true sovereignty. The paradox of seeking economic independence by finding a patron had heightened rather than reduced Bolivia's dependency, and had led to frustration and finally to hostility. Yet the paradox remained, and soon after his speech to the COB, Siles privately told U.S. officials that he feared the riots would curtail future aid. "All we can do," he told embassy officials, "is hope for the best and prepare for the worst."[47]

When peace returned, the embassy publicly blamed the rioting on Communists, knowing that doing so would leverage the Siles government into further anticommunist action and reduce criticism of Bolivian policies back in the United States. But the embassy's confidential assessments of the affair pinned the blame squarely on Siles, Guevara, and Andrade, recognizing that the Siles administration's "all-too-intimate" collaboration with the United States made such men even more resentful of the United States than were many common Bolivians.[48] For both sides, it seemed time to reevaluate the collaboration.

Reevaluating and Renewing the Unequal Partnership

In 1955, after a visit to Central America, Vice President Nixon told a meeting of the National Security Council (NSC) that Latin American affairs probably seemed "small potatoes" when compared "to the weighty matters thus far discussed." Even so, he continued, the region should not be taken for granted.[49] Three years later, violent disruptions of his South American tour in Lima, Bogotá, and Caracas brought that fact vividly home to the vice president and his country. When Nixon returned to the NSC to report on his 1958 trip, he did not need to begin with deprecating apologies. Communism threatened Latin America, he told the council, and neither the democratic system nor the system of private enterprise provided a safeguard.⁵⁰ In direct response to this wake-up call, President Eisenhower expanded aid programs, agreed finally to fund a regional development bank, and pledged support for a new Social Development Fund. Eisenhower, his advocates claim, took the first steps toward the new policy that his successor would name the Alliance for Progress, and in doing so drew on U.S.-Bolivian precedents. When Fidel Castro came to power in Cuba, the administration offered him an assistance package similar to the one it had offered President Paz and chose Bonsal as ambassador.⁵¹

The irony, of course, is that at the same time the Eisenhower administration began to draw on its Bolivian experiences, it began to *withdraw* from Bolivia. Through the rest of 1959 and 1960, Washington dismantled the servicios, withdrew North American personnel from Bolivia, and cut funding for fiscal year 1960 by one-third. But no one in an influential position seems to have considered the larger implications of the problems in Bolivia.⁵²

The discussion at the NSC meeting following Vice President Nixon's trip is revealing. The vice president stated that the answer to U.S. problems in Latin America "was certainly not just better publicity"; however, the discussion that followed focused almost entirely on just that. Nixon wondered how foreign investment could be more effectively presented as a way to raise living standards, and thus counter arguments that private capitalists exploited Latin America's resources. The president thought that perhaps the United States should try to coin a new phrase to replace the term *capitalism,* with its connotations of imperialism; and Dulles suggested that U.S. personnel increase person-to-person contacts. Nixon closed the discussion by stating that the United States must counteract the ideological appeal of communism as an economic system by reminding Latin Americans that, politically, Soviet-style communism meant dictatorship and foreign control.⁵³

If top Eisenhower officials had followed the shock of the Nixon trip by taking a closer look at their Bolivia experiment, they might have realized that the problems in Latin America were too fundamental to be solved by mere repackaging. The MNR had agreed that communism meant dictatorship and foreign control, and in a monumental gamble had turned to the United States to achieve the development it believed was a prerequisite to reducing its dependency on tin. The result instead was enough foreign interference in Bolivia's internal affairs to justify later claims that it represented a "particularly pure form of neo-colonialism."[54] Bolivians also had gambled that private foreign investments and the capitalist path meant improved standards of living, not exploitation; yet the results so far—to paraphrase Bonsal—were decreasing employment and increased sacrifice. The Bolivians had accepted a deluge of experts, analysts, and assorted goodwill ambassadors from the United States. In return, the face-to-face contact that Dulles favored had resulted in an unprecedented wave of anti-Americanism. In short, the Eisenhower administration had tried its new packaging in Bolivia, and the *Time* incident proved it wanting.

As the United States backed away from its special partnership with Bolivia in late 1959 and 1960, Bolivia also retreated. Before the 1960 elections, Víctor Paz renewed a populist revolutionary alliance by taking Juan Lechín as his running mate. The new administration restored anti-imperialism to its nationalist agenda, and Paz strengthened Bolivia's ties to the nonaligned movement by opening relations with the United Arab Republic, inviting Yugoslavia's President Tito and Indonesia's President Sukarno to visit Bolivia, and sending observers to the Belgrade Conference of nonaligned nations.[55]

The Paz government also initiated closer contacts with the socialist bloc. Bolivia sent a series of official visitors to the Soviet Union, defiantly exchanged visits with Communist China, opened a legation in Czechoslovakia, and reaffirmed ties to Cuba despite that country's growing problems with the United States. Soviet premier Khrushchev responded to initiatives from La Paz by offering the Paz government $150 million in direct assistance. In December 1960, four members of the Supreme Soviet visited La Paz and confirmed Khrushchev's offer of funds for YPFB, loans for road and railroad construction, and technical and financial assistance to build a tin smelter—something Bolivians had long coveted but their North American patrons had always argued was unnecessary.[56]

The vigorous domestic debate that ensued created a moment of opportunity for Paz to either shift patrons or take advantage of the new international context to mark out a nonaligned position that would allow him to play off the great powers against each other. Instead he chose a third option. Paz used the Soviet offers to convince U.S. policy makers to reconfirm their commitments to his country. In May 1961, soon after announcing the Alliance for Progress, President John F. Kennedy sent Paz a letter that offered to make Bolivia a "full partner" in this new inter-American venture. Lauding the MNR government, Kennedy stated that "this great revolution, has blazed a path for others to follow," and then went on to outline an eight-point program of increased assistance to Bolivia.[57] The following month, Paz signed agreements renewing and deepening the special relationship. Days later, his government uncovered a communist plot to seize control of Bolivia, imprisoned PCB leaders, and expelled the Cuban chargé d'affaires; and soon afterward the president postponed a commission planning to visit Moscow to study the Soviet offer. It would never leave.[58]

The sudden shift from multilateral bargaining that included a flirtation with the Soviets back into a tight bilateral partnership with the United States is as disconcerting to observers as the rapid shift from vehement anti-Americanism to careful compliance with U.S. wishes back in April and May 1953. But again, as then, the underlying continuities are more important than the apparent shifts. Paz had never seriously considered shifting patrons because to do so would weaken his own position domestically. Further, he did not trust the Soviets. In 1958, while he was the ambassador to Great Britain, Paz had negotiated with the Soviets for three months on tin matters, only to see Moscow renege at the last minute.[59] He probably would have preferred to accept assistance from both superpowers; "Poland does it, so can we," he once told the press.[60] But Paz understood that the United States was a jealous patron and that Bolivia had limited importance and could easily overplay its hand, so he used Soviet offers to expedite a shift that he astutely realized was in progress in Washington—a coming to terms with state capitalism. In late 1959 the Eisenhower administration had finally devised a way to indirectly assist YPFB despite its long-professed opposition to supporting state-run oil companies. The more troubling question of assistance to COMIBOL was still pending, however, when the Kennedy administration took office.[61]

In 1961 the nationalized mining company lost about $500,000 a month, making it an all-consuming maw into which U.S. assistance inevitably disappeared. The country's mines required too many workers, who used obsolete equipment to extract ores of negligible tin content—all in the context of a general market slump.[62] President Paz sent representatives to Europe to seek assistance on both sides of the Iron Curtain, and he used Khrushchev's offer in late 1960 to wrest further concessions from the lame-duck Eisenhower administration. One observer of hemispheric affairs commented that "the international spotlight focused briefly on the nationalized tin mines in Bolivia and found the United States and Russia standing at the edge of the circle of light bidding for the right to subsidize the collapsing [mining] industry."[63] The new Kennedy administration was the dubious victor. Soon after the new administration took office in Washington, Andrade—who was again ambassador—cabled Paz that the "atmosphere under the Democrats" seemed much more favorable for a quick conclusion of an aid package to COMIBOL. Paz dispatched Lechín to Washington to negotiate directly and assure the Kennedy administration that he was not a Communist. He kept the Soviets at arm's length despite growing pressures from the left to accept Moscow's offer of aid.[64]

In early June, with Lechín in formal compliance, Bolivia, West Germany, and the United States agreed to a package of aid aimed at completely overhauling the nationalized tin industry. The so-called Triangular Plan envisioned a COMIBOL made competitive again, and linked new investments to cost-cutting measures that included wage cuts, layoffs, and a definitive end to subsidized mining-camp stores.[65] The "communist plot" exposed a week later had obvious parallels to the "Nazi putsch" of 1941, when similar charges rid the Bolivian government of a troublesome German presence, provided an opportunity to crack down on domestic opponents, and solidified the country behind the Allied war effort. This time the charges rid Paz of a troublesome Cuban presence, provided an opportunity to crack down on the PCB, and solidified the country behind the Triangular Plan. The difference this time, of course, was that Paz and the MNR were the protagonists instead of victims of what were probably equally spurious charges.

Déjà Vu

With relations between the United States and Bolivia once again running smoothly, it was natural that Bolivia became something of a showcase for the Alliance for Progress. The Kennedy administration increased aid to Bolivia by 600 percent between 1960 and 1964—sending a total of $205 million in economic aid and an additional $23 million in loans from the Inter-American Development Bank.[66] The first Peace Corps volunteers arrived in Bolivia in early 1962: thirty-five young North Americans who, the Bolivian press approvingly noted, "came with no immunities or special privileges."[67] The new ambassador, Ben Stephansky, reflected Washington's changed approach. A naturalized American of Russian parentage, Stephansky specialized in labor issues, enthusiastically supported the objectives of the MNR, and strongly advocated the Kennedy administration's new development thrust.[68]

Bolivia's economy had finally recovered from the traumas of revolution, stabilization, and world recession and for the first time since the 1952 revolution registered moderate growth. The recovery was fostered in part by increased U.S. assistance, but derived more directly from the rebound in mineral prices. By 1964, the price of tin had risen to $1.70 a pound—double the lowest price of a decade before.[69] With revenues up, Bolivia needed less of the U.S. budgetary support that sustained the MNR through the 1950s, and a greater proportion of aid now went directly into investment. Productivity rose in the mines, and the country exported small amounts of petroleum and lumber as well. Instead of spending $38 million yearly for food imports, Bolivia now supplied more of its own basic foodstuffs. Between 1961 and 1964 the GNP grew at an average of 5.7 percent annually, with the percentage increase in 1963 being the highest in Latin America.[70] To top off the good news, in April of that year, Bolivia won the South American soccer title by defeating World Cup champion Brazil. Even though Brazil played without Pelé and the finals took place in La Paz, where the altitude gave the home team a distinct advantage, the victory was an international triumph for a country with all too few of them.[71]

President Paz visited Washington a few months later, the last official guest of John F. Kennedy. At the time, Bolivia had the appearance of a development success story, and Kennedy cited it as an example of what the Alliance for Progress could accomplish.[72] On 21 November, the day before Kennedy's tragic assassination, *El Diário's* editorial cartoonist depicted the North American president and a distinctly infantile Paz locked in embrace. The image and the caption, "The prodigal son," succinctly captured several important elements of the new partnership: the renewed bonds after a period of estrangement, the continuing inequality and paternalistic elements of the restored relationship, and the degree to which it depended on these two extraordinary men.[73]

Kennedy redefined U.S. Third World policy, turning away from the negative task of fighting communism to set in motion a decade of development that would reduce the attractions of that ideology. The Americas were to be the focus of such policies, and Kennedy genuinely admired pragmatic, nationalist reformers like Paz. The U.S. president once told Cheddi Jagan of British Guiana (a reformer Kennedy considered neither sufficiently pragmatic nor sufficiently nationalist to receive U.S. support): "We are not engaged in a crusade to force private enterprise on parts of the world where it is not relevant. If we are engaged in a crusade for anything, it is national independence. That is the primary purpose of our aid."[74]

Increased national independence through statist development had always been Paz's primary goal, although the means to achieve it posed his dilemma. In a speech given soon after the aid relationship was reconfirmed in mid-1961, Paz identified two chief obstacles in his way: anarchic political and labor forces within the country, and bureaucratic forces outside it.[75] Kennedy and Stephansky, by embracing Paz's state capitalist goals, helped reduce bureaucratic obstacles in Washington and thus fostered Paz's illusion that, with generous U.S. support, he could maneuver around the domestic obstacles. During Paz's second term, instead of balancing forces and parceling out decision making and rewards, as he had done from 1952 to 1956, he instead surrounded himself with technocrats and relied on aid-stimulated growth to transcend the highly factionalized polity bequeathed him by Siles.[76]

One casualty of this shift was the long-nurtured symbiotic relationship with Juan Lechín. The labor leader had renewed an alliance with Paz in 1960 on the understanding that labor would again participate in setting national policy and that he would be the MNR candidate in 1964. Now, the premises had changed and Lechín found himself among those against whom Paz maneuvered. Not long after the aid relationship with the United States was reconfirmed, Lechín was forced to answer trumped-up charges of cocaine trafficking. After briefly resigning as vice president, he accepted quasi exile as ambassador to Rome.[77] While Lechín was gone, the Triangular Plan undermined his labor support and Communists made headway among rank-and-file miners. Meanwhile Paz threatened massive layoffs in the mines to meet Triangular Plan requirements and in August 1963 revoked *control obrero* (worker oversight of COMIBOL administrators). Communist union leaders immediately called a strike that eventually involved twenty-eight thousand workers. Together these developments illustrated the multiple forces threatening Lechín.[78]

Lechín arrived back from Rome in early November 1963 to shore up his position, and relations between the two old political rivals quickly deteriorated. Paz later claimed that he did not decide to continue as president until U.S. officials made clear while he was in Washington that Lechín would be unacceptable as his successor. But since Paz had been positioning himself for possible reelection since 1961, when Bolivia's congress amended the constitution to allow successive terms, it is likely that what he heard in Washington merely reconfirmed his preferred course.[79] In any case, U.S. policy effectively undermined Lechín's role as broker. At the national congress of mine workers in early December, the union leader tried to revive his legitimacy with the rank and file by attacking both the United States and Paz. An open break came on 5 December when Lechín supporters resigned from Paz's cabinet.

Paz lashed out verbally at Lechín, then jailed several labor militants.

Miners at Catavi immediately seized hostages, including four U.S. citizens, and for several days world attention focused on the disintegrating relationship between the MNR government and the miners.[80] Paz surrounded Catavi with peasant and military forces, with the full support of Lyndon Johnson, who was facing his first international crisis as president.[81] U.S. officials whom Lechín had visited during his pilgrimages to Washington appealed to the union leader to see that the hostages were freed, and, as he had done so often in the past, Lechín played a mediating role that settled the hostage crisis without casualties.

The larger significance of the hostage affair was not lost on those who knew their history. In 1942, a massacre at Catavi began a long, often tense, but mutually beneficial relationship between miners and the MNR. In 1963, that relationship ended at Catavi, and the party's revolution came full circle. Labor and government were again adversaries, with the military offering crucial support to an increasingly isolated regime.

At the MNR convention in January, Paz made the split with Lechín definitive. His address to the convention repeated a now familiar theme, though with a new twist. Development was the essence of nationalism, for only through development could Bolivia reduce its dependency. "U.S. assistance is still essential and we are very thankful for it," the president observed, "but we must try very hard to get to the place where we can do without it."[82] This might have been a major theme of Paz's third term—if he had been allowed to serve it. But his illusions of relatively autonomous action in the quest for development were about to be shattered on the realities of Bolivian politics.

In the midst of Paz's break with Lechín, the local press noted that the president was visibly moved when army commander Alfredo Ovando Candia affirmed the full support of the army for the Paz government and for democracy.[83] Actually the military was deeply committed to neither, and by 1964 was even less willing to play its assigned role as Paz's protector and enforcer. Air Force general René Barrientos Ortuño was the focus of new political dynamics in which the military itself became another interest group in the complex Bolivian polity. Barrientos, a flamboyant *cochabambino*, mixed ambition with machismo and the ability to speak Quechua with a facility at cultivating close contacts with U.S. military advisers. His political profile rose steadily through 1963 as he visited mines and brought peace to warring parties of campesinos. In mid-1963, peasant leaders declared Barrientos their choice for vice president, and in October Barrientos threw his hat into the ring.[84]

Paz clearly did not wish to share the ticket with a man as blatantly ambitious as Barrientos, and in January the party convention rejected the general in favor of Federico Fortún, a loyal party functionary whose choice confirmed Paz's desire for increased autonomy. But Barrientos continued to politick so shamelessly that Paz gave him an ultimatum to either withdraw from the political arena or resign from the military.[85] The next day a bomb exploded at Barrientos's home. Two days later, on 25 February, an unknown assassin fired a "magic bullet" that nearly killed the general—"magic" not only for being fortuitously deflected by the U.S. Air Force wings that Barrientos wore, but also for the way it revived his moribund vice-presidential candidacy. The assassination attempt unified the military behind Barrientos, and within days Paz (sensing the shifting political winds) unceremoniously dumped Fortún and named Barrientos as his running mate. The authors of the attempts on Barrientos's life were never identified, but one of Barrientos's military colleagues commented years later that "there always remained the suspicion that these attempts might have been fabricated by the general's own followers as demonstration that he was a man of destiny, protected by the gods."[86] What is certain is that, in the words of analyst William Brill, Paz had "traded a loyal, unthreatening man of the party apparatus for a man who was a power in his own right—one who was not about to be relegated to a nondescript role."[87]

U.S. officials assessed Paz's faltering presidency and withdrew their support even as their policies exacerbated his problems. Lyndon Johnson accepted his predecessor's essential policy premises and objectives, but in Latin America as in Vietnam, the new president brought a subtle but significant shift to their emphasis and execution. Johnson's diplomacy was an extension of his domestic political gamesmanship and involved less advocacy and encouragement and more arm-twisting and pressure. Thomas Mann, Johnson's chief spokesman on hemispheric affairs, was a tough, pragmatic Texan with long experience in the region and a perhaps justified sense that he knew more about Latin America than the revolving-door academics and idealists who preceded him under Kennedy.[88] Kennedy had already increased U.S. support for hemispheric security forces as a parallel theme to the Alliance for Progress. Johnson and Mann shifted the emphasis ever so slightly, but significantly, further in this direction. The new emphasis on security became apparent in early April 1964 when the United States supported the Brazilian military coup against populist president João Goulart. Soon afterward, Mann announced that the United States would no longer automatically sanction de facto governments.[89]

Events in Brazil coincided with growing U.S. fears that Paz could not maintain order or survive (perhaps literally) a third term. Both the embassy and the State Department had serious fears that Paz would be assassinated before the election, making Lechín president unless he were directly implicated. Washington asked the embassy to monitor Lechín's actions closely and to prepare a list of possible courses of action for such a contingency.[90] The final report, approved by the National Security Council days after the coup in Brazil, made it clear that Lechín would be unacceptable: at best he would be like Goulart—ineffective and unstable; at worst he could create a government of the "Castro-communist mode." As action items the embassy's report proposed more military assistance and direct U.S. intervention if requested.[91]

Just before the elections, a high Bolivian military official (probably Ovando) asked the visiting head of the U.S. Army's Southern Command how the United States would react to a coup. He was told that this was a Bolivian internal matter.[92] Thus, in a number of less than subtle ways, U.S. officials revealed their waning commitment to civilian democracy. One of the more blatant cases was a U.S. military adviser's introduction to a Bolivian military pamphlet published in early 1964: "The military . . . is perhaps the only institution endowed with the organization, order, discipline, and self-sacrificing attitude towards objectives for the common good. Should political and economic institutions fail . . . then there is a real possibility that the military would move in against graft and corruption in government."[93]

With U.S. policies helping to undermine his position, Paz faced constant domestic uproar during the period between his reelection in May and his fall in November 1964. Bolivian newspapers carried daily accounts of the mounting disorder, and the *New York Times* carried no fewer than forty-two articles on the strikes, riots, kidnappings, beatings, and bombings. Beneath this chaotic surface, factional leaders from Lechín on the left to the FSB on the right cynically encouraged the military to intervene. Barrientos, for his part, entertained all comers, implying to each that they would have a special place in a military regime. By October, all he and Ovando awaited was the opportune moment when they could seize power without sharing it.[94] Both had been actively plotting ever since Paz rejected Barrientos at the convention in January, and Ovando's apparent wavering in the days prior to the revolt was only a ruse. Ovando later told the press that he and Barrientos had "acted together" all along. He had played the loyal soldier while Barrientos kept the political waters stirred until conditions were right.[95] Conditions were right in late October, when disturbances caused by striking teachers spread to students and miners. When Paz called on the army to quell a miner uprising outside Oruro, Ovando and Barrientos decided that there was no reason to wait any longer. On 3 November the coup began, and on 4 November 1964 the revolutionary nationalist regime and the U.S. experiment to support it ended.[96]

Evaluating the Unequal Partnership

El Diário headlined its blow-by-blow account of the coup "Twelve-Year Regime Crumbles in a Few Hours." Of course, the demise of the revolutionary regime had been in progress far longer than that. The original task facing the MNR was immense, and ultimately the party failed to complete its revolution. The reasons for the failure do not relate primarily to U.S. aid; the key factors in the MNR collapse were internal. The party faced a thorny dilemma posed by conflicting demands to redistribute scarce resources for short-term political purposes and to allocate them to investment and diversification for long-term development. It approached this immense task with the support of a shaky and contradiction-filled coalition and without a clear ideological vision.[97] The revolution's leaders had been dealt a bad hand, and though they did not play that hand perfectly, they successfully enlisted a powerful outside patron to help them consolidate revolutionary gains and develop and diversify Bolivia's economy. The strategy did not differ greatly from the one employed by Fidel Castro; only the patrons were different. Now that the end of the cold war has reduced the mythic appeal of Cuba's revolution and the collapse of Soviet communism appears to have removed alternatives to the capitalist path to development that Paz and his colleagues pursued, perhaps it is time to look more closely at why Paz's strategy was no more successful than Castro's.

U.S. assistance failed to resolve Bolivia's dilemma, although it did buy time for the MNR center to maintain power through twelve difficult years and to institute a basic and significant core of necessary reforms that began to open the Bolivian social system to the modernization both partners sought. But the MNR's position steadily deteriorated through those twelve years, and U.S. aid contributed to the process. The quid pro quos the United States attached to aid, many of them unnecessary and degrading, helped erode the party's political support, and the aid did not bring sufficient compensating economic gains to keep competing interest groups loyal to the party. The process and its resolution are succinctly summarized by Sergio Almaraz Paz, an early supporter of the revolution but later one of its most cogent critics:

> In 1953 came the first North American food aid. In 1957 the monetary stabilization plan was imposed. A little later came the reorganization of the army. North American advisers were accepted into key administrative organizations. The petroleum code was passed. One thing led to another and in this complicated game, surrender alternated with defense. It is not that there was no understanding of the situation: "we yield over here in order to hold firm over there." "This is more important than that." Yet these choices, products of given circumstances, led quickly to loss of control. In 1953 the government was willing to grant certain concessions in exchange for U.S. aid, but would have thought it madness to accept a plan like the one imposed by the International Monetary Fund four years later. In 1957

no one would ever have thought that to receive credits for the nationalized mines, force would be used against workers. . . . One concession led to the next in a sequence that made it impossible to tell the seriousness of each new step. . . . The revolution did not crumble from a single blow, it fell bit by bit, piece by piece.[98]

Almaraz adds that the final piece, the coup itself, was "a shot fired into a corpse."[99]

It is difficult to ascertain whether U.S. objectives were met by the denouement of November 1964. Some analysts argue that it was always the goal of U.S. policy to moderate the revolution and to prop up the MNR only until more stable and dependably conservative pro-U.S. forces had recovered strength.[100] But U.S. policy is neither so clear nor so cynical, and the story of U.S. aid to Bolivia is not just the story of a powerful and self-interested nation destroying a revolution in order to restore a docile satellite. It is also the story of an idealistic people progressively disillusioned by their inability to reshape another in their own image. Robert Packenham argues that through the 1950s and 1960s, U.S. development policy in the Third World was guided by four premises rooted in America's liberal tradition: change and development are easy and result from an evolutionary rather than a revolutionary process; change is cumulative and positive: economic change leads to social change, which leads to political change, which results in decreased social and political tensions and finally in democracy; radicalism and revolution, therefore, are bad because they destabilize, confuse, and endanger the evolutionary progress of modernization; and power is better distributed than accumulated—an implicit faith in the "unseen hand."[101]

Bolivia was, in some ways, a distinctly favorable place for the United States to test these premises. Well-entrenched elites ensured an underlying continuity to Latin America's legendary political instability, and the hegemonic interests of the United States, particularly during the cold war, favored stability, no matter how far the terms of such stability diverged from the American ideal. But for a time in Bolivia, neither norm held true. The revolution destroyed the old ruling caste with remarkable ease and little bloodshed and brought to power men genuinely interested in modernization along capitalist lines. For historical reasons, the driving force of their nationalism was not directed against the United States and their ideological vision was more liberal than Marxist.[102] Perhaps most important, Bolivia's revolutionaries acknowledged their place in the hemispheric system and sought U.S. assistance. Thus the United States gave them qualified support, and two nations with highly unequal resources and very different motives and objectives sought mutual accommodation, though on unequal terms. The United States and Bolivia became patron and client.

U.S. policy during the first phase of the relationship (1953–55) reflected the first and third premises identified by Packenham—modernization was relatively easy; and since the core of MNR leaders were moderates interested in evolutionary, capitalist-oriented change, they deserved at least limited U.S. support. When the complacency and optimism behind this initial assessment proved ill founded, the United States in 1955 inserted itself more directly into the modernization process by acting on premises 2 and 4. Bolivia could be made more secure if economic growth fostered social and political stability, but economic growth required closer adherence to the development model of the United States: market-responsive, open to private initiative and foreign investment, and demonstrating faith in the driving logic of individual initiative and the hidden hand.

Packenham observes that "the first two liberal premises make the United States excessively optimistic or utopian; the third liberal premise often makes us counterrevolutionary and even reactionary; and the fourth assumption inclines us toward a special kind of pretentiousness and arrogance."[103] Such criticisms are clearly borne out in the case of Bolivia. By 1959 disillusionment was high on all sides. The relationship foundered for a time; then both sides recommitted to an aid relationship that, on the surface, was more generous and less ideologically confined than before. The four premises continued to guide U.S. aid policy under the Alliance for Progress, but North Americans had learned enough during the 1950s to qualify at least three of them somewhat. Development was not as easy as once thought, and the Kennedy administration understood that a certain amount of social restructuring—of a type that made sense within the context of America's own history—might be prerequisite to development in Latin America. Nor was faith in the hidden hand and private initiative as unqualified as before, since Kennedy brought a twentieth-century liberal Democrat's awareness of the crucial guiding and regulatory role of the state in the modernization process.

But premise 3—that radicalism and revolution were harmful to U.S. interests and would derail Bolivia's own development process—remained as strong as ever. And when instability grew in Bolivia despite massive U.S. assistance, the conservative interests of a hegemonic power and the idealistic protestations of a nation that continues to fancy itself something of a revolutionary model to the world no longer cohered. Stability was paramount, and State Department adviser Adolph Berle, who at the beginning of the decade prophesied that the Alliance for Progress would raise the standard of living of every Latin American by 50 percent, succinctly explained why Paz fell: "he was unable to keep the peace."[104] Washington now condoned and even supported authoritarianism in the name of national security and, because of a lingering sense that Latin Americans were perhaps ultimately unfit to follow the U.S. model, decided in Bolivia and elsewhere to give militaries a chance to bring progress with order.

6   The National Security State and the Limits of Hegemony

Wan from a night without sleep, Víctor Paz Estenssoro appeared at the door of his office on the morning of 4 November 1964 and in a low voice told gathered reporters he was "off for a little drive to inspect defenses." There *were* no defenses; Paz was on his way to the airport and to exile in Peru. Nevertheless, inside the armored car that had been sent for him, Paz flashed the V-for-victory sign—one of the few recognizable symbols his muted revolution had produced. General René Barrientos Ortuño, who in 1952 piloted the plane that brought Paz from Argentina to assume the presidency, now ended the twelve-year civilian revolutionary experiment by escorting Paz back out of the country.[1]

During the intervening years, officers like Barrientos had carefully resurrected a military that had been decapitated and nearly destroyed by the 1952 revolution. Over those twelve years, the United States actively supported military reconstruction, believing that the armed forces could ultimately guarantee capitalist progress and noncommunist order in Bolivia. The military would rule Bolivia for most of the next two decades, but over time it became apparent that North American advice and assistance were no more successful at shaping the Bolivian military into an instrument of friendly order and progress than they had been at molding Paz and his revolution into an Andean reflection of democratic and capitalist America.

The Restored Military
and the *Revolución Restauradora*

The April 1952 revolution transferred the balance of armed power from the traditional military to armed militias. When key officers failed

147

to join the MNR revolt and then fled to Peru with the collapse of the an-
cien régime, Bolivia's military went into eclipse. Immediately after the
revolution, Víctor Paz slashed military spending by 50 percent and,
conceding to labor's demands, closed the military school in La Paz. Over
the next five years his government cashiered three hundred officers,
slashed army manpower from twenty thousand to five thousand, and
cut military spending from 22 percent of the national budget before the
revolution to 6.7 percent in 1957.[2] The leaders of the Central Obrero Boliviana argued that Paz should completely replace the traditional army
with worker militias, but he never seriously entertained that option.
Mistrusting any scheme that gave the labor-left a monopoly of armed
power, Paz instead preferred to create a new "nationalist" army that
could counter the militias. In mid-1953, as part of his campaign to enlist
U.S. assistance, Paz officially reorganized a trimmed-down army; reopened the military school, saying that it was now prepared to train an
army loyal to the revolution; and created a special engineering corps
charged with assisting Bolivia's economic development.[3]

Washington monitored these developments closely. Reassured by
Paz's moves, the State Department encouraged the Department of Defense to assist Bolivia's engineering corps. The Pentagon initially hesi-
tated because Bolivia was still in arrears for earlier military missions but
by 1956 had begun to reconsider the role Latin American militaries
might play in larger cold war strategies. After the MNR left dominated
the raucous party convention in early 1956, Paz, Siles, and Andrade approached the U.S. embassy to ask for help to rebuild the army. The
request struck a responsive chord in Washington, and in early February, a month after the convention, a memo circulated through the State
Department suggesting a contingency plan to strengthen the military
"should political chaos come to Bolivia through a collapse of, or an unfavorable reorientation of the MNR regime":

> It appears so far that we have been putting our energies into the formula-
> tion and application of [current policies to support the MNR] and have not
> yet developed alternatives or something in the way of secondary insur-
> ance. Such insurance might be provided if there were an organization or

agency in Bolivia which might act as a balance and having the right capacity and orientation, be able to step into the breach in extreme circumstances. The only organization in Bolivia which, if strengthened, might be
able to take the kind of action required is the Bolivian Army.[4]

The author of the memo, Officer in Charge of West Coast Affairs Ernest
Siracusa, admitted the sensitive nature of the recommendation and
added that "tact, timing, and approach" would be the secrets to its
success.

As to timing, Siracusa's memo could not have been more opportune.
Less than a month after he wrote it, miners at Huanuni seized a nearby
military arsenal and angry officers demanded that the Paz government
either strengthen the military and use it effectively or disband it completely. Paz entered closed-door conversations with key military officers and U.S. embassy officials and made plans to increase budget
allocations for the armed forces at the very time the U.S.-sponsored stabilization plan drastically cut government spending in other areas.[5]

President Hernán Siles initially was cautious about strengthening
and politically reengaging the armed forces because he realized that to
do so would be to cross a Rubicon of sorts. In mid-1957, with the showdown with the COB over stabilization looming for the MNR government, the United States offered Siles arms and military training for a
Presidential Escort Battalion that could bolster his influence. Siles refused, saying that the timing was not right. As economic conditions
worsened, however, the president desperately sought support from any
quarter and accepted the offer. Direct U.S. military assistance began in
April 1958—initially a modest $417,000 worth of equipment, materials,
and services. For the United States, the small investment was an aspect
of a contingency plan and a larger shift in emphasis toward enlisting
the Latin American militaries in the cold war struggle. The military
now weighed heavily in Siles's increasingly complicated balancing act.
For the military, the U.S. aid was a new source of legitimization and
influence.[6]

The Rubicon had been crossed, as domestic events soon made clear.
In late 1958, regional resistance to MNR policies exploded in Santa

Cruz, and for the first time since the revolution the government used the military to restore domestic order. In March 1959 Siles secured the streets of La Paz with military patrols during the *Time* incident riots. A few months later he sent the military to intervene and bring peace to rival campesino organizations in Cochabamba; and in March 1960 he used the army to put down a carabinero revolt. Military expenditures rose steadily as Siles added two new army divisions to help maintain order in the increasingly fragmented polity over which he presided.

Rumors abounded before the 1960 elections that Siles might turn power over to a military junta, but the elections went smoothly.[7] Nevertheless, on returning to power, Víctor Paz embraced the armed forces even more fully than Siles, who had always nurtured antimilitary sentiments. Paz's inaugural parade on 7 August 1960 prominently featured marching soldiers; and when, after a year in office, Paz decided to marginalize labor-left support and return more fully to the U.S. orbit, the army assumed a political role that matched its new visibility. By the close of Paz's second term in mid-1964, the military was back to its prerevolutionary strength. It matched the militias in total manpower for the first time since the revolution, and its new equipment was far superior. The army was also back as an autonomous political actor, helped to that position by the fracturing of the MNR and the political role Paz asked that it play.[8]

After Castro assumed power in Cuba, U.S. strategic thinking began to crystallize into national security doctrine, and Bolivia became a laboratory to test ideas regarding the new role Latin American militaries might play in U.S. efforts to secure a friendly and developing hemisphere and avoid other Cubas. While John Kennedy augmented economic and development assistance to the region, he also increased military assistance by 50 percent—by 800 percent in the case of Bolivia, where both wings of Kennedy policy came together in a program called Civic Action. The Bolivian military was given new development functions under Civic Action: constructing roads and airstrips, providing air service to remote areas, assisting in agricultural and industrial work projects, building schools, clearing land for colonization, conducting literacy campaigns, and providing medical services. By 1964, a major portion of U.S. development assistance was administered through Civic Action and one-fifth of the Bolivian army's man-hours was allocated to the program. Civic Action closely tied the military to MNR goals but, paradoxically, also undermined the regime it served by convincing many in Bolivia and the United States that the army might more effectively advance the revolution's development goals than Paz himself.[9]

In the eyes of the Pentagon, the Bolivian army's development role was linked, but subordinate, to its security role. Training of Bolivian military personnel at the School of the Americas began in 1958. By 1962–63, the school had prepared 659 Bolivian officers. In 1963, the entire senior class at the Bolivian military academy was schooled at the U.S. jungle warfare facility in Panama, and Bolivia had more graduates from the U.S. Army Special Warfare School at Fort Bragg than any other nation in the hemisphere. In addition to new equipment and training methods, U.S. military officials also introduced new ideas that made the Bolivian military a guardian of national security under cold war conditions with a new language of raids, ambushes, counterambushes, "annihilation zones," and "hammer-and-anvil operations."[10]

The increased levels of U.S. aid and contact with Bolivian military officers made the Department of Defense a new patron with different— and in many ways more direct and higher-priority—links to a potentially more powerful Bolivian client than the MNR could ever be. By 1964 the Pentagon wielded as much influence in Bolivia as the State Department, and the November coup received "the unmistakable support of the Pentagon," according to one Bolivian officer.[11] Rumors abound, still unsubstantiated, concerning the role of U.S. air attaché—and CIA station chief—Lieutenant Colonel Edward Fox. Fox knew and had worked closely with Barrientos since coming to Bolivia in the 1950s and grew personally close to the air force general during a course for senior officers in Oklahoma. Fox was at Barrientos's side after he was struck by the "magic bullet" and escorted the general to the U.S. Air Force plane that whisked him from El Alto airport in La Paz to Panama for treatment. Nine months later, Fox met with Barrientos on the eve of the coup. And when the coup was over, Fox clearly had few regrets.[12]

The State Department viewed the coup more equivocally because it had invested heavily in the MNR over the previous twelve years. Nonetheless, the department and the MNR itself were also architects of the coup. When, with active State Department encouragement, Siles and Paz embraced the military as an ally in internal struggles that U.S. policy had helped to engender, Siracusa's 1956 State Department memo became a self-fulfilling prophecy: "That we adopt and put into effect a line of action with respect to the Bolivian army for the deliberate purpose of seeing the formal military so strengthened that there would be some responsible body from which leadership might emerge should political chaos come to Bolivia through a collapse of or an unfavorable reorientation of the MNR regime." [13]

By 1964, although the "decade of development" was less than half over and the Alliance for Progress was barely on its feet, Washington was disillusioned with both programs. Many in the United States were inclined to agree with Barrientos's own assessment: "If the MNR had done what it claimed it would do, the military would still be in its barracks." [14] In the aftermath of his coup Barrientos stated that he did not plan to roll back the revolution: "We never threw the Bolivian National Revolution aside. . . . We made a revolution within the revolution. . . . We achieved the restoration of the revolution." In Barrientos's words, his was a *"revolución restauradora."* [15]

Ñancahuazú and Its Paradoxes

Barrientos's claim rings true when his policies are measured against the trajectory Bolivia's revolution had assumed by Paz's second term. The new military president maintained the emphasis on economic development, deemed necessary to increase national autonomy, and further diversified Bolivia's economy by opening it to foreign investors. Bolivia's GDP grew an average of 6.2 percent annually over the course of his regime, with only 5 percent annual inflation. Richard Thorn notes that the new president pulled off two coups that the MNR had never managed: a tin smelter funded by private German capital and an agreement with Argentina and Bolivian Gulf Oil to build and finance construction of a gas pipeline from Santa Cruz to the Argentine frontier.[16]

Also like Paz, Barrientos attempted to co-opt the popular masses while pursuing policies that primarily satisfied newly emerging economic elites. But Barrientos augmented the limited populist tools that Paz and his party possessed—demand satisfaction and low-key appeals to nationalism—with the force of his personality and charisma. His contacts with peasants were direct and paternalistic: he spoke Quechua with them and visited their villages unexpectedly to dispense schools, soccer balls, and public works. In 1966 he formalized his special bonds to the peasantry in the Pacto Militar-Campesino, and he relied heavily on peasant votes to win the 1966 election with a 62 percent majority—the last Bolivian president to muster a majority.[17] His ability the following year to isolate and eventually eliminate the legendary international revolutionary Ché Guevara and his guerrilla band only seemed to corroborate Barrientos's contention that he had kept the revolution on track and was more popular and effective than Paz or Siles had ever been. The *New York Times's* assessment was that "Guevara found Bolivia barren ground for revolution precisely because the campesinos believed in a President who spoke their Quechua tongue, identified with their interests, and gave them an expanding role in the country's embryo democratic processes."[18]

The Barrientos government first became aware of the presence of big, bearded foreigners at a place called Ñancahuazú in southeastern Bolivia in late February 1967. In March, police in the nearby oil town of Camiri apprehended two young Bolivians who were trying to sell an expensive gun. Under interrogation the men quickly revealed that they had deserted a guerrilla operation supported by Fidel Castro and that the bearded men were Cubans. Even more shocking, they claimed that Ché Guevara was the leader of the guerrilla band, a fact verified soon afterward when Bolivian authorities found documents in an abandoned jeep that linked Ché to a wider international conspiracy.[19]

Official U.S. observers initially doubted that Guevara would launch a guerrilla movement from eastern Bolivia and thought Barrientos was exaggerating the situation to attract additional economic and military assistance. But after a clash between the army and the guerrillas in late

April, Washington sent two U.S. Army officers and twenty Green Berets to train a special Bolivian anti-insurgency unit at a camp north of Santa Cruz. The CIA also dispatched two agents to Bolivia—both Cuban nationals who would not easily be identified as U.S. operatives.[20]

Through the Bolivian winter the army tightened its circle around Guevara and his band. On 31 August the Bolivian army destroyed the guerrillas' rearguard, which had been out of communication with Ché's main force since mid-April. By then the guerrillas were so famished that they killed and ate the mule that Ché was compelled to ride because of his deteriorating health. In late September, with Guevara's insurrectionists on the run, the U.S.-trained Rangers were brought into the operation zone. On the night of 7 October, a man watering his potatoes saw Ché's straggling band and informed the army. The Rangers moved into place that night and the next afternoon captured the legendary guerrilla leader. The following day, 9 October, Guevara was first interrogated by Bolivian military officers and CIA agent Félix Rodríguez and then executed by a Bolivian sergeant under orders from La Paz.[21]

Ché had wagered both his theories and his life on the premise that Bolivia was ripe for revolution, a premise based in part on his experiences there in the 1950s. In 1953, fresh out of medical school, Guevara and a friend took a train across the continent from Buenos Aires to La Paz, arriving just in time to witness the revolution's crowning achievement—agrarian reform. While in La Paz, Guevara lived a curious double life, enjoying meals and parties at the homes of well-heeled Argentine exiles by night and immersing himself in the continuing fervor of Bolivia's revolution by day. He was fascinated by the quest of an impoverished nation to reorder itself to the national good, but disappointed by Bolivia's growing rapprochement with the United States and ultimately disenchanted by the lingering elitist attitudes of Bolivia's revolutionary leaders. On visiting the Ministry of Campesino Affairs after the land reform, Guevara observed that Indians who came to claim lands were dusted with white powder because, he was told, it was impossible to teach Indians to be clean. "The MNR is carrying out the DDT revolution," was Ché's caustic comment.[22]

Although there is no indication in his diary or his letters that Guevara was aware of it at the time, it was on 26 July 1953, while Ché was in Bolivia, that Fidel Castro led his failed attack on the Moncado barracks. The MNR revolution ultimately disappointed Guevara, who proceeded on to Guatemala and was present for the overthrow of President Arbenz in June 1954. These experiences progressively radicalized Guevara and brought Fidel and him together. In 1967 Ché returned to Bolivia precisely because he was convinced that its revolution had been thwarted.[23]

The ease with which Guevara was subsequently defeated seems to refute his interpretation of Bolivia and to verify the lingering significance of the 1952 revolution. Bolivia's revolution had consolidated enough reforms to limit Ché's appeal, had maintained sufficient nationalist credibility to leave Ché and his international revolutionaries exposed, and had broadened the benefits of the system enough to reduce the appeals of communism. Fortified by U.S. assistance and training, the once moribund Bolivian military had defeated a near mythical revolutionary. The victory over Guevara seemed to affirm U.S. support of necessary reforms while confirming the role Latin American militaries could play as instruments of national and regional security.

But all was not as it seemed. "Bolivia, which has resisted most efforts to change it," journalist Eric Lawlor later observed, "defeated one of guerrilla warfare's greatest theoreticians."[24] But Bolivia would just as successfully thwart the objectives of the Western Hemisphere's most wealthy and powerful nation. Subsequent events were to reveal that Bolivia's military no more conformed to objectives established by U.S. advisers and military strategists than its masses and Communist party had played the roles scripted for them by Ché's revolutionary dogma. One problem not apparent to U.S. advisers, because the military has never played a direct political role in the United States, was the political liabilities of a military regime. James Malloy and Eduardo Gamarra note that under Barrientos, "as the country developed economically, it regressed politically."[25] Barrientos had no political base beyond his own personal connections and charisma and his patronal influence over other military officers. Peasants were his primary numerical base of political support, although Barrientos was more interested in the image of peasant support than in actually improving their living conditions.[26]

As Siles, Paz, and now Barrientos retreated from the populism of Paz's first term, growth-oriented development strategies required that the costs of investment be allocated, and workers were the primary losers. Unlike his predecessors, Barrientos made no pretense of including workers in his coalition, in part because, unlike civilian politicians, he had recourse to the army when coercion was necessary.[27] Barrientos adhered religiously to the Triangular Plan to restructure COMIBOL, and during his regime, six thousand miners lost their jobs and the remainder took pay cuts averaging from 40 to 50 percent.[28] When in May 1965 miners resorted to their traditional weapon, the strike, the new president sent troops to the mines, disarmed the militias, seized and deported Juan Lechín, disbanded the Federación Sindical de Trabajadores Mineros de Bolivia and the COB, and declared the mines a military zone.[29] Military discipline and rebounding world prices meant that Bolivia's mines turned their first profit since nationalization in 1966, but tensions remained high.

In mid-1967, Guevara's guerrilla army reanimated the miners' resistance, and on 24 June, the morning of the festival of San Juan, eighty miners were killed when soldiers attacked a clandestine union conference. In the midst of the military's quest to close the circle on Ché's guerrillas, top military units were pulled from the guerrilla zone to reoccupy the mines.[30]

While Barrientos was cutting miners' wages and occupying the mines, he cemented support within the military by doubling army budgets, increasing officer salaries by 70 percent, and adding a host of new officer perquisites.[31] Gary Prado, the officer who led the Ranger unit that captured Ché, later observed that despite such efforts, the military was much less united under Barrientos than it seemed. In fact, the army became increasingly polarized between those intending to use the military's power to push the country forward and those in it for more narrow institutional and personal advancement.[32] This division would progressively destabilize and weaken military rule over the fifteen years that followed.

The underlying weakness of the Barrientos government and the role the United States played in fostering that weakness came to sharp international focus in mid-1968 when Fidel Castro announced that he would publish the diary of Ché Guevara. Since the Barrientos government held the original diary and all existing copies except for one kept by the CIA, it was apparent that either foreign agents had somehow purloined a copy of the document or someone inside the government had sold a copy to the Cuban leader without authorization. Soon evidence pointed incontrovertibly to one of Barrientos's friends and advisers, Minister of the Interior Antonio Arguedas.[33] Barrientos closed congress and declared a state of emergency in response to the resulting round of criticism, and all the civilians in his cabinet resigned in protest. Arguedas subsequently resurfaced in Lima, claiming that he had been pressured to become a CIA informant, and that "to destroy the imperialist entanglement into which Bolivia has fallen" he had given (not sold) his copy of the Guevara diary to Castro. Arguedas went on to name CIA agents in Bolivia, including Barrientos's old friend Lieutenant Colonel Fox. A *New York Times* correspondent commented that, if true, the Arguedas declarations "would indicate that the Bolivian government for the past three years has been little more than a mouthpiece for the United States, notably the CIA."[34]

Although Arguedas's charges were not entirely credible, they contained enough truth to disrupt the U.S. security apparatus in Bolivia for a time, and charges of U.S. manipulation had sufficient resonance with the Bolivian public to alter the domestic political balance. Alive, Ché Guevara the guerrilla had scarcely affected the popular Barrientos, but in death, Ché as symbol exacted his revenge by making the president's close relationship with the United States a political liability. To counter his predicament, Barrientos improved relations with the Soviet Union and supported reaccreditation of Cuba in the Organization of American States against U.S. opposition.[35] Naturally, as Barrientos distanced himself from the United States, he lost support in Washington; at the time of his death in April 1969 he was losing ground both internally and externally. The *New York Times* called him an "unusual Latin strong man" committed to democratic reforms and with a grasp of development economics, but an itemized list of Barrientos's property revealed that the impoverished orphan was worth $10 million when he died. Still later,

U.S. Senate testimony revealed that the helicopter in which he died while on a lightning visit to a peasant rally near Cochabamba had been a gift from Gulf Oil. These revelations tarnished Barrientos's revolutionary credentials and raised questions about the flamboyant president's exact political trajectory.[36]

Vice President Adolfo Siles Salinas, half-brother of former president Hernán Siles Zuazo, filled the presidency briefly after Barrientos's death, though with little popular appeal and much less political acumen than his brother. It became immediately apparent that real power continued to reside in the military, specifically with General Alfredo Ovando.[37] A conjunction of local and international issues pushed Ovando and the military sharply to the left in 1969. The domestic issues included the public revulsion and anti-U.S. feeling stirred by the Arguedas revelations and the power shift in the military after Barrientos's death. The international issues included the changing geopolitical calculus in Latin America created by the rise of the left in both Peru and Chile and the general decline of U.S. hegemonic influence in the midst of the Vietnam War.[38]

But perhaps of greatest significance was the fact that the United States no longer exerted the direct leverage on the Bolivian government that it once did. The paradoxes are obvious, but a combination of military success in "disciplining" labor, rising world tin prices, and belated benefits from agrarian reform meant that in 1968, for the first time since 1953, the United States provided no direct budget support to the Bolivian government. Aid now shifted from grants and food aid to interest-bearing dollar loans, which carried restrictions that only exacerbated Bolivians' resentment. Through 1969 Bolivians complained bitterly about "additionality clauses" in loan contracts that required their country to spend an amount equivalent to all loans received on U.S.-made products. The requirement, designed to ease mounting U.S. balance-of-payments problems, forced Bolivia to pay up to three times more for American goods than for comparable goods produced in Japan or Europe. Ironically, additionality clauses increased the operating costs of COMIBOL, which the United States had just spent millions to make profitable. Bolivians were also quick to note that the United States would actually receive more than two dollars in return for every dollar loaned—one immediately with the purchase of American goods, and the second plus interest when the loan was repaid.[39] Such resentment helped to wean Bolivia from aid dependency and gave the military freedom to distance itself from direct U.S. pressure.[40]

On 26 September 1969, apparently to avoid the scrutiny that his less-than-consistent revolutionary nationalism might raise in an open election, Ovando seized power. He quickly made clear the revolutionary-nationalist-statist focus of his new regime in radio addresses and a revolutionary manifesto issued the day of the coup. This was a revolution for international autonomy, domestic freedom from import dependency, and a recommitment to agrarian reform, he claimed. "Fundamentally, our revolution is the same as Peru's," he told the Bolivian people by radio.[41] A month later, on the anniversary of the nationalization of the Big Three, Ovando withdrew the military from the mines (where he had helped to put them four years earlier) and allowed the COB to reorganize. In pursuit of a more independent foreign policy Ovando opened the first ambassador-level contact with the Soviet Union and deepened relations and trade agreements with the Eastern bloc. These ties reduced the leverage of U.S. oil interests. At the urging of ambitious young socialist reformers in his government such as Marcelo Quiroga Santa Cruz, Ovando abrogated the 1955 petroleum code; negotiated a $27.5 million loan for oil exploration from the Soviets; and, on 7 October 1969, nationalized Bolivian Gulf Oil properties in Bolivia.[42]

The anti-American feeling engendered by the CIA, the Arguedas affair, and additionality clauses had spilled over against Bolivian Gulf Oil. Gulf entered Bolivia after the 1955 petroleum code was written and explored extensively in Santa Cruz. In 1966 it began to produce petroleum for export, and by 1968 its share of Bolivian petroleum exports was 80 percent. Relations between Bolivian Gulf and Barrientos were cozy, and the company's profits soared, but public opinion turned when Barrientos granted further concessions to Gulf in exchange for its help to finance the gas pipeline to Argentina.[43]

Like the earlier nationalizations of Standard Oil and the tin mines, nationalizing Gulf caused a brief surge of nationalist approval but in the long term only further underscored Bolivia's dependency. The Nixon administration cut U.S. grants and credits by more than one-half, and an international oil boycott cost Bolivia another $14.4 million in lost revenues and also delayed completion of the gas pipeline.

By early 1970 Ovando and his revolutionary program were in retreat. Santa Cruz, which received an 11 percent royalty on all Gulf Oil revenues, opposed the Gulf seizure, as did a powerful new interest group, the Confederación de Empresarios Privados de Bolivia (CEPB). Over the years that followed, the CEPB would exert increasing influence on Bolivian state policy in the interest of the emerging private sector. With opposition rising inside and out, Ovando sacked reform ministers in early 1970, assigned military radicals to obscure posts, and agreed to pay Gulf Oil $78 million in compensation.[44] Pressure from within the officer corps also grew, making Ovando back off from plans to close the U.S. military mission and withdraw from the Inter-American Defense Council. Charges surfaced that Barrientos and Ovando had been involved in a lucrative but illegal arms deal with Israel and had profited from an illicit slush fund generated by the sale of PL-480 food assistance from the United States. Journalists who made the charges died mysteriously, and fingers pointed at people close to Ovando.[45]

Ovando's programs polarized the military. On 4 October 1970, rightist officers attempted a coup that dislodged the president but failed to eliminate all his support. Backed by labor and feigning air raids on key positions held by the golpistas, General Juan José Torres emerged on top at the end of a confusing day during which six men had been president.[46] Torres, unlike Ovando, was a genuine reformer—the product of an impoverished background (as a child he sold candy on the streets of Cochabamba) and a representative of the new "revolutionary classes" around whom the MNR had attempted to rebuild the military. But Torres also had risen through the military ranks by dint of loyalty and hard work and was as much a child of the institution as he was of his class or of the 1952 revolution. Torres had authored Ovando's revolutionary manifesto the year before, then was sent into retirement in July to appease the military right. He now reemerged to salvage the military reform position. At his swearing in, the new president voiced the contradictions that were to haunt his brief tenure as president. His words, "My people and my army, I swear to put myself totally and completely at your service," revealed no understanding that the two would make conflicting demands on him.[47]

At a meeting of the Inter-American Defense Council while Ovando was president, Torres had denounced the council as a tool of the United States and called formal democracy a sham. Now in power, Torres issued a call to establish "an organ of workers' and popular power" that would serve as a more authentic voice of the people than did the formal legislature. The Popular Assembly, as it was called, opened on 2 July 1971, dominated by labor representatives. Through several stormy sessions the Assembly approved resolutions to open a workers' university, oust the Peace Corps, and nationalize the remaining mining enterprises. It argued vociferously over reinstating popular militias and creating popular tribunals with legal jurisdiction over all "crimes against the working class," but delayed final passage of those measures.[48]

Whatever its lofty intents or merits as a grassroots forum, the Popular Assembly set in motion a confused and confusing phase during which interest groups buffeted the ineffectual Torres government from all sides with competing and largely impossible demands. The Assembly was a product of the mobilization that had accompanied the 1952 revolution, but it also graphically illustrated the failure of the revolution to create institutions that could channel mobilization effectively. Since it had no power except to confront and propose, the Popular Assembly came quickly to symbolize the anarchy that threatened constantly to reemerge in Bolivia.

The Popular Assembly also revealed once again the mixed legacy of U.S. assistance and was accompanied by new expressions of the anti-Americanism latent in Bolivia since the 1930s. During the weeks following Torres's rise to power, student protestors seized U.S. government properties in La Paz and other Bolivian cities and did more than $36,000 worth of damage. Juan Lechín, as always a bellwether of pragmatic leftist calculation, became more outspoken in his anti-U.S. views than at any other point in his long career, reflecting the general Bolivian frus-

tration, his own need to move left to retain control of the labor movement, and his awareness of declining U.S. hegemony and influence.[49]

Torres improved Bolivia's relations with the socialist bloc and sent
observers to the Conference of Nonaligned Nations in Lusaka, Zambia.
In more direct challenges to the United States, his government nationalized the American-owned Matilde Mining Corporation, closed the
U.S. military's satellite-tracking station on El Alto above La Paz (known
as "Guantanamito" to its Bolivian critics), expelled U.S. labor organizations, and in May 1971—at the behest of the Popular Assembly—
ousted the Peace Corps on charges that it carried out racially motivated
contraception and sterilization campaigns in the Bolivian countryside.
Popular revulsion to the purported Peace Corps role was further stirred
by one of Bolivia's first internationally recognized films, *Yahwar Mallcu*
(Blood of the condor), a film that through powerful symbolism linked
birth control to the castrating presence of the United States in Bolivia.[50]

On the surface, the Nixon administration continued to remain calm,
but off the record U.S. officials described Bolivia as more of a threat to
hemispheric security than next-door socialist Chile because of military
divisions and the potentially explosive tensions from below. An old fear
resurfaced in the U.S. business community: concern that Torres and the
Popular Assembly were goading Bolivia's Indian peasantry into an explosion that would be difficult to contain.[51] As in Chile, the Nixon administration undermined the Torres government by blocking and delaying loans and isolating Bolivia internationally. *Prensa Latina* later
reported that during an OAS ministers' meeting, Secretary of State
William Rogers told Bolivian foreign minister Huascar Taborga, "This
time you have gone too far. Let me tell you that we have every intention
of seeing that Torres is overthrown." The statement, even if apocryphal,
accurately reflects the Nixon administration's position.[52]

An irony of this military challenge to U.S. hegemony was that the ambassador to Bolivia during the period was Ernest Siracusa—the same
Ernest Siracusa who had written the 1956 memo suggesting that the
United States support the military as "a responsible body from which
leadership might emerge."[53] Now Siracusa dealt with a military government that was no stronger or more unified than MNR governments

had ever been, was less "responsible" than the United States was willing to tolerate, and that, like the MNR, had come to resent the heavy hand of the United States.

Central premises of U.S. security doctrine were that Latin American militaries would be more dependable allies against communism and more authoritative and disciplined guarantors of orderly, capitalist-oriented evolutionary development than civilian democracies, buffeted as they were by populist demands. But the Torres government conflicted with each premise because the Bolivian military was never more than tangentially the reflection of U.S. security doctrine and North American training. It was a product of revolutionary upheaval, linked both to the MNR's legacy of reform and to the fragmented cliental system that emerged out of the confusion of the revolutionary era. Officials in Washington were tempted to see the military as the only institution that could bring order to this disrupted system, but in fact, Bolivia's military reflected these divisions rather than transcending them. The new officer corps was as socially mixed and politically factionalized as the civilian party it succeeded, and being in power only exacerbated the factionalism. In the words of political scientists James Malloy and Eduardo Gamarra, "the military began to reproduce within itself the conflicts ripping at civil society, and the result was internal fragmentation, undermining of the chain of command, and the beginning of decomposition."[54]

Finally, the military remained a product of Bolivian dependency and its cliental relationship with the United States, and U.S.-Bolivian military relations manifested the same dynamics of attempted cooperation, rising expectations, U.S. impositions, Bolivian resistance, and escalating conflict as had the MNR's relationship with the State Department the previous decade. One of the most authentically institutionalist reformers within the military, General Gary Prado Salmón, has commented that in its weakness, Bolivia in the early 1970s was buffeted between the tendencies in Peru and Chile, on the one hand, and the *linea dura* of Brazil and Argentina, on the other. It was further buffeted between the rising popular anti-imperialism that marked that troubled period in world affairs and the continuing influence of the United States in the Western Hemisphere in general and in Bolivia in particular. In Bolivia, those forces resolved themselves not in synthesis, but rather in increasing levels of conflict and rising political and social atomization. Revolutionary Marxism of the type brought by Ché had limited appeal in postrevolutionary Bolivia, but military rule made Bolivia no more the stable, friendly client of the United States than had the MNR. By 1971, Bolivia was almost a paradigm of what political scientist Samuel Huntington calls a praetorian system, in which "social forces confront each other nakedly; no political institutions, no corps of professional political leaders are recognized or accepted as the legitimate intermediaries to moderate group conflict. Equally important no agreement exists among groups as to the legitimate authoritative methods for resolving conflicts."[55]

The Ephemeral Banzer Boom

The coup against Torres surprised no one. His own minister of interior called the Torres regime "ten months of emergency." Military plotting had become constant, but the coup that finally toppled Torres began in Santa Cruz on 19 August 1971. Slowly, military units across the nation fell into line, although strong civilian opposition made the death toll unusually high for a Bolivian coup. The Red Cross listed 98 dead and some 506 wounded in fighting at the university in Santa Cruz alone. The death toll would have been higher if Torres had released arms to civilian militias as Juan Lechín and other labor leaders urged, but the president refused, unwilling to risk further bloodshed or the possibility of armed conflict between military units.[56]

The exact role Ambassador Siracusa and the United States played in the coup has not been fully determined. U.S. military advisers were close to the victor, Hugo Banzer Suárez, and allowed his supporters to use U.S. military communications facilities to maintain radio contact with rebel units. The U.S.-trained and -equipped Ranger battalion spearheaded the coup, and tanks purchased with U.S. aid were first battle-tested by the rebels, indicative of the indirect support the United States offered. The United States quickly recognized the new regime, and when calm returned, Ambassador Siracusa met with new president Banzer to assure him that several projects delayed under Torres would now proceed. U.S. aid jumped 600 percent during Banzer's first year in power and Bolivia received more military assistance than any other country in Latin America.[57]

Banzer himself had long connections to the United States. The grandson of German immigrants, Banzer survived the military purges of 1952 and rose in the hierarchy as an expert in logistics. He served as minister of education and military attaché to Washington under Barrientos and received advanced training at various U.S. military installations. James Dunkerley notes that Banzer's connections to the Bolivian civilian and military right and his strong links to the United States made "the diminutive Machiavellian . . . the perfect leader for the new Bolivian counter-revolution"—and the kind of military leader U.S. officials could again trust.[58]

Brazil openly supported the coup, at least in part as a surrogate of the United States, although the South American giant also had its own agenda. Before the coup an editorial in *O Estado* of São Paulo expressed those interests baldly: "Brazil cannot lose its image as a great power. If the situation worsens in Bolivia, Brazil is quite capable of assuming a role as guardian of democracy on the continent and asserting, by force if necessary, the fundamentals of Western, Christian civilization."[59] In December 1970 and January 1971, Brazil's outspoken ambassador to Bolivia, Hugo Bethlem, openly assisted several unsuccessful rightist coup attempts before being deported. When Banzer's coup succeeded, Bethlem returned to head a Brazilian business consortium. Trade ties between the two countries strengthened as a result of bilateral agreements, and subsequent border revisions gave Brazil an additional thirty-nine thousand square kilometers of Bolivian territory.[60]

Banzer now shifted from a Peruvian to a Brazilian military model, one emphasizing depoliticization of the masses and a capitalist, technocratic approach to development. His government moved quickly and hard against the left, even against such symbols of counterculture protest as long hair and beards. Police and military units roamed the streets of the major cities, detaining those whose personal appearance was not to the regime's liking and administering forced haircuts to longhaired youths. Banzer crushed remaining guerrilla movements in eastern Bolivia and expelled one hundred diplomats from the greatly expanded Soviet embassy staff.[61]

The repression that followed was aimed at demobilizing the left and muting protests against unpopular investor-oriented reforms. In the aftermath of a steep devaluation of the peso, mandated by the International Monetary Fund in late 1972, living costs jumped 39 percent while wages rose at half that rate. Banzer followed with a second shock in early 1974 when he removed state subsidies on many basic consumer items, allowing their prices to nearly double. Workers struck and peasants near Cochabamba set up roadblocks. When negotiations failed, Banzer sent the army to clear the roads. The clash that followed, known as the Massacre of Tolata, took the lives of more than one hundred peasants.[62]

Banzer, Christopher Mitchell observes, "crystallized . . . middle-class-based populism in Bolivian politics," but without a base of co-opted peasant support.[63] The new president tried to renew the Pacto Militar-Campesino, but he lacked Barrientos's charismatic links to the peasantry, and the pact was bereft of even a hint of legitimacy. Without ties to the popular classes Banzer was afraid to test the political waters in direct elections. Instead he relied heavily on the military, Santa Cruz agribusiness, owners of the private mines, the CEPB, and a group of young middle-class technical experts. This new generation of technocrats was the product of twenty years of significant investments in education, but also of the difficult years at the beginning of MNR rule—the years of political imprisonment, bread lines, and unruly peasant and labor militias—and populist nationalism repelled them.[64]

Víctor Paz and his loyalists in the MNR initially joined Banzer out of distaste for the disorder and radical turn of the Ovando-Torres interim. Paz hoped he could use the alliance as a vehicle to reassert his own popular legitimacy and return to power, but Banzer quickly recognized the threat the old revolutionary leader posed and thwarted Paz's attempts to build an independent base. Two months before the Massacre of Tolata, Paz broke with Banzer and went back into exile in time to keep intact at least some of his credibility with peasants.[65]

Banzer's failure to develop strong popular support and the growing criticism of his government's methods from the Catholic church and human rights organizations convinced several young institutionalist officers that the military should withdraw from politics. Their attempted coup failed, further hardening Banzer's resolve to stay the course as Augusto Pinochet was then stating he would do in neighboring Chile.[66] The economic news was reassuring; growth averaged 6.8 percent between 1973 and 1975, and earnings on all key exports were up. Oil led the way, as a percentage of total export earnings rising from 5.7 percent in 1970 to 31.6 percent by 1975. But tin also rose—total export value up from $113 million in 1972 to $374.4 million in 1978—and agricultural export earnings rose by 600 percent between 1970 and 1974.[67]

Bolivia was far different in 1974 that it had been in 1952 when it imported 35 percent of its food and exported unrefined raw materials to Europe and the United States. The Banzer government sold Bolivia's first smelted tin, and by 1974 tin metal accounted for 9 percent of total export value. Bolivia's trading partners also became more diversified; Latin America now received more than one-third of all exports, Europe received one-fifth, and the United States just one-third. As late as the mid-1960s the United States and Europe together had purchased 90–95 percent of all Bolivia's exports and provided 70–75 percent of its imports.[68]

In short, by late 1974 Banzer felt both sufficiently pressured and sufficiently independent to dispense with all constitutional trappings and go it alone. On 9 November 1974, after another abortive coup attempt in Santa Cruz, the president decreed the cessation of all political activity and again put labor organizations under direct government control. When workers protested, Banzer sent the army to occupy striking factories and mines; the occupation lasted four years.[69]

But while Banzer was shifting to Pinochet's political model, his economic policies continued to adhere more closely to Brazil's military-dominated, state-capitalist approach. There were no Chicago Boys in Bolivia to oversee a drastic reduction of state expenditures. Instead Banzer's *autogolpe* increased the dominance of the state sector as rising export earnings made it both easy and tempting for the tenuously situated president to spend and borrow in order to build political support. Government payrolls increased sixfold between 1970 and 1977, and the foreign debt quadrupled from $782.1 million in 1971 to $3.1 billion by 1978—with 43.1 percent of the debt held by private foreign banks at high market interest rates.[70]

In the short run, social indicators improved: unemployment was down and life expectancy rose from forty-three years in 1960 to fifty-one years by 1980, although it was still the lowest in the hemisphere. Education opportunities increased, illiteracy was down from 61 percent in 1960 to 37 percent in 1980, and food production per capita increased 15 percent. But the gap between poor and rich also grew. During the 1970s, the upper 20 percent of Bolivian society saw their share of the national income rise from 41 percent to 46 percent while the bottom 40 percent of income earners saw their share decline from 22.1 percent to 19.4 percent. Despite the revolution, income distribution was less equitable in Bolivia than in most of Latin America and getting worse.[71]

By early 1978, the limits of Bolivia's "economic miracle" were apparent. Although the balance of payments had been favorable through the mid-1970s, by 1975 imports were again rising faster then exports; at the end of Banzer's regime, government deficits had risen by a factor of ten. Tin and petroleum shared serious structural weaknesses. Bolivia's tin continued to be the most expensive in the world to produce, but investments went to increase refining capacity rather than to improve the productivity of the mines. Meanwhile, policies that kept the domestic price of petroleum well below the world market price resulted in rising consumption at home and a loss of exportable surpluses. By 1978 oil exports were less than one-fourth of what they had been in 1972. Meanwhile, overall growth fell far short of rates projected in the 1975 five-year plan—by 1980 growth was only 1.2 percent rather than the projected 8 percent.[72]

Politically, the Banzer regime was not as strong as it seemed. The growth of the state sector during the *banzerato* revealed the continuing cliental dynamics of a praetorianized society, and the military never completely closed ranks behind Banzer. Gary Prado, a critic from within the military, comments that while officers received higher wages and better social benefits under Banzer, these benefits isolated the military from the people, who increasingly viewed them as a privileged sector.[73]

In addition, the rising benefits created a clique of officers interested in power solely for personal gain. Attempts to exclude the popular sectors and proscribe political organization and expression generally work only briefly, even in countries where the repressive powers of the state are far greater than Banzer's and where popular sectors are less organized. In Bolivia, labor, peasants, and the political parties were never fully silenced or made impotent by Banzer, and they waited impatiently in the wings to reassert their demands.

The changing U.S. posture also undermined Banzer. Presidents Nixon and Ford were supportive, but with Bolivia prospering during the 1970s, U.S. assistance played a different role than before. Instead of trying to stimulate basic growth, U.S. assistance was finally geared to helping the benefits trickle downward more effectively. With agribusiness booming, U.S. development assistance shifted toward programs that benefited the peasants. When Banzer tried to subordinate labor to state control in November 1974, the American Institute for Free Labor Development (AIFLD) moved in with labor education programs and a variety of social projects designed to loosen the grip of the COB on the labor movement. The AIFLD organized and funded cooperatives, small housing projects, schools, and the like, and in a few cases even served as something of a mediator between proscribed unions and the government. Although the role of U.S. aid was to assist Banzer and provide alternatives to traditional leftist-oriented peasant and labor organizations, shifts in the focus of aid gave North American officials in the field a new and better grasp of the problems facing Bolivia's popular sectors.[74]

Thus when Jimmy Carter came to office with a plan to emphasize human rights and democratization, the change resonated at the field level and was not just the idiosyncratic preference of an idealistic president. A growing number of North Americans both in Bolivia and in Washington were convinced that the Banzer experiment in military authoritarianism should end; and because Bolivia was both peripheral to U.S. interests and particularly susceptible to leverage, it seemed an ideal location to test the new human rights emphasis. In May 1977 Carter sent Assistant Secretary of State Terence Todman to Bolivia to clarify to

Banzer that the United States would now give preference to countries with democratic governments. In September Carter himself reinforced that point when Banzer flew to Washington to attend the signing of the revised Panama Canal treaty.[75]

A month later Banzer announced that he would hold elections in July 1978, although he did not yet remove restrictions on political organization and expression. At the time, observers thought it an astute move that would humor President Carter and capitalize on the lingering prosperity from the mid-1970s boom. By calling elections so soon but not reopening the political system, Banzer apparently planned to minimize the ability of the parties to organize, thus putting himself in position to better control the outcome. But Banzer's grasp on power was far more tenuous than most outside observers realized. By the close of 1977 it was clear that whatever political base Banzer hoped to have consolidated during Bolivia's six years of prosperity was rapidly crumbling. In December the wives of four exiled miners initiated a hunger strike that quickly expanded into a general strike to pressure Banzer to fully reopen the political system. In mid-January Banzer announced unrestricted amnesty for all political exiles and prisoners and promised that no reprisals would be taken against the hunger strikers and their supporters.[76]

What had begun as controlled liberalization that would keep Banzer in power had gone out of control, and he withdrew from the race. His bureaucratic national security state, of the type then in vogue in southern cone countries and Brazil, had proved surprisingly fragile in Bolivia. Banzer's economic boom and Bolivia's surface stability and growth had been ephemeral. Bolivia was now about to enter a particularly tumultuous period of its tortured history.

The Failed Transition to Democracy and the Cocaine Coup

It quickly became clear that the military candidate who stepped in for Banzer, Juan Pereda Asbún, was too independent to be the faithful lackey that Banzer wanted, but too lackluster and wooden to be a true political force on his own. Banzer briefly thought of delaying the elections, but the process was already in motion, and both the military and the Carter administration made it clear that delay would be unacceptable.[77] Political parties had little time to form coalitions to oppose the military candidate, yet on election day it was obvious that Pereda held the crucial rural vote only through massive and blatant fraud, and the electoral court had little choice but to annul the elections. Banzer announced on 19 July that he would hand power to a military junta, thereby setting in motion a preemptive coup by Pereda.[78]

From the outset, Pereda found himself isolated. The coup embarrassed the Carter administration, and Ambassador Paul Boeker informed Pereda that he would lose $70 million in assistance unless new elections were called immediately. More ominous for Pereda, the military failed to unite behind him. His ill-starred regime lasted only four months before it was overthrown by young officers led by General David Padilla. Convinced that it was time for the military to get out of politics for good, Padilla immediately called elections for early July 1979 and began to simplify electoral procedures to remove opportunities for fraud. This time the elections went smoothly, on schedule, and with relative honesty. The judgment of La Paz's leading newspaper, *Presencia,* was that Padilla had done nothing, "for which he deserved the profound gratitude of his people."[79]

Padilla's presidency had been a holding action—a half-year preparation for one of the cleanest elections in Bolivia's history. Unfortunately, much of the business he left pending during that time badly needed doing as the country's economy lurched ever closer to crisis. The world price of oil rose precipitously in 1979, but Bolivian oil exports were nil due to a lack of new discoveries and high domestic demand fostered by controlled prices. The jump in world prices that accompanied the return of a world oil shortage only increased the effective subsidy to domestic consumers and provided further incentives to smuggle oil products to neighboring countries. An increasingly overvalued exchange rate further discouraged exports and subsidized imports and smugglers. Bolivia's debt burden was crushing, and new credits were difficult to obtain except at increasingly exorbitant interest rates.[80]

Nonetheless, Bolivia's old political veterans fought each other for the chance to contend with these problems. Hernán Siles Zuazo, leader of a left-center coalition party called the Unión Democrática y Popular (UDP), won a plurality of popular votes in the election, but Víctor Paz Estenssoro's right-center MNR coalition controlled the legislature, which would choose the president from among the top vote getters. Siles, Paz, and their followers locked horns in partisan intransigence, with neither side willing to find common ground. Hugo Banzer, now a civilian and head of the third-place Acción Democrática Nacionalista (ADN), proved equally inflexible unless promised a major voice in either government. The legislature deadlocked, and Rosalyn Carter was forced to cancel her plans to attend the inauguration when it became apparent that no one had emerged to whom Padilla might transfer power. Finally, in late-night sessions, Senate president Wálter Guevara Arze, third in the old MNR triumvirate, was selected as interim president until new and definitive elections could be held.[81]

Without a mandate of any kind, it was now Guevara's unpleasant task to guide Bolivia through IMF-mandated monetary stabilization. Meanwhile, Socialist party senator Marcelo Quiroga Santa Cruz, who as minister of mines and petroleum under Ovando had authored the decision to nationalize Bolivian Gulf Oil, picked that moment to launch a high-visibility inquest into the Banzer government. The investigation served primarily to strengthen the position of those in the military who were convinced that it had been a mistake to turn power back to civilians.[82]

In late October, just two months after Guevara took office, the hemisphere's attention focused on La Paz, where the Ninth General Assembly of the Organization of American States was meeting. Amid strong affirmations for Bolivia's experiment in democracy, the OAS passed a resolution affirming Bolivia's right of access to the sea, with only Chile and Paraguay voting against. But while OAS delegates were praising Bolivia's return to democracy, a military plot was under way to abort it. On 31 October Guevara appealed to Paz and Siles to form a coalition government, but they refused. That night, while OAS delegates enjoyed closing festivities, Guevara slipped into hiding. Early the next morning, with many OAS delegates still in the city, tanks and armored cars rolled through the center of La Paz in what initially seemed a relatively peaceful if oddly timed coup.[83]

The goals and purposes of the coup's leader, Colonel Alberto Natusch Busch, the nephew of former populist military president Germán Busch, were as incomprehensible as his timing. Natusch's stated purpose was to end the impasse between the executive and legislative branches, but his *golpe* did that only by uniting them in opposition. Natusch further claimed to be a leftist, but he was bitterly opposed by every authentic leftist group in the country. He stated he would deal decisively with Bolivia's economic problems, but his initial plan to raise the wages of all Bolivian workers seemed closer to demagoguery than to decisive action. His claim to popular support was belied by the immediate popular resistance and the heavy human cost Natusch was willing to pay to quash it. In short, he seemed a man with few real goals or standards other than a desire and ambition for power.

The major parties and the COB refused to collaborate with Natusch. Meanwhile, Guevara and former president David Padilla led a courageous and effective resistance in hiding. Three days into the coup, Natusch ended his appeals for popular support and unleashed tank units to quiet challengers inside the military. He sent air force planes and a helicopter commandeered from a North American construction company to silence civilian opponents in the working-class neighborhoods of the capital. The toll mounted—200 people dead, 125 disappeared, and 200 wounded.[84]

International pressure on Natusch's government was intense. Virtually all the OAS nations refused to consider recognition, and the Carter administration, miffed that Natusch had openly defied Cyrus Vance's counsel at the OAS meeting to give democracy a chance, immediately severed diplomatic relations and froze $60 million in aid. The coup acutely embarrassed many Bolivians and was yet another reversal for the beleaguered Carter—though one receiving far less attention back home than did the assault on the U.S. embassy in Teheran and the capture of hostages by Islamic fundamentalists, which occurred in the midst of the Natusch fiasco. With military support tenuous at best, and isolated both at home and abroad, Natusch finally agreed to step down. His only face-saving request was that the presidency not be returned to Guevara, who had stood as a rallying point throughout the coup attempt, but instead should pass to the presiding officer of the House of Deputies, Lidia Gueiler Tejada, Bolivia's first and, as of 1998, only woman president.[85]

Gueiler, a longtime MNR militant most recently linked to Siles, faced an even more impossible task than had Guevara. Bolivia's deteriorating economy basically shut down during the two-week coup attempt, and speculation against the peso now made an economic package imperative. Two weeks after taking office, Gueiler devalued the peso by 25 percent and removed all subsidies on domestic oil consumption. Immediately the prices of transportation and most basic consumer goods rose precipitously, and striking peasants, workers, and the powerful transport union paralyzed the nation. Gueiler was forced to retreat, and renewed speculation against the peso began. Meanwhile, the combination of popular mobilization, deepening economic crisis, and the apparent impotence of the Gueiler government played into the hands of military hard-liners, who consolidated their control of the military even as they surrendered control of the government. Now led by President Gueiler's cousin, Luis García Meza Tejada, and García Meza's close associate Luis Arce Gómez, the hard-liners shared the convictions that democracy was premature and that military honor had been besmirched by Quiroga Santa Cruz's inquest.

García Meza, a stocky and humorless bully, was born into a military family in La Paz. He rose slowly through the ranks and survived the purges in the early 1950s largely because, at the time, he was suspended from the army for excessive hazing of cadets. His first important political position came under Natusch as head of the army.[86] Luis Arce Gómez brought a sinister new interest in paramilitary forces to supplement the military's internal security role. Arce Gómez was something of a protégé of ex-Nazi Klaus Barbie, the "Butcher of Lyon." After World

War II, Barbie escaped to South America, assisted by U.S. intelligence officers who believed him to be an important source of information. Barbie came to Bolivia in 1951, took the name Klaus Altman, and became a Bolivian citizen. Barrientos involved Barbie/Altman in state security, and the ex-Nazi became a close confidante of Arce Gómez, who once called him "my teacher."[87] Arce Gómez had been expelled from the army in 1960 on charges of raping the daughter of a superior officer, but Barrientos reinstated him in 1964 because he was useful at getting things done and silencing troublesome opponents. As chief of military intelligence under Natusch, one of Arce Gómez's first acts was to seize and destroy all damaging security files that Quiroga Santa Cruz might use in his inquest.[88]

With popular mobilization rising in the aftermath of devaluation, García Meza and Arce Gómez engulfed Bolivia in a new and disturbing reign of terror. When Jesuit priest Luis Espinal and his weekly newspaper *Aquí* began a series of articles on military involvement in the drug trade, paramilitary forces bombed Espinal's office. Two weeks later the priest was found tortured and killed. García Meza made loud and specific threats against those who "wished to harm the military." In response, labor, church, and political leaders—including Paz, Siles, Guevara, and Lechín—set aside their differences to create the Comité Nacional de Defensa de la Democracia (CONADE).[89]

The violence escalated prior to the third election in as many years. A plane chartered from a private aviation service partly owned by Arce Gómez crashed, killing several high officials of the UDP. Siles was to have been on the plane but canceled at the last minute. The only survivor was vice-presidential candidate Jaime Paz Zamora, who escaped by leaping from the burning plane. Sabotage was widely suspected.

When the *Washington Post* broke the story that U.S. ambassador Marvin Weissman had intervened to avert a coup attempt by the hardliners, Arce Gómez detained the *Post* correspondent. Arce Gómez demanded that the reporter reveal his sources, and the case became a cause célèbre for rightists opposed to elections. Paramilitary provocateurs accused Weissman of imperialist intervention, and in the resulting uproar García Meza demanded that Gueiler postpone the upcoming elections. Gueiler declined. The anti-Weissman campaign escalated when a band of paramilitary thugs invaded government buildings in Santa Cruz; shot the governor, his aide, and a newsman; and attacked U.S. property. If military hard-liners hoped that the anti-Weissman campaign would derail election plans, they were disappointed. The general public, even in conservative Santa Cruz, seemed to interpret Weissman's act as no more and no less than a defense of the democratic process, and the furor died as quickly as it had flared.[90]

The hubbub only consolidated support for the leftist UDP coalition, and on June 29, after much ado, many threats, and seemingly inevitable violence, the elections came off in relative peace with Siles increasing his plurality from the year before. The two and one-half weeks following the election were also quiet as CONADE worked to prepare the way for Siles to take office. Paz sealed the matter by announcing that he would not stand in the way of his old political rival.[91]

Then, unexpectedly at noon on 17 July, the tanks rumbled again and García Meza and his cronies seized control. His explanation had the ring of parody: His purpose was "to save Bolivia from communism" in the name of national security and "to defend Bolivia's sovereignty from outside intrusion" in the service of the continuing national revolution. Later events confirmed Laurence Whitehead's assessment that the coup was mostly about drugs and the basest of self-interest.[92]

Most Bolivians accepted the coup passively, some because they felt powerless to resist it and others because the coup seemed to promise the order and security that had been missing during the tumultuous months of democracy that preceded it. Others were less resigned. Miners continued their resistance sporadically for several months, and the tense internal situation kept the nation under martial law for the duration of García Meza's regime. Unlike the Natusch fiasco, this time the military and paramilitary repression was fierce and immediate. On the day of the coup, armed men in civilian clothing broke into an emergency meeting of CONADE at the COB building on La Paz's main avenue, killed Marcelo Quiroga Santa Cruz and two union leaders, and took the rest prisoner. Paramilitary squads roamed cities, towns, and even the countryside, seizing union and political leaders and demoralizing the opposition with unprecedented brutality.[93]

The new government now shifted to the Argentine variant of national security doctrine, a Latin American refinement of security principles taught by U.S. military advisers. Argentina was just emerging from its "dirty war," and shadowy figures from that country joined Barbie to "advise" the official and unofficial security forces working under Minister of Interior Arce Gómez. These ominous developments made Bolivia, a place historically of much political turmoil but relatively little violence or brutality, one of the worst human rights offenders in the hemisphere.[94] Its policies in Bolivia a shambles, the Carter administration immediately recalled Ambassador Weissman and canceled nearly all military and economic aid. Over the next fifteen months, Bolivia lost $125 million in assistance from the United States and another $40 million from Venezuela, which led the Andean Pact nations in a determined effort to isolate the new Bolivian regime.[95]

Rumors and hard evidence of García Meza's connections to Bolivia's burgeoning cocaine industry quickly surfaced. Arce Gómez was first cousin to Roberto Suárez Gómez, Bolivia's richest and most flamboyant drug trafficker—a man who fostered a Robin Hood image by equipping hospitals, paving roads, and providing low-income housing, and who was rumored to be rich enough to pay off Bolivia's international debt by himself. In May, just before the elections and while the Weissman case was occupying Bolivia's attention, the U.S. Drug Enforcement Agency (DEA) launched the biggest sting operation in its history against Suárez. Although the Bolivian drug lord managed to elude the net, one of his close associates was captured in Miami. Rumors circulated that Suárez feared the pressures the United States could exert on a relatively weak civilian government and financed the 1980 coup with the understanding that his cousin would be given a key position from which to protect Suárez's business interests.[96]

As the García Meza government consolidated its position, the DEA pulled out of Bolivia and became the source of many of the rumors linking the regime to cocaine traffickers. Arce supposedly squeezed small traffickers out of the Santa Cruz market and received a 10 percent cut from all who were allowed to continue the trade. García Meza was charged with taking millions of dollars from traffickers to buy the active support—or at least the silence—of key military officers. General Wálter Bernal, head of the Bolivian air force, was said to receive payments of $10,000 weekly to permit the transport of cocaine through Bolivian airspace. And a new tax on truckloads of coca went straight to the pockets of García Meza, Arce Gómez, and other functionaries. A DEA official, when asked the degree of corruption, said: "It is impossible to calculate the money they made. Think of a preposterous figure, double it, and know damn well that you've made a gross underestimate."[97] Arce indeed improved his standard of living during his brief year in power, obtaining three mansions, four luxury apartments, five ranches, a milk-processing plant, and a number of new aircraft. The assessment of one State Department spokesman was that "for the first time the mafia has bought itself a government."[98]

In 1956, Ernest Siracusa suggested that the United States "adopt and put into effect a line of action with respect to the Bolivian army for the deliberate purpose of seeing the formal military so strengthened that there would be some responsible body from which leadership might emerge should political chaos come to Bolivia." To that end, Siracusa recommended that the United States strengthen its military mission, increase its training of Bolivian officers, encourage civilian leaders to increasingly rely on the military, and devise means "to enhance the prestige of the Bolivian military."[99] Over the twenty-four years that followed, the United States pursued each of those policies, yet by 1980 the Bolivian military was dominated by outlaws who were neither responsible nor secure.

Back in Washington, Jeane Kirkpatrick was receiving public exposure—and subsequently gained a high position in the incoming administration of Ronald Reagan—for arguing that Carter's emphasis on democracy and human rights was naive, particularly in this hemisphere. Kirkpatrick claimed that by conflating all nondemocratic regimes Carter ignored the substantive difference between the "authoritarianism" of the right and the "totalitarianism" of the left, and that Carter's reforms played into the hands of Communists. Again as so often before, Bolivia had too low a priority and seemed too easy to manage to merit close scrutiny. If U.S. policy makers had more closely examined the trajectory of Bolivia's military regime since 1964, Kirkpatrick's renewed defense of right-wing military authoritarianism might also have been called into question as naive.

7 Frontier Myths, Cocaine Dependency, and Limits to the American Dream

When Lieutenant Lardner Gibbon visited Bolivia in the early 1850s he was struck, as were many of the North American visitors who followed him, by the undeveloped potential of Bolivia's eastern frontier. On observing an Indian sucking juice from a *totora* rush on the shores of Lake Titicaca, Gibbon noted in his journal: "We cannot understand why the population of those mountains have not cleared more lands at the base of the Andes, where their children would find beautiful flowers, and the men the real sugar-stalk; where they might tickle their noses with the fragrance from rich pine-apples and oranges, and where their tables might be loaded with the choicest vegetable productions."[1] As Gibbon proceeded down the Chapare, Mamoré, and Madeira Rivers to the Amazon, he saw only silence and neglect. The inhabitants of that region seemed singularly devoid of ambition and energy to Gibbon, who thought the people of Santa Cruz "the most indolent in the world." Few there seemed willing to "exert themselves beyond what is absolutely necessary," he observed. And although a typical *cruceño* "would love to see a steam vessel on the rivers of the east, yet when asked what he might want to buy from the world market, it is seldom that he thinks of anything he wants."[2]

Gibbon inevitably contrasted the "neglect" and "death-like silence" of the Bolivian wilderness with the frenetic activity on the frontier back home. The United States had just straddled a continent. Thousands had already pushed their way into California, and energetic entrepreneurs were busy planning railroad routes to span the newly acquired territory. In contrast, Gibbon's observations and report gave further confirmation to the North American image of South American beggars seated passively on benches of gold.[3]

It was an image with deep cultural resonance for North Americans. To the citizens of the United States, the frontier was both actual and metaphysical; it was a place where men and women were renewed and made whole by immersing themselves in nature, subduing it, and making of it and themselves something better. The frontier was the birthplace of American exceptionalism, and in the words of Wallace Stegner, "an American, insofar as he is new and different at all, is a civilized man who has renewed himself in the wild."[4] Fredrick Pike adds that in the view of many Americans, "Latin Americans remained only half alive, because of their failure to undergo comparable experiences." More deeply, the paucity of apparent energy clashed so graphically with America's own frontier spirit that it shaped a host of cultural valuations. "Americans," Pike says, "have suspected that only serious deficiencies of virility could account for the Latin Americans' willingness to leave virgin land unviolated."[5]

For almost a century, North American entrepreneurs, visionaries, and finally the U.S. government worked to rouse Bolivia to recognition of the potential wealth of its eastern hinterland. In the eyes of visitors, the continuing slumber of the Bolivian frontier served as silent rebuke to the lethargy and lack of vision of those who inhabited and administered it, and called for the energy of those who could better tap its potential. Ironically, when Bolivia's eastern hinterland and the entrepreneurial energy of its inhabitants finally awoke in the 1970s and 1980s, that awakening created new conflicts in U.S.-Bolivian relations. American dreams, the Bolivian frontier, and a traditional Bolivian crop—coca—blended in unexpected ways to create new strains on the relationship between the two nations, yet the continuing realities of hegemony and dependency and the underlying clashes of power and culture led to familiar patterns.

American Dreams, the Bolivian Frontier, and Coca

Moving from mythology to fact, it should be noted that the search for El Dorado took intrepid Spanish explorers deep into the heart of Bolivia long before the British mainland colonies in North America even existed. By the mid-sixteenth century, Spanish priests had established missions in areas of eastern Bolivia where highways and railroads still have not reached today. The difference that underlay Americans' and Bolivians' approach to their respective frontiers was never a matter of energy or virility. Through the colonial period and after, coca and sugar production pulled Bolivians east of the Andes; and through the nineteenth century, the lucrative search for cinchona bark and rubber sent hardy Bolivian adventurers to the country's remotest regions. Nor was ambition or entrepreneurial spirit inherently lacking. In the late nineteenth century, Nicolás Suárez, an ancestor of drug lord Roberto Suárez, possessed enough of both to create a veritable trade empire in the northeastern interior of Bolivia and controlled the exploitation of rubber over an area the size of Missouri.[6]

Nonetheless, at the end of the nineteenth century a widely traveled North American could still report: "When one compares its possibilities with its performance, except for a few, very limited exceptions, one gets the impression in South America of a vast continent almost literally going to waste."[7] This North American abhorrence of "waste"—defined as the failure to tame the land and put it to productive use—led to several attempts, already described, to apply American energy and entrepreneurial skills to the Bolivian lowlands. Yet each time they tried to tap the wealth of the Bolivian *oriente*, U.S. citizens faced a bewildering combination of official apathy or outright obstruction that only confirmed pejorative stereotypes. From Colonel Church's railroad scheme through Standard Oil's explorations, energetic, profit-seeking North Americans gained concessions from an apparently enthusiastic Bolivian government, only to subsequently run into a host of bureaucratic and other stumbling blocks—or, in the case of Standard Oil and later Gulf Oil, outright confiscation.

A story more symbolically important than actually so is that of William H. "Alfalfa Bill" Murray, a former congressman and future governor of Oklahoma. Murray was a staunch prairie populist convinced that the area south of Santa Cruz could become "America's new frontier"—a place to restore traditional pioneer virtues and re-create America as it had been and ought still to be. More than two hundred colonists, mostly Oklahomans, left for Bolivia in 1923. After being stranded at the railhead on the harsh altiplano, the colonists finally straggled into the zone reserved for them, only to find it already occupied. After Murray's group struggled more than a year with the harsh environment and the suddenly uncooperative Bolivian government, the U.S. State Department set up an emergency fund to help most of them return home. Bolivia, once again, had been the deathbed of American frontier dreams; and once again the hopes of Bolivians raised by U.S. visionaries were overwhelmed by the fears and resentments aroused by the actual foreign presence.[8]

As was true of many aspects of U.S.-Bolivian relations, the frontier theme underwent a significant transformation during World War II. As noted in Chapter 3, Bolivia's tin, rubber, and quinine drew unprecedented attention from the U.S. government during the war, and the latter two products rekindled interest in Bolivia's frontier east. Knowing that the demand for all three Bolivian products would diminish when peace returned, the United States sent Merwin Bohan to Bolivia to formulate what today would be called a plan of sustainable development. The essence of Bohan's plan was to develop the agricultural potential of the east, reduce Bolivia's food imports, and thus reduce dependency on the foreign exchange generated by mining. To that end, the United States initially committed $25 million. The subsequent Bolivian development strategy, particularly that of the MNR, adhered closely to Bohan's plan.[9]

MNR policies encouraged capital-intensive "agricultural enterprises" in Santa Cruz. Such enterprises were exempt from land reform; thus the impact of agrarian reform in Santa Cruz was precisely the opposite of its effect in the highlands. In the east, agrarian reform allowed large landholders to consolidate and formalize land tenure while U.S.-funded agricultural assistance programs helped owners clear land and mechanize and provided credits to expand production. U.S. assistance also helped complete the all-weather highway connecting Santa Cruz to Cochabamba in 1954. A year later, eleven thousand trucks a month plied the new highway. Toward the end of the decade the number climbed to nearly fifty thousand. With access to the national market, Santa Cruz increased sugar production from 34,000 tons in 1950 to 1.95 million tons in 1964; rice production rose from 10,000 to 123,500 tons in the same period. By the early 1970s Bolivia was self-sufficient in sugar, rice, cotton, beef, lumber, and corn; Santa Cruz was the country's fastest growing city and region; and much of Bohan's dream seemed well on the way to fulfillment.[10]

Internal colonization was the counterpoint to this emphasis on agribusiness, though it received lower priority from both the MNR and U.S. advisers. One of the six stated objectives of agrarian reform was to encourage highland peasants to relocate to the underpopulated east, but initially this was a paper commitment only. In 1954 a team of U.S. advisers revealed long-held prejudices by asserting that highland Indians were unsuitable for colonization purposes because they were "people who themselves require development"—and could not, therefore, be agents of development.[11] The MNR shared U.S. preconceptions that native highlanders were unsuitable colonists and focused instead on attracting foreigners.[12] With the advent of the 1956 stabilization plan, however, both the Siles government and the United States came to see the east as a potential social safety valve for miners separated from COMIBOL. An objective of the budding Civic Action program was to develop both the frontier and the young highland army recruits who manned the new "revolutionary" army by sending them east to build roads and clear land in colonization areas. Each soldier would then receive a plot when his term of service ended.[13]

Few highland soldiers or miners settled permanently in Santa Cruz or other colonization zones during the 1950s, and official U.S. and Bolivian priorities and funding remained heavily skewed toward agribusiness.[14] Under the Alliance for Progress, however, colonization became an institutionalized feature of U.S. development strategy in Bolivia. A joint U.S.-Bolivian pamphlet on colonization put out in 1965 makes explicit the parallels both participants drew and the hopes those parallels fostered:

> This Eastern country is the area of greatest potential development today. In fact, Bolivia's east is at this moment in the country's history almost the

exact equivalent of the North American Far West of about 150 years ago—
wild, untamed, undeveloped, and much of it virtually unpopulated. It is a
land of promise which offers a challenge to those venturesome souls who,
like the rugged pioneers who developed the great West of the United
States, are willing to face the unknown and assume risks and hardships in
an effort to improve their lot and extend their country's frontiers.[15]

While much of eastern Bolivia remained a relative backwater in 1970,
the boom in Santa Cruz seemed a portent of what lay ahead as Bolivians, under U.S. tutelage, awakened to the full potential of their frontier.
Then, in 1971, Santa Cruz formally seized political power. General
Banzer and six of his ministers were cruceños, and the new government
further increased support for agribusiness. At the time, a combination
of unusually dry weather and artificially high world prices made cotton
the "white gold" of Santa Cruz. Hectares under cultivation increased
tenfold in less than five years, and foreign banks pumped more than
$11 million in loans to cotton growers. A fivefold increase in the world
price of petroleum and a sixfold rise in sugar prices, also products of
Santa Cruz, followed hard on the cotton boom. The Banzer government
subsidized all three products with easy credits, generous write-offs for
speculative loans that often could not be repaid, state-owned support
services, and—in the case of sugar and oil—increased state-financed
refining capacity.[16]

The burgeoning commercial agricultural sector demanded labor, in
chronic short supply in Santa Cruz; the obvious labor pool was the highlands. Contractors went to the altiplano and valleys to find workers and
bring them to the oriente to work in the cotton and sugar harvests. By
the mid-1970s, almost sixty thousand seasonal laborers arrived in Santa
Cruz each year. Once in the lowlands, many of the contracted workers
were lured to stay by the availability of land, a high and relatively stable
market for rice (a crop with low input costs other than labor, making
it easy for small farmers to grow), and the spreading highland peasant networks in the oriente. By 1975 an estimated fourteen thousand
to twenty thousand highlanders relocated to Santa Cruz each year.[17]
Tradition-bound highland Indians had become mobile and energetic
petty capitalists.

The new cruceño entrepreneur had little in common with his "indolent" ancestor, whom Gibbon described a century before as seldom exerting himself "beyond what was absolutely necessary." Both highland colonist and cruceño agribusinessman now coveted ever more of the things the world market offered: bicycles, radios, watches, stereos, televisions, video cassette recorders, and sport utility vehicles, as resources allowed. Both colonists and agribusinessmen were products of the transforming power of Bolivia's frontier boom as well as two decades of U.S. policies, and the expanding Santa Cruz economy seemed to corroborate North American frontier myths—even in a country as distant and different as Bolivia.

When the cotton boom collapsed in the mid-1970s, some cotton growers shifted to sugar. Others, as journalist René Bascopé has documented, began to see the merits of an even more lucrative product—cocaine paste.[18] When sugar followed cotton into decline in the late 1970s, even more cruceños diversified into cocaine paste production, encouraged by coinciding factors that brought new commercial importance to coca, a very old Bolivian product. During the 1970s, the coca derivative, cocaine, became the drug of choice for an increasing number of consumers in the industrialized world—a high-priced plaything of the rich that, when snorted, brought near-instant euphoria without unduly affecting performance. By the late 1980s, North Americans alone spent $28 billion a year on the drug. Colombian traffickers, already well connected to the U.S. underworld as suppliers of marijuana, now came to Santa Cruz to buy the semiprocessed paste, which was refined into finished cocaine in Colombia. The logic that drew them was simple: a kilo of cocaine had the same street value in the United States as a ton of Colombian marijuana and was much easier to smuggle.[19]

Most of the coca came from the Chapare, a colonization area just northeast of Cochabamba whose acidic soils produced a coca too bitter for traditional mastication but with a high alkaloid content that made it a potent source of cocaine.[20] Chapare colonists were quick to see the advantages of coca: it yielded four to five harvests a year, had limitless demand, provided at least three times the income on a hectare of land as any other crop, barely needed pesticides, flourished in acidic rain-leached soils, and required little up-front investment. Add to these attractions the fact that rather than having to market the crop, buyers sought out peasant producers, and one had a near-ideal crop for struggling colonists![21]

For the landless, the new crop provided abundant employment opportunities: as fieldworkers; as *pisadores* or *pisacocas,* who stamped the coca in a vile mixture of kerosene, lime, and sulfuric acid to release the alkaloid; or as *zepes,* a lowland Indian name for the leaf-cutter ant but now applied to the peasants who carried fifty-pound loads of coca leaf along forest trails to well-hidden, low-technology processing centers located well beyond the eyes of any authorities who might care. An enterprising peasant could buy a liter of kerosene in Cochabamba and sell it for fifty times the purchase price in the Chapare. Even toilet paper, used in the processing of cocaine paste, increased in value by a factor of ten when smuggled into the Chapare.[22]

Coca-cocaine was an industry with a booming market in which Bolivia had a clear comparative advantage. Coca production provided an outlet for energetic and entrepreneurial Bolivians, and transformed traditional peasants into modern consumers and a highly energetic, mobilized, and even politically militant citizenry. Coca was a wonder crop that filled many of the ambitions long held for Bolivia's eastern frontier. But cocaine was also illegal. From the 1970s until the present, the United States worked unstintingly to discourage and destroy the miracle crop, a campaign that created a new and difficult coca-cocaine nexus at which U.S.-Bolivian relations would reconnect.

The Cocaine Nexus

Sidney Mintz writes that for the modern capitalist industrial nations, "cocaine sins thrice: It interferes with labor productivity; the profits it garners are not made by 'respectable' capitalists; and the state, in addition to what is spent to control and harass the purveyors, has trouble claiming its share."[23] Kevin Healy develops a longer list of "sins" for dependent cocaine-producing countries like Bolivia: Cocaine contributes to market distortions, reduced food production, overconsumption of luxury goods, higher school dropout rates, increased inflation and general cost of living, drug addiction, rising prices for traditional coca users, and ecological damage. Further, it pulls peasants into an underground economy within a political framework that severely sanctions those caught—particularly those without connections.[24]

Many of these problems could be resolved by the simple act of legalizing cocaine, but for a host of reasons—many of them sound—that is not likely to occur soon, if ever. One reason the United States will probably never support the legalization of cocaine and other illicit drugs is that drug addiction exposes deep paradoxes in American society that most North Americans prefer to deny. Bolivian writers see those paradoxes, and with some merit one of them states that "cocaine addiction is the natural product of a society that puts profits before people, material values before the spiritual, and measures success by the accumulation of things."[25]

For U.S. consumers in the 1970s and early 1980s, cocaine powder was at once a measure of status and worth in a world of conspicuous consumption and an indicator of the ultimate hollowness of such standards of success. As cocaine became cheaper during the 1980s and filtered down through the socioeconomic levels of U.S. society, its crystallized derivative, crack, became a particular scourge in urban ghettos, feeding violence and crime and providing yet another indication that the American dream was still foreclosed to many except during brief moments of chemically induced euphoria.

In part because cocaine and other illicit drugs raise such difficult and culturally loaded issues, it has been easy for Americans and U.S. policy makers to externalize the drug threat, particularly since most drugs traditionally come from foreign sources. When cocaine began to trouble the United States in the early 1980s, many Americans were quick to make it a national security and foreign policy issue. In the words of Congressman Stephen Solarz: "If intercontinental ballistic missiles were being fired on U.S. cities from Peru and Bolivia, surely our government would have devised a plan to knock out the enemy. Why then should we treat the threat posed by the international cartels so lightly?"[26]

Such externalizing of a problem that is fundamentally North American inevitably rouses Bolivians' resentment. Bolivians first react to the way North Americans conflate coca and cocaine and have made the eradication of both their objective. *Coca no es cocaina,* they argue, and a political tract presents that position succinctly:

- Coca is an Andean product, whose domestication and use date back four thousand to six thousand years.
- Cocaine is a European invention of 130 years ago.
- Both products stimulate the cultural values of their respective societies: Coca enhances community, sociability, and the communal spirit. Cocaine is the maximum expression of so-called "Western" individualism; it isolates the individual, not only from other people, but from all reality.[27]

Furthermore, the fact that the ratio of the price of coca leaf in Bolivia to that of derived cocaine on the streets of New York is on the order of one to five hundred arouses old resentments of dependency and exploitation that make even Bolivians deeply opposed to the drug trade resist attempts to shift the locus of blame to their impoverished country. Finally, in the rush to solve its own problems in Bolivia, the United States has perpetrated actions that arouse a deep sense of wounded sovereignty that transforms drug traffickers into perverse cultural heroes and coca growers into powerful symbols of Bolivian victimization and resistance.[28]

But because coca and cocaine expose deep ethnic, class, and power conflicts in Bolivia, it is just as tempting for Bolivians to moralize and externalize the problem as it is for North Americans to do so. Cocaine is not just a North American problem, as the growing number of *basuco* smokers attests.[29] While the cocaine trade reveals the inequities of the international system, it also exposes inequities in Bolivia. Major traffickers make millions of dollars while peasant coca producers make just enough to survive. A popular and well-connected Cochabamba race driver receives a slap on the wrist for cocaine trafficking while the poor receive stiff sentences for smuggling a few pounds of the leaf. When traffickers are caught, they can often escape indictment on legal technicalities; peasant producers sometimes spend years in jail awaiting trial.[30] Well-heeled traffickers buy protection from government officials who posture before the United States and their own constituents as enemies of the trade. Meanwhile, corruption eats at the heart of the already fragile Bolivian political system. All these reasons make coca-cocaine a particularly volatile issue in U.S.-Bolivian relations.

Coca issues have not always been framed in such stark, moralistic terms. Coca is a very old crop, perhaps one of the first plants domesticated in the Andes. Early Spanish attempts to control coca use failed, and in 1573, Viceroy Toledo reached a pragmatic decision that later leaders would find difficult to make—state interests would be better served by legalizing coca production and placing it under state control than by unsuccessfully trying to suppress it. Coca rations were an integral feature in the mita system, and coca producers were important members of Bolivia's agricultural elite. Through the nineteenth century, coca production was just a business. British observer Joseph Pentland called it "the most important branch of interior trade" and noted that it was the principal source of income for the most wealthy La Paz merchants.[31]

Because it was a lucrative trade, coca production inevitably drew the interest of North American entrepreneurs. In 1885, responding to a request from Washington, the U.S. consul general in La Paz filed a lengthy report detailing where the best varieties of coca were found and how North Americans could better take advantage of the trade.[32] That same year, John Styth Pemberton introduced "French Wine Coca," a wine laced with coca extracts, to the U.S. market. A year later, Pemberton added his own variant, called Coca Cola, which combined coca and caffeine in what he called a "remarkable therapeutic agent." The only coca leaves still legally imported into the United States go into Coca Cola as a flavoring agent, after the alkaloids are carefully and completely removed. But the alkaloid was not always forbidden in the United States. Cocaine was first isolated by German scientists earlier in the nineteenth century, and was introduced to the U.S. market as a local anesthetic; an ingredient in medicinal tonics, ointments, and sprays; and an occasional additive to shots of whiskey.[33]

At the turn of the century, as the national mood shifted toward government activism and controls over food and drugs, progressive reformers launched a campaign that linked coca and cocaine as narcotics. Both were banned from the United States in 1914, and after World War I the League of Nations—and later the United Nations—pressed for international controls and suppression. Bolivians consistently resisted these laws, and the United States applied only sporadic pressure. One U.S. ambassador—a political appointee—determined soon after arriving in Bolivia that coca was the source of most of Bolivia's problems. He suggested that the solution was "plain American chewing gum," which could be donated by U.S. gum manufacturers and distributed free at embassy-sponsored motion picture shows. The State Department's response was sensible. Coca was used, the ambassador was informed, to "withstand discomfort, hardship and near starvation, especially among those laboring at extreme altitudes." The answer, the department spokesman commented, was not chewing gum but education and improved standards of living.[34]

With the United States applying leverage by threatening to withhold aid, Víctor Paz ratified the 1961 United Nations Convention on Drugs, which classified coca as a narcotic. But neither Paz nor subsequent military governments did much to enforce the convention.[35] The United States did not take issue with Bolivia's failure until the 1970s, when cocaine use in the United States began to rise. During that decade, Bolivia signed a series of bilateral agreements with the United States to control coca production and develop alternative crops—agreements solidified in meetings between President Banzer and Secretary of State Kissinger in 1976. Between 1976 and 1979 Bolivia received the first U.S. assistance earmarked for the control of coca production and trade.[36]

Cocaine became a central issue in U.S.-Bolivian relations only after the García Meza coup. Despite the regime's trumpeted anticommunism, Ronald Reagan refused to lift U.S. sanctions because of the García Meza's drug connections. In the face of unrelenting pressure from Washington, García Meza sacrificed Luis Arce Gómez in early 1981, in part because of a pending exposé of the "cocaine minister" on the CBS television program *60 Minutes.*[37] Nevertheless, international opposition continued unabated. Under García Meza the Bolivian political system devolved to a kind of parasitic looting and brutality that brought to mind the worst of the nineteenth-century caudillos. That assessment is graphically illustrated by the scandal that erupted when a Santa Cruz newspaper revealed that García Meza and his closest cronies took bribes from a Brazilian company to smuggle gems worth millions of dollars from public lands. A flurry of unsuccessful coups finally culminated in late July 1981 when García Meza resigned and turned power over to a three-man junta.[38]

By late 1981 both the United States and the world were in a deep recession, and Bolivia's legitimate export earnings declined steeply. The U.S. government drove up interest rates as it borrowed to meet its own deficits, then, in June and July 1981, sold 5,920 tons of stockpiled tin, which caused tin prices to drop precipitously.[39] Two interim military governments, stages in the armed forces' long and reluctant retreat from power, failed to halt stagnation and inflation; and by mid-1982 the per capita GDP was decreasing by 1.8 percent annually. The military's flagging political support deteriorated even more rapidly, and in early October 1982 massive demonstrations called by the Central Obrero Boliviano put 100,000 protestors on the streets of La Paz to demand an immediate return to civilian rule. Congress was convoked on 5 October, and five days later Hernán Siles Zuazo and Jaime Paz Zamora were finally installed as president and vice president.[40]

After two chaotic years of military rule, Bolivia returned to democracy, more because of exhaustion than anything else. Politically, the moment was auspicious; conditions had converged in such a way as to make support of civilian rule a near-national consensus. But economic conditions made the new government's task daunting. During his final month in power, García Meza bounced $10 million in Bolivian government checks to pay the foreign debt; even a long-awaited $220 million infusion of cash from the IMF after he resigned failed to halt the deterioration of Bolivia's economy.

The IMF, with strong U.S. backing and powerful support from the Confederación de Empresarios Privados de Bolivia, pressed for an austerity program that, as usual, would place the highest costs on organized labor and the popular sectors. On the other hand, those sectors, just freed from two years of harsh military repression, fought to achieve long-postponed demands—demands made the more poignant by the physical toll El Niño took soon after Siles took office. Drought devastated much of the highlands, and unseasonal floods decimated crops in Santa Cruz. Hundreds of starving peasants descended on La Paz. Relief agencies estimated that under normal growth conditions, it would take until 1989 for Andean farm families to return to 1981 subsistence levels, but unfortunately, growth was nowhere near normal levels.[41] The GDP deteriorated 5.6 percent in 1982 and another 7.3 percent the following year. As the conditions of the popular sectors worsened, their anger mounted.[42]

Caught in the middle was Siles, frail in appearance, gentle by nature, and committed to consensus at a time when the brutal clash between the political imperatives of populism and the economic requirements of ongoing dependency and pending economic collapse made consensus impossible. For the second time in his political career, he faced the onerous task of allocating losses in a negative-sum game, and again his personal political philosophy was at odds with the changing times. From 1956 to 1960 he had championed austerity and orthodox economic policies at a time when Third World challenges and the rise of Fidel Castro were making even Dwight Eisenhower rethink that approach. Now transformed over the years into the leader of the MNR left, Siles and his coalition brought a faith in populism and democratic socialism at a time when much of the world was ready to shift hard right toward neoliberalism. Having been through it all before, Siles refused this time to play the role assigned him by the United States and the IMF and relive the late 1950s. The result was impasse and further deterioration of the economy.[43]

Over the next two years the Siles regime launched six economic packages, each a compromise between what Bolivian popular sectors demanded and what the United States and the IMF would allow. The COB was finally in the ascendancy but maintained an autonomous position that gave it primarily a disruptive, vetoing power that contributed to the country's growing disarray. In 1986, two friends of labor, James Dunkerley and Rolando Morales, sadly commented that the labor-left had failed decisively "to produce anything remotely resembling a coherent answer to the gravest economic crisis in Latin America."[44] For his own failure to lend coherence or offer effective leadership, Juan Lechín finally and permanently went into retirement.

Hyperinflation began in May 1984. By the first half of 1985 it averaged 11,750 percent; it topped out at a stupefying 25,000 percent at the end of Siles's term in office. Paper peso bills printed in West Germany, Brazil, and England were the country's third-largest import item, and the volume of bills needed to buy a car weighed more than the car itself. The total national debt stood at well over $5 billion and would have required all the country's legitimate foreign exchange earnings to service had not Siles already defaulted in May 1984 to set off the hyperinflation. Meanwhile, export earnings steadily declined from $912.4 million in 1981 to $724.4 million in 1984, and slid below $500 million the following year when the International Tin Committee collapsed and OPEC failed to maintain a price floor for petroleum.[45]

At a time when Bolivia's dependency was manifest on all fronts, the Siles administration attempted to institute a relatively independent foreign policy. The Siles government established relations with Nicaragua and Cuba and improved relations with the Soviet Union. Siles won international support for seizing Klaus Barbie and allowing him to be extradited to France to face war crimes charges.[46] Meanwhile, the Reagan administration kept its distance, unsympathetic to Siles's attempts at independence and disturbed by the increasing flow of drugs from Bolivia. Washington put intense pressure on Siles to combat the drug trade more effectively. In response to a visit from Attorney General William French Smith in April 1983, President Siles signed a series of secret agreements that called for a five-year coca eradication plan and the creation of a specialized antidrug police force, the Unidad Móvil Policial para Áreas Rurales (UMOPAR), to coordinate with the DEA. In return, the United States provided $14.2 million in aid.[47]

The agreements promised far more than the Siles government could deliver at a time of rising turmoil and crisis. By late 1983, large parts of the Chapare were a "wild east" where fortunes were easily made and lost in a lawless environment beyond government control. For many Bolivians the Chapare was the bonanza in the midst of an almost unbearable crisis, and the region's population mushroomed from 40,000 in 1980 to 215,000 seven years later. One day in early 1984, the price per hundredweight carga of coca hit $800—the highest it would ever reach—a figure so outrageous that it gave the peasant owner of a few hectares in the Chapare the earning potential of his former landlord back in the highlands with hundreds of acres.[48] To defend their bonanza, coca growers took advantage of the democratic opening to organize and display a militancy reserved in an earlier era to miners. In fact, with the collapse of the mining industry, some of the "peasants" *were* former miners, and attempts by the newly created UMOPAR and the DEA to attack their livelihood led to violent clashes and a strong identification between the coca producers and the COB.[49] The United States exerted pressure on Siles from without, and with the U.S. Congress threatening sanctions, Siles reluctantly sent the military into the Chapare to restore a semblance of order and national control. In May 1985 Siles promulgated a decree to regulate coca production and marketing and to provide legal authority for eradication, but two months later, when he left office, no coca had been destroyed and new plantations were proliferating at an accelerating pace.[50]

Siles resigned a year ahead of schedule, turning to the church to broker an early-exit plan that kept democracy and a semblance of his own dignity intact. Hugo Banzer and his Acción Democrática Nacionalista won a plurality of nearly 30 percent of the popular vote in the June 1985 elections, but Víctor Paz and the MNR again held more seats in congress and controlled the electoral court. Banzer protested vociferously but with the country in the grips of its worst domestic crisis, made the calculated decision to accept the results and find common ground with the new president. It was, James Malloy and Eduardo Gamarra note, a historic decision: "To accept defeat and remain in the political fray according to the existing rules is one of the more crucial ethics of a democratic system."[51] As for Siles, he also gained stature in his final days by peacefully turning power over to a new party for the first time in Bolivia's history. This was the good news in the midst of a great deal of bad.

Cocaine Dependency and the
Return of Víctor Paz Estenssoro

On 6 August 1985—the 160th anniversary of Bolivia's independence—Víctor Paz Estenssoro became president of Bolivia for the fourth time. Paz had spent most of the previous two decades in exile, and doubtless he had changed. Perhaps he had taken on some of the conservatism that often accompanies advancing years, even though his old party *compañero,* Hernán Siles, had moved in precisely the opposite direction. Now, after a disastrous *trienio,* Siles handed power to Paz for the third time in his own political career, having inadvertently made Paz's task somewhat easier by clearly demonstrating what did *not* work.[52]

Once in office, Paz moved quickly. Before the end of his first month he adopted a drastic stabilization plan called the New Economic Policy (NEP). When the COB struck, Paz declared a state of siege, seized the leaders, and briefly exiled more than a hundred of them to Bolivia's eastern jungles. A month later, Paz signed a "Pact for Democracy" with Hugo Banzer Suárez that strengthened his center-right coalition and guaranteed that his policies could clear congress. Paz also solidified U.S. support by shifting from Siles's reformist populism toward "neoliberal" economic policies that pleased the Reagan administration, and by distancing himself from Siles's independent nonaligned position and returning to close international conformity to the United States.[53]

Although the initiative for the NEP clearly came from Paz, in consultation with Banzer's ADN, it also had a certain "Made in the USA" stamp about it. Its primary architect was Jeffrey Sachs, a bright, brash, young Harvard professor whom the *Los Angeles Times* called "the Indiana Jones of economics." Its domestic manager was Planning Minister Gonzalo Sánchez de Lozada, a businessman who had spent so much time in the United States that he spoke Spanish with an accent.

Sachs, who was barely thirty at the time, claims that he told the septuagenarian Paz, "What you have here is a miserable, poor economy with hyperinflation; if you are brave, if you are gutsy, if you do everything right, you will end up with a miserable, poor economy with stable prices." But if he did not do it right, Sachs warned Paz, the country would not survive. The warning resonated with Paz, who told the nation in his 29 August speech announcing the NEP: "Either we have the moral courage to make sacrifices necessary to put in place a radical new policy, or quite simply, Bolivia will die."[54]

Paz indeed was gutsy—even draconian—and Sánchez de Lozada later recalled that the president would quote Machiavelli—"Do bad things all at once and do good things little by little"—as he pushed constantly to take the hard line. "If you are going to do it, do it now. I can't operate twice," he told his advisers.[55] Two months after Paz took office the tin market collapsed. All through the 1980s, tin production and prices had declined while the International Tin Committee desperately stockpiled the metal to bolster prices. Meanwhile, the Reagan administration unloaded its own tin stocks, seemingly bent, in the words of one commentator, "on spurring its free market bronco right through the fabric of international understanding on tin."[56] In October 1985, just after the announcement of the NEP, the ITC could no longer maintain supports, and overnight the price of tin declined by one-half, reaching an eventual low of $2.43 a fine pound, down from $7.61 at the beginning of the decade.

Despite this disaster, the NEP halted hyperinflation within ten days. Annual inflation fell from almost 12,000 percent for 1985 to between 10 and 15 percent in 1989; tax revenues increased fourteenfold; the debt was down, as were servicing requirements; and after several years of steadily declining GDPs, real economic growth reached 2–3 percent by the end of Paz's administration. At the same time, export earnings finally rebounded, almost doubling by the end of the decade, and such efficiency was restored to the public sector that already in 1986 the government deficit was reduced to levels that Bolivia's mentors in Washington could not match. Paz's acts were those of a man at a point in his career where a place in history ranked ahead of politics. His goal was not to "disappear the state" but, as Catherine Conaghan puts it, to make it "leaner and meaner" and more able to exert authority across a limited range of issues.[57]

The social costs of Paz's actions were immense. Breaking radically from his earlier belief that populist redistribution and capitalist development might be compatible, Paz passed the costs of stabilization on to the lower classes. In the new era, the ever pragmatic Paz looked to Sachs and Machiavelli, even if doing so meant reversing nearly everything his first presidency had accomplished. The statistical details roll by too quickly for an outsider to fully grasp the human costs. In 1986 the purchasing power of the average Bolivian was down 70 percent from the beginning of the decade. Minimum salaries stood at $6 a month, and per capita income fell from $1,178 in 1980 to $789 in 1987, with peasants averaging only $140 annually. Unemployment reached 20–25 percent, and nearly all social welfare benefits to workers were swept away. One source calculated that with annual rates of 3.5 percent economic growth, it would take forty years to restore per capita incomes to 1978 levels. Meanwhile, in the aftermath of the tin shock, twenty thousand of COMIBOL's twenty-seven thousand workers were laid off. Miners lacked their traditional recourse, the strike, because closing the mines and leaving tin in the ground would now save the country money. An era was over, Paz proclaimed. Tin no longer reigned, and neither, by implication, did the long powerful mine workers.[58]

Again Bolivia's great nationalist—the pragmatic politician with an eye to history—faced a paradox. Bolivia was starved for capital; its key traditional exports were in steady decline, and its shock-treated economy was in deep recession. The country's only growth industry through the 1980s was coca-cocaine, an industry that was both illegal and strongly opposed by the United States. Paz understood the problems that coca-cocaine posed to Bolivia. In his inaugural address he lashed out at the corroding impact of the industry on the nation—the increased crime, the decomposition of national society, and the sullying of Bolivia's international image.[59] But coca-cocaine also provided a safety net for Bolivians dislocated first by hyperinflation and then by stabilization. Between 1983 and 1987 some forty to sixty thousand Bolivians lost jobs in the state sector alone. Only coca-cocaine and the burgeoning informal sector, often linked to unofficial dollar sources, could absorb them at a time when official unemployment rates hovered near 25 percent. Coca-cocaine also provided foreign exchange when other sources of exchange were in decline. Although the value of Bolivia's legal exports in 1987 was about $400 million below what it had been in 1980, the decline was more than compensated for by the $600 million (conservatively estimated) in coca-cocaine earnings that entered and remained in the country annually in the late 1980s—about 15 percent of the GDP.[60]

Paz, an economist, understood the significance of these figures, and the NEP included features that brought more of the foreign exchange generated by the drug trade into Bolivia's formal economy. The plan reduced disclosure requirements, provided tax amnesty for repatriated assets, and competed with the parallel market by allowing the Central Bank to auction dollars directly to the public. The NEP also reduced import restrictions and tariffs, thus allowing drug traffickers to launder dollars while providing imports to the country. By the late 1980s a Japanese-made television often cost less in La Paz than in Tokyo. President Paz denied that these were deliberate policies to capture cocaine revenues, but a bank official acknowledged that cocaine was a cushion preventing social explosion. Without cocaine, it is a distinct possibility that Paz's talk of the "death of Bolivia" might have been more than rhetorical hyperbole.[61]

For Bolivia, the coca-cocaine industry was both palliative and addictive, sustaining and destructive. For Paz, it was the two-edged sword that it was for all who touched it. He could not allow Bolivia to be branded a pariah state as it had been under García Meza, but because of the developing war on drugs in the United States, the industry gave Paz negotiating assets. The United States needed his cooperation to stem the flow of cocaine and was willing to pay for it. But because of the realities of power, a supposed partnership could easily devolve into hegemonic imposition. Paz certainly understood this—who better than he, having been through it all before. As was true of his first two terms, relations with the United States were an essential factor in his political calculus.

When he took office, Paz immediately faced sanctions imposed because Siles had failed to live up to his coca eradication commitments. The NEP bought time from the newly sympathetic Reagan administration, but in June 1986, with virtually no eradication accomplished during Paz's first devastatingly difficult year in office, Congress convinced Reagan to suspend $7.2 million in aid.[62] A month later, Paz signed off on an unprecedented joint U.S.-Bolivian military exercise against drug traffickers called "Operation Blast Furnace." Three oversized U.S. cargo planes descended on the Santa Cruz airport carrying helicopters, troops, and DEA operatives. The numbers put up by Blast Furnace were unimpressive, to say the least—one prisoner, virtually no cocaine captured, and only twenty-one labs decommissioned—while the political costs were high. Because Paz had not previously cleared the operation with congress, it was easy to charge that he had allowed a secret yanqui invasion of Bolivian territory. The Bolivian congress launched an inquest, and Paz's personal popularity plummeted.[63]

It would be a mistake, however, to view Operation Blast Furnace as a political miscalculation or a sign of Paz's abject submission to U.S. leverage. Under adverse bargaining conditions, Paz shifted the emphasis of joint action from eradication of peasant-owned coca fields—a volatile political task—to interdiction of cocaine and coca paste and the destruction of labs. Further, he authorized the exercise only after being assured that U.S. sanctions would be lifted and that aid would be restored, and, in what was likely the most important U.S. concession, only after the IMF and the U.S. government withdrew their demands that Bolivia begin servicing its defaulted debt and accepted Paz's argument that loan repayment at this point would endanger the NEP.[64]

Paz, as was his tendency, worked to balance opposing forces: pressures from below—pressures rooted in Bolivia's economic dependency—and pressures from the United States and its hegemonic instrument, the IMF. Still, as before, his shrewdness grew out of a perception of Bolivia's weakness, which in turn made him subject to further pressures. The U.S. Congress blamed the modest accomplishments of Operation Blast Furnace on Bolivian corruption and again threatened sanctions. Paz responded this time by agreeing in 1987 to a three-year plan that would eventually destroy 70 percent of Bolivia's known coca fields. Paz explicitly connected the plan to increased cooperation to fight traffickers and more U.S. assistance to help peasants shift to alternative crops. Washington, for its part, stipulated that assistance would automatically cease if eradication goals were not met by an agreed deadline, and Paz pushed the deadline safely past the date his term in office ended.[65]

Meanwhile, the United States kept up its pressure. An official U.S. report on drug measures in Bolivia criticized rampant Bolivian corruption and "the unwillingness or inability of the government of Bolivia to introduce and implement effective coca control." Sanctions, said Florida congressman Larry Smith, were the only way to gain even minimal cooperation and action, so once again the United States threatened sanctions.[66]

Fernando Illanes, Bolivia's ambassador to Washington, a wealthy businessman and the former head of the CEPB, offered a spirited rejoinder. "There seems to be a false perception around Washington," he told a Senate caucus in July 1987, "that all Bolivia wants is U.S. money. . . . This is not so." Total possible U.S. sanctions would amount to no more than $30 million, Illanes pointed out, while the estimated value of the cocaine trade to the Bolivian economy that year was $600 million. Sanctions, Illanes charged, only poisoned the atmosphere, weakened the alliance between the two countries, and played directly into the hands of traffickers. The key issues were not will and backbone, as U.S. critics implied, but rather power and resources. The United States had a clear preponderance of both, so ultimately it was Washington that determined the degree and level of cooperation between the two nations, not Bolivia.[67]

It was an infuriating state of affairs for Bolivians, many of whom undoubtedly wished their country could sanction the United States for failing to reduce demand for a drug Bolivia was sanctioned for supplying. But even in this brave new free-market world that Paz had boldly entered, the old power system continued to operate. U.S. sanctions could foreclose bilateral assistance, endanger crucial credits from multilateral lending agencies, end IMF assistance to keep the country's economy stable, and again stamp Bolivia as a renegade nation. Yet U.S. support was a pittance compared with the coca dollars that sustained Bolivia's battered economy. Unable to threaten sanctions of its own, all Bolivia could do was feign cooperation, resist U.S. impositions, and bargain for the best terms possible. It was, one study observes, a complex and intricately choreographed dance between two very unequal partners.[68]

Facing new sanctions in mid-1988, the Paz government cooperated with the DEA to finally net Roberto Suárez. Soon after, Bolivia passed a tough antinarcotics law that made all coca except for that produced in the traditional Yungas region illegal and subject to eradication in stages. Neither sprung on the Bolivian people by executive fiat like the NEP, nor rubber-stamped by congress after the fact like Operation Blast Furnace, Law 1008 was the product of several months of often acrimonious debate that provided the imprimaturs of dialogue and constitutionality to a controversial measure. The law had two features that revealed peasant and labor input: it did not outlaw all coca, and it clearly attached Bolivia's efforts to eradicate excess coca to effective indemnification and alternative cropping programs that required outside assistance. The law was tough, but it destroyed no coca immediately, outlawed the use of herbicides (to the chagrin of some North American officials), and tied eradication to appropriate levels of U.S. assistance. Although passed in July, it was not promulgated until December, after Washington promised more money.[69]

The dynamics of the U.S.-Bolivian dialogue were familiar, as were the levels of U.S. imposition and rising Bolivian resistance. Soon after Law 1008 was passed, peasant producers seized a police station in the Chapare and demanded that DEA officials be removed from the zone. A month later, a bomb exploded along the motorcade route of visiting Secretary of State George Schultz, who noted in his speech that the bomb brought home the significance of the struggle jointly waged against drugs. It also brought home the dangers of escalating domestic strife and made manifest the building resentment of Washington's perceived stinginess and its meddling in Bolivian affairs. At the news conference after Schultz's speech, several reporters challenged the secretary to explain why only 11 percent of the committed U.S. assistance had so far gotten to Bolivia. But while Bolivians complained that the United States was not keeping its word, coca cultivation continued to expand—more than 20 percent in 1988 alone according to U.S. government sources. It was indeed a complex and intricate dance.[70]

Déjà Vu All Over Again

In 1989, the now octogenarian Víctor Paz successfully completed a constitutionally mandated term for the third time—a feat unmatched in Bolivia's history. Further, his party, the party that administered neoliberal "shock therapy," won the next election as well. The MNR candidate, Minister of Planning Sánchez de Lozada, won a narrow plurality in what was essentially a three-way dead heat, but the presidency went to third-place finisher Jaime Paz Zamora of the Movimiento de Izquierda Revolucionaria (MIR). Paz Zamora became president after making a deal with runner-up Hugo Banzer Suárez that gave Banzer's ADN the vice presidency, a majority of the cabinet slots, and a pledge from the MIR to back Banzer in 1993. Since both opposition parties had already promised to retain the essence of the NEP, the elections, in any case, reaffirmed Paz's program.[71]

The imprint of Víctor Paz Estenssoro on the last half century of Bolivia's political history is undeniable, but the exact nature of his legacy will be long debated by historians. One aspect of that legacy that is particularly open to debate is his tendency through four administrations to forge close cliental ties to the United States. As a pragmatic and essentially liberal nationalist, Paz accepted the reality of Bolivian dependency and worked to turn it to his advantage, manipulating as often as he was manipulated, bargaining shrewdly, and utilizing all the "weapons of the weak" to successfully link the resources and influence of Washington to policies he favored all along. But the weapons of the weak are nonetheless the products of weakness, and Paz's successors would not wield them as effectively as he.

Paz reshaped drug control relations with the United States and avoided U.S. sanctions despite making little or no progress in efforts to reduce the flow of cocaine from Bolivia. The essence of the new relationship can be summed up as follows. Bolivia agreed to eradicate all excess coca beyond the twelve thousand hectares deemed necessary to meet the demands of traditional users. Since more than fifty-eight thousand hectares was under coca cultivation at the time Paz left office, by agreement with the United States, Bolivia would destroy between five and eight thousand hectares each year until all excess coca was eradicated. The United States would, in turn, pay compensation to Bolivian peasants who destroyed their crops and would develop alternative crop and marketing strategies to help peasant producers replace their coca income.

The latter points were the rub. Bolivian officials wanted the United States to ante up sufficient assistance to truly give coca growers an option, or, alternatively, to eliminate U.S. demand sufficiently to remove the price incentives for coca production. If the United States did either, Bolivia's political and economic costs would be minimal. But the United States was unwilling to foot the costs of either alternative, and instead used more limited assistance and the threat of sanctions as carrot and stick to encourage Bolivian compliance. This limited commitment triggered Bolivian resentment and fostered indirect or passive resistance to U.S. pressures. Since the United States preferred to exert its power rather than expend its resources, the apparent partnership again became conflict ridden. These are the essential dynamics of the new, but actually very old and already familiar, relationship that Paz forged with the United States around the cocaine nexus.

The new president, Jaime Paz Zamora, was Víctor Paz's nephew. He had briefly studied for the priesthood but left the seminary during the ferment of the late 1960s to receive guerrilla training in Albania. He returned to Bolivia in the midst of Popular Assembly mobilization to form the MIR, a party modeled on its radical Chilean counterpart. A year later, he was forced into exile by Banzer, the man with whom he now formed a "Patriotic Accord." He returned in 1980 as Hernán Siles's running mate, then nearly died in the suspicious plane crash that left his ruggedly handsome face permanently scarred.[72]

Paz Zamora's alliance with Banzer was indeed strange considering the political trajectory of each man, but the changes sweeping the world made both somewhat flexible. In June 1989, as Bolivia held elections, Chinese reformers marched in Tian'anmen Square, Lech Walesa and Solidarity swept to power in Poland, and by year's end the Berlin Wall had been breached. The United States agreed to negotiate an end to conflicts in Central America, then reconfirmed its continuing hegemony with a lightning invasion of Panama in December. Both Paz Zamora and Banzer were sufficiently pragmatic to understand that the days of populism, militarism, state capitalism, and revolutionary socialism were past. Paz Zamora in particular understood that free-market capitalism was the only real game left, and, pursuing policies that were if anything more orthodox than those of his uncle, he won the support of international bankers and effectively erased Bolivia's debt.[73]

With the cold war ending and economic stability restored, drugs loomed larger than ever in U.S.-Bolivian relations. While campaigning in the Chapare, Paz Zamora had hung a garland of coca leaves around his neck and promised to defend traditional coca usage, a show of apparent defiance that did not please the U.S. embassy. In September 1988, Robert Gelbard replaced Edward Rowell as ambassador to Bolivia. Rowell had served in the La Paz embassy during the 1950s and knew Paz, Bolivia, and the history of U.S.-Bolivian relations as well as anyone in the State Department. Gelbard, the highest-ranking department official ever sent to Bolivia as ambassador, came to the position with a different set of credentials. He had served in the Peace Corps in Cochabamba in the 1960s, then had become the department's key drug war strategist for the Andean region. More advocate than diplomat, and more activist than analyst of Bolivia's nuanced history, Gelbard devoted almost single-minded attention to narcotics matters. His goals were to make Bolivia a showcase, to keep pressure on traffickers and the Bolivian government, and to smooth and expedite the flow of assistance deemed necessary to snuff out the drug trade and keep the Bolivians cooperative. To meet those goals he was more than willing to insert himself deeply into Bolivian affairs.[74]

Gelbard and his approach to the drug problem reflected changes in

Washington. On 5 September 1989, a year after Gelbard arrived and soon after Paz Zamora took office, President George Bush gingerly held up a small plastic bag before an American television audience and told them it contained crack cocaine purchased in Lafayette Park across from the White House. It was time, Bush said, to escalate the war on drugs, and in a speech filled with martial allusions he outlined a comprehensive plan to reduce drug supplies in the United States by 15 percent in two years and by 60 percent within ten. Soon after his speech, Bush outlined an initiative that would win the cooperation of the Andean nations. And early the following year at a drug summit in Cartagena, Columbia, the U.S. president laid out plans to enhance economic, military, and law enforcement assistance at an estimated cost of $2.2 billion over five years.[75]

At the United Nations, a few weeks after Bush's speech, Paz Zamora outlined his own proposal to fight the war on drugs, calling it "*coca por desarrollo*—coca for development." Paz Zamora explicitly reversed the terms of the debate and linked Bolivian efforts to fight drug traffickers to increased international assistance for alternative development.[76] The Cartagena Declaration seemed to endorse Paz Zamora's approach, but privately both Gelbard and the State Department put intense pressure on the Bolivian president to increase eradication and expand the coercive role of the Bolivian military.

In the face of that pressure, Paz Zamora signed an assistance package in May 1990 that included a separate annex making $32.2 million contingent on involving the Bolivian military in the fight against drugs. Back in La Paz, he denied militarizing the drug conflict to a Bolivian populace justifiably wary of reinserting the army into domestic matters, but when U.S. sources revealed the wording of the annex, President Paz Zamora was forced to retract.[77] The affair revealed a pattern in U.S. relations with Paz Zamora that is succinctly described by Eduardo Gamarra: "Counternarcotics activities were planned by the United States with little or no Bolivian input. The Bolivian government agreed to implement policies in secret to avoid political costs. All 'secret' initiatives inevitably became public, revealing that most were unconstitutional."

That process, Gamarra adds, undermined the democracy that U.S. officials vehemently claimed to support and kept Paz Zamora off balance and made him increasingly resentful.[78]

In 1990 Bolivia met and exceeded eradication targets for the first time, although less as a result of U.S. pressure or military involvement than because of the temporary drop in the market price for coca caused by a crackdown on the Medellín cartel. Low coca prices led Chapare growers to weigh the advantages of destroying old coca plantings and taking the $2,000 per hectare in compensation offered from U.S. assistance while waiting to gauge future market conditions. Unfortunately, alternative cropping programs were not well established, and plans to award technical and credit assistance to Bolivian farmers to grow soybeans and citrus were abandoned when U.S. producers of those products lobbied against the program in Congress. When coca prices rebounded in 1991, most Chapare peasants replanted coca.[79]

Meanwhile, Paz Zamora's policies remained erratic. In late 1989 he allowed DEA agents to seize Luis Arce Gómez and take him to the United States, despite the lack of a formal extradition treaty. Then, in early 1991, he chose a military officer with unsavory ties to Arce Gómez and known drug connections as head of Bolivia's antidrug agency. Gelbard was incensed. The man many Bolivians now called "Viceroy Gelbard" immediately got Washington to agree to freeze $120 million in aid and leaked information to the *Miami Herald* concerning the Bolivian government's drug connections.[80]

With Paz Zamora reeling and again reversing himself, Gelbard and Washington increased the pressure to militarize the drug conflict. It was probably inevitable when Reagan and later Bush declared their war on drugs that pressures to militarize the metaphorical war would increase. The image of war carried with it a concept of victory that was difficult to achieve against drugs. As pressures to produce results intensified in Washington, it became easy to focus on repressive rather than educational aspects of the war and external rather than internal strategies to win it because both shifts seemed to promise quicker and more measurable results. Bush himself proclaimed, "The logic is simple. The cheapest and safest way to eradicate narcotics is to destroy them at their source. . . . [W]e need to wipe out crops wherever they are grown and take out labs wherever they exist."[81]

The logic was not nearly so simple to Bolivians. In April 1991, Bolivia's congress gave permission to U.S. military advisers to train Bolivian forces in antidrug tactics nine hours after those advisers were already on Bolivian soil. In June, Bolivian military and U.S. and Bolivian antinarcotics forces engaged in the largest military counternarcotics operation ever undertaken in Bolivia. The campaign, timed to coincide with Gelbard's return to Washington as the number two man in the State Department's Latin American division, culminated in late June when combined forces descended on the little town of Santa Ana de Yacuma—"Bolivia's Medellín"—and began a house-to-house search. The international press observed closely, while Bolivians were forced to read translated accounts from the *Miami Herald* to learn about this foreign-directed campaign on Bolivian soil. In September, with eradication targets far from met, the new U.S. ambassador, Richard Bowers, announced to the press that the Bolivian army would begin forced eradication and that he himself was ready to wield a machete.[82]

Bowers's announcement set off another firestorm of protests and complaints of wounded sovereignty. Caught between outside and inside pressures, Paz Zamora again backed away from involving Bolivia's military in the drug wars. U.S. officials were also reconsidering the wisdom of involving U.S. or Bolivian troops in so politicized an environment, a concern brought home when a combination U.S. Army training mission and civic action project to build schools and latrines in the Beni fostered rumors that the United States planned to bury nuclear waste on Bolivian soil, build a huge military base like the one in Panama, or perhaps begin trafficking in Bolivian children.[83] By the end of 1991 the plan to militarize the drug war was officially laid to rest, although not before revealing a lingering U.S. bias: when it came to money, U.S. officials found it easier to trust militaries than peasants. In one year the aborted program to involve the Bolivian armed forces in the drug wars received more U.S. funds than coca growers received the previous eight years to try alternative crops.[84]

Once again latent Bolivian resistance had thwarted preferred U.S. policy, and the escalating anti-Americanism gave Paz Zamora room to distance himself from the United States. In mid-1991 he promised that drug traffickers who turned themselves in would not be extradited to the United States, and seven drug lords accepted his offer.[85] Over the balance of his administration the president increasingly celebrated the positive virtues of coca, and "Coca no es cocaina" became his new slogan. Paz Zamora's campaign to change the way the world saw coca began in April 1992 when Bolivia sent a supply of coca leaf tea to Seville to serve visitors at its World's Fair pavilion. Bolivian national pride was wounded when Spanish customs agents impounded the shipment, but unlike the United States, which often seemed to act as if Bolivia had no pride to wound, Spain softened the blow. Queen Sofia herself went to La Paz to apologize to the Bolivian people and to sip a cup of coca tea with Paz Zamora. She had respectable precedent. When Pope John Paul II visited Bolivia in 1988, the press gave daily accounts of the number of cups of coca tea he consumed.[86]

In early 1993, with a change of presidents in the United States and a similar change pending in Bolivia, there were hints that the drug war was coming under reappraisal. In December 1992, ABC television anchorman Peter Jennings visited Bolivia and on national television pronounced the drug war lost. Jennings challenged incoming president Bill Clinton to stop wasting U.S. funds fighting drugs in Bolivia and to instead focus on eliminating the problem at home.[87] The new administration announced in mid-February that it planned to reduce the size of the DEA, cut aid linked to eradication from $66 million in 1992 to $40 million in 1993, and turn its focus to curbing U.S. demand for cocaine. The reality, as the new administration was quick to point out, was that Bush's war had failed. Antidrug budgets swelled from $6.6 billion in 1990 to $11.9 billion in 1992, but even official U.S. government sources admitted that the price, purity, and availability of cocaine on the streets of U.S. cities were virtually unchanged.[88]

Then, within weeks, in a pattern that was to become familiar, the Clinton administration reversed itself. Administration spokesmen announced that the United States could not abdicate its leadership in the struggle against drugs or abandon its Latin American partners. The administration's reversal was in part the result of the political dangers facing a noninhaling president who appeared soft on drugs, and in part the result of considerable bureaucratic momentum now built into the antinarcotics campaign. Yet another factor in the reversal was Latin American governments' protests of the cuts. Bolivia's interior minister called the cuts "an error," and the minister of agriculture added it was a decision that Bolivia "cannot accept." Antidrug assistance was as addictive as crack cocaine.[89] By the time Bolivia's June elections arrived, the Clinton administration was again suggesting the need for military involvement, and observers saw U.S. policy coming back full circle to early Bush positions.

The victor by a wide plurality in the 1993 presidential election was the MNR's Gonzalo Sánchez de Lozada. The U.S.-born and -educated former planning minister and architect of the NEP seemed a good fit with patrons in Washington. On coca-cocaine, however, "Goni," as Bolivians often called him, initially sounded much like Paz Zamora. He explicitly rejected the United Nations position that all coca production should be made illegal and echoed Jaime Paz that "coca no es cocaina." He further criticized U.S. policy as unimaginative and inflexible and charged that the Clinton administration was increasing pressure at the same time it reduced funding. "They want coca to disappear without it costing them anything," Goni complained.[90]

In confronting the same conflicting pressures on his regime that had faced his predecessors, Sánchez de Lozada responded with less art and artifice than Paz, and less fluctuating defiance and retreat than Paz Zamora. In mid-1994, in the midst of an ambitious and increasingly unpopular reform program and with his public approval ratings already falling, Sánchez de Lozada began forceful eradication of coca plantings in the Chapare. Coca eradication had steadily decreased from a high of 8,100 hectares eradicated in 1990, and it was only with an extensive DEA and police presence that 1,058 hectares was destroyed in 1994.[91] Fresh from victories against the Colombian cartels, Clinton officials feared that Colombians were finding refuge in Bolivia. In May, after repeated denials that he would militarize the Chapare, Sánchez de Lozada sent in troops; and on 13 July he began the largest antidrug offensive in years with the support of the DEA and several U.S. military aircraft.[92]

Again coca moved to center stage in Bolivian domestic politics. Coinciding with the offensive in the Chapare, a highly publicized inquest into the previous administration's drug connections began in La Paz. Jaime Paz was accused of receiving $500,000 in campaign funds from a Bolivian drug lord connected to the Medellín cartel.[93] As drug-related conflicts again began to escalate, coca growers, with close press coverage and broad national sympathy, began a five-hundred-kilometer march from the Chapare to La Paz to protest for "coca, dignity, and national sovereignty."[94] Meanwhile, Sánchez de Lozada developed his own radical plan to finally halt the dynamics set in motion a decade earlier by his mentor, Víctor Paz. In November the president announced a "zero option policy." Bolivia would eradicate the entire coca production of the Chapare if the international community would ante up $2 billion to relocate and compensate current residents. All land in the Chapare would revert to the state and be converted into either a national park or an industrial zone where private entrepreneurs could provide a base for sustainable, alternative development. Since the industrialized nations would foot the bill, they presumably would decide if new investment possibilities or the environment should come first.[95]

Zero option was an ironic punctuation to a half century of development strategy in the Chapare. Since 1942 and the Bohan mission, the United States had supported opening the Chapare as part of a larger plan to develop the potential of the east, believing that in doing so Bolivians would discover their nation's and their own potential, just as Americans had. Fifty years later, however, the United States was dissatisfied with the unintended consequences of its development strategies in the Chapare. Sánchez de Lozada, tired of the constant pressures he received from all sides and unwilling to play the two-faced game Paz Estenssoro had played so well and Paz Zamora so poorly, challenged the international community to put up or shut up. Believing it was time for radical surgery—to do bad things all at once, as Machiavelli and

Víctor Paz had counseled—the president pressed the United States and other developed nations to provide sufficient funds to wipe the slate clean. Again foreigners would have a chance to make things right.

The plan drew immediate and furious public reaction from Bolivians and a quick negative from Washington. Growers promised civil war if Sánchez de Lozada tried to dislodge Chapare residents; and the new U.S. ambassador, Curtis Kamman, quickly made it clear that Bolivia would receive no increase in the $30–$40 million already budgeted by the United States for antinarcotic activities.[96] It was business as usual, a point made clear in March when Washington announced that annual aid to Bolivia would be cut by one-third because of Bolivia's continuing failure to meet coca eradication targets. Washington also wanted Bolivia to sign a long-delayed extradition treaty. Revealing a tenuous grasp of geography as well as of international law and inter-American relations, Congressman Dan Burton—the Republican chairman of the House Western Hemisphere Subcommittee—suggested that the United States anchor an aircraft carrier off Bolivia's coast, send in helicopters to spray coca plantations, and snatch known drug traffickers unilaterally.[97]

The United States got its extradition agreement in 1995, but the building pressure from the North revealed the paradox in the "gringo" persona Sánchez de Lozada purposefully cultivated. He maintained his English accent, he once admitted, in order to produce "confidence in my ability and my honesty."[98] But when he appeared subservient to U.S. interests instead of his own constituents, as was true during his escalation of the drug war and when he signed the extradition agreement despite widespread opposition from his constituents, then the same Americanized features that had been part of Goni's appeal became foci of resentment. In the midst of the conflict over forced coca eradication, an opposition deputy said of him: "The way he talks disgusts us . . . and his groveling attitude towards a foreign economic power disgusts us even more." Goni's public approval ratings plummeted from 70 percent at the outset of his presidency in 1993 to 19 percent by its end in 1997, revealing that many Bolivians shared those sentiments.[99]

The immediate crisis over sanctions was averted when Hugo Banzer came out of retirement to facilitate a deescalation of the rhetorical warfare between Goni and the coca growers. The purpose, Banzer made clear, was to arrive at the consensus necessary to satisfy U.S. demands and keep international assistance flowing. As a result of both internal compromise and outside pressure, Bolivia met eradication targets in 1995 for the first time since 1990. Eradication stayed on target through early 1996 as coca growers cooperated to meet U.S. requirements. The U.S. embassy feared that the coca producers' fierce protection of their new plantings and nurseries revealed a lack of commitment to the underlying purpose of eradication. In light of the continuing paucity of viable alternative crops, the embassy was undoubtedly right.[100] Meanwhile, a shipment of finished cocaine chlorohydrate seized in Lima led to subsequent revelations of a full-fledged La Paz cartel capable of producing up to forty tons of finished cocaine annually, marketing it through Mexican middlemen, and with tentacles extending deep into Bolivia's antinarcotics police and high into the Sánchez de Lozada government.[101] The drug wars became an ever more complex and elaborately choreographed dance.

Robert Gelbard, now assistant secretary for international narcotics and law enforcement affairs in the State Department, issued a report in mid-1996 that expressed cautious optimism. Gelbard claimed that cocaine seized the previous year had a street value equal to the entire U.S. antidrug budget, thus more than justifying President Clinton's commitment to a source-country strategy. In the Chapare, legal crops now occupied twice the acreage of coca. In his report Gelbard reconfirmed his own commitment to eradication strategies. While he acknowledged that successes in one area tended to cause the problem to spill over into new areas—the so-called balloon effect—Gelbard believed there was nonetheless a light at the end of the tunnel.[102] He did not use those exact words—the Vietnam analogy would have been too painful.

Total cocaine output in the late 1990s, at the time of this writing, is about twelve to fifteen times larger than it was when Ronald Reagan first declared war on drugs in the early 1980s, and drug prices are down 80 percent. A United Nations report suggests that more than half of Bolivia's export revenues still come from drugs; and the U.S. embassy estimates that despite more than half a billion dollars in U.S. assistance, the area under coca production has increased by 27 percent since the 1987 agreement that was to have destroyed all excess production within a decade. Waltraud Queiser Morales suggests that, as in Vietnam, the United States "should just declare victory and go home to fight the drug war at its real source."[103]

In a candid moment in the midst of his conflict with the coca growers, just as he was about to publicly announce the zero option proposal, Sánchez de Lozada told Voice of America that he personally believed that drugs should be legalized because prohibiting substances for which there is high demand does not work. His dilemma, of course, was that to advocate such a position officially could make him an international pariah.[104] Compounding that dilemma is another: experts generally agree that, at least in the short run, Bolivia would suffer from either legalization or a successful conclusion to the drug war.[105] While the illicit drug trade by definition produces criminals, smugglers, mafias, and a host of attendant social problems, Bolivia's economy in the late 1990s has still not found an economic sector equally vibrant and able to provide employment, or any equivalent source of leverage to encourage international transfer payments. LaMond Tullis observes that if cocaine were suddenly legalized, big planters would drive small peasant producers from the market, the price of coca would fall, and Bolivia would receive no more assistance to suppress production. The combination of factors, he adds, would increase the impoverishment of at least 20 percent of the population and add to Bolivia's political conflicts.[106]

So, Bolivia fights the drug war with a great deal of ambivalence. Its own essential drug problems—despite proliferating crime, corruption, and drug abuse—are the old ones of poverty and of people struggling to survive. Strong market signals make coca growing attractive to many, and cocaine production and trafficking attractive to a few. Political gains since the 1952 revolution have made growers articulate and well organized, while the revolution's economic failures and Bolivia's ongoing underdevelopment and persistent rural poverty make it difficult for politicians to attack growers with real vigor. A U.S. official admitted to British journalist Clare Hargreaves that the Bolivian politician has no real incentive to fight cocaine, "as it doesn't win him a single vote. . . . The only people who want him to do anything are those at the U.S. embassy." In fact, the new emerging democracy in Bolivia provides even fewer incentives for politicians to attack drugs. In 1993, the major political parties each spent between $15 and $20 million on elections, and drug barons inevitably help fund costly campaigns in an impoverished country. Another U.S. official candidly told Hargreaves that "if the drug industry didn't pay off government officials, it would be the only industry in Bolivia that didn't." [107] Thus it is not surprising that few in politics care to establish close federal election oversight. Nor is it a surprise that in a country where the per capita income is $700 and the rural per capita income is one-third that, the opportunities and corruption that accompany the lucrative drug trade make the drug war difficult to win. In battling drugs in Bolivia instead of fighting them more forcefully in the homes, schools, and streets of the United States, U.S. officials face a host of cultural and political barriers that make this seemingly logical point of attack quite difficult. Even the economic logic is faulty. One study notes that it takes only $700 worth of coca leaf to produce a kilo of cocaine with a street value of $15,000. With that profit margin, raising the cost of producing the leaf has little impact on cocaine supply.[108]

A coherent U.S. policy in Bolivia continued to be limited by deep ambivalence. When Vice President Al Gore visited Bolivia in March 1994, he extolled the model Bolivia provided in almost rhapsodic terms. "The entire world is marching on the Bolivian road," he announced, placing Bolivia "at the vanguard of social, economic, and political reforms." But those words had less impact on Bolivians than the image of the smiling vice president suddenly turning serious and quickly shedding the garland of coca leaves placed over his head when the ambassador whispered in his ear what it was.[109]

To U.S. officials such as Gore, Bolivia was both a compelling model of neoliberal and democratic reform and the epitome of the intractability and frustrations of the drug war. Rather than see the connections between these two views of Bolivia, it was easier to keep them separate. The average North American may have connected Bolivia to drugs but knew or cared little about reforms. Champions of neoliberal capitalist and democratic models embraced Bolivia as a success story but uncomfortably avoided examining how coca-cocaine revenue and jobs helped keep neoliberal democracy afloat.[110] It was easier, too, for the frontline U.S. soldiers in the drug wars to focus on victory with little apparent awareness of the capitalist logic that made coca-cocaine so lucrative, the Bolivian cultural norms their policies violated, or the way their flaunting of Bolivian sovereignty slowly undermined democracy and political stability.

At a deeper level, few Americans seem even yet to understand the way U.S. policy contradicts long-held American myths about hard work, the sanctity of profits derived from the soil, the compelling logic of the marketplace, or the regenerative power of frontier opportunity. In a host of ways, coca-cocaine brings to sharp focus the disparities of power and wealth that sabotage true partnership between the United States and Bolivia, and reveals the conflicting myths and values that keep Americans and Bolivians at arms' length.

Epilogue

This crowd of young, free-market-oriented reformers has managed to push [Bolivia's] inflation . . . to levels lower than in Chile or Mexico, and it's the first time South America has seen single digits in a generation. Growth clocked in at a middling 3.8 percent for 1992, [b]ut . . . is headed for a 5 percent increase this year. These are the latest items in a solid eight-year trend, and it's not being done with bankers' mirrors. It's being done by the kind of give-and-take democracy that has never been in fashion in South America. This may sound embarrassingly starry-eyed. . . . However, there's no question that the kind of stability that Bolivia has achieved over the past several years is tied directly to consensus politics.

Nicholas Asheshov, *Wall Street Journal*, 11 June 1993

[I]t was one more piece of Bolivian folklore he had picked up in prison from Claude who understood the place better than any three historians of the world put together. To understand Bolivia you had to live it, live in it the way you lived in your skin only closer, tighter, scarier. You had to live it in a place like [the prison in La Paz], where the terror of being totally vulnerable, totally weak, totally a victim, worked its way into your system and made you into a different kind of person. . . . Bolivia makes a joke of the entire bourgeois world . . . all that ridiculosity about working hard and saving money and being monogamous and cultivating the aesthetic virtues and praying to God on Sundays. Tell me what relevance all that has to a place like Bolivia.

Mark Jacobs, *Stone Cowboy*, 86, 88

Since James Buchanan wrote his letter of instruction to Chargé John Appleton 150 years ago, two distinct American visions of Bolivia have been at odds—Bolivia, America in the making, and Bolivia, antithesis of all that is American.

Starkly differing Bolivian views of the United States also conflict.

Raul Barrios, an astute observer of U.S.-Bolivian relations, describes two distinct subcultures. Bolivian anti-imperialists view the United States as a powerful nation-state conspiring malevolently against their country's sovereignty and sabotaging its progress. To anti-imperialists, Bolivian identity is negation of all things American and resistance to all U.S. pressures. On the other hand, pro-Americans regard the United States as a model and turn to its people as mentors. They embrace all things American—from Disney World to democracy—partly out of genuine affection and admiration but also out of assumptions rooted in lingering dependency and weakness.[1] The unequal and limited U.S.-Bolivian partnership does not merit study because Bolivia is particularly important to the United States—it is not. Or because the United States has the solutions to Bolivia's problems—it does not. Rather this relationship merits attention because the ways that Americans see Bolivians and Bolivians see Americans provide valuable clues to how each of these peoples see themselves and help explain why the history of U.S.-Bolivian relations has run in cycles.

Neither American nor Bolivian views are static, and the apparently dichotomous attitudes each has of the other are perhaps better understood as pendulum shifts. Admiration and envy, patronage and resentment are manifestations of a Bolivian weltanschauung that is rooted in historical frustration as well as in the continuing realities of poverty and relative powerlessness. Barrios notes that neither of the manifestations he describes allows Bolivians to fully understand the United States or its people, or to create effective modes of bilateral discourse that could lead to more authentic partnership.[2] Extreme American views are also connected. An American desire to uplift, model, and instruct can quickly turn to scorn or to a frustrated sense that Bolivia remains indecipherably distant and intractably other. Views of Bolivia are the product of U.S. power and of an American weltanschauung that assumes a tutorial role for the United States in the hemisphere—particularly in a country as different and distant as Bolivia. To loosely paraphrase a point made by Eldon Kenworthy in *America/Américas: Myth in the Making of U.S. Policy toward Latin America*, Americans (including U.S. policy makers) too often have projected on Bolivia their own values and myths and then assessed it accordingly.[3] The ways that Americans and Bolivians see themselves have consistently fostered patron-client dynamics that limit true partnership and poison true friendship between these different and distant, but generally well-disposed peoples.

But anyone who has watched Bolivia over the past two decades knows how suddenly and how dramatically old patterns can be broken. In a book provocatively titled *The Devil Is Dead: Democracy in Bolivia*, Bolivian scholar Javier del Granado argues that nothing in Bolivia's history precludes it from now establishing an enduring democracy.[4] Compelling evidence to support his thesis is that while this epilogue was in initial draft, Bolivians, for the fourth time without interruption, went to the polls on 4 June 1997 to peacefully select a president—a notable feat for a country that until 1985 was notorious for having averaged better than a coup attempt per year since independence. Hugo Banzer Suárez, the man selected, led one of those coups a quarter century ago, but since then has waited patiently through six failed attempts to regain the presidency constitutionally—his patience itself compelling evidence of change.[5]

Symbols of change and of a new Bolivian spirit of compromise and healing were particularly evident in the 1993 campaign. That year Banzer chose Oscar Zamora, previous guerrilla head of the Maoist Partido Comunista Marxista-Leninista, as his running mate. Zamora had been forced into exile when Banzer seized power in 1971, but now the old enemies from opposing ends of the political spectrum shared a ticket. The MNR fielded candidates who bridged an even older and wider chasm. Presidential candidate Gonzalo Sánchez de Lozada, Bolivia's wealthiest private mine owner and archetype of the Hispanic elite that traditionally has dominated Bolivia, chose indigenous leader Víctor Hugo Cárdenas to be his vice president. Goni grew up in the United States, graduated with a degree in philosophy from the University of Chicago, and not only talked but thought like a "gringo."[6] Cárdenas was born in a mud hut near Lake Titicaca and headed a party named for Túpac Katari, the legendary Aymaran guerrilla chieftain who during the rebellion of Túpac Amaru tried to eliminate the ancestors of men like Sánchez de Lozada from his homeland. The vice presidential candidate's wife wore the bowler hat and *pollera* skirts of an Aymaran *chola,* and Cárdenas's Spanish was as colored by Aymará as Goni's was by English.[7] Modernity and tradition, gringo and indio, conqueror and conquered, dictator and guerrilla: the election symbolized the synthesis of old Bolivian dualities into a new and satisfying consensus.

Against the backdrop of the elections, Bolivia's Supreme Court reached a verdict in the long trial of Luís García Meza; a trial that lasted six years longer than the general's benighted regime. Found guilty on thirty-three criminal counts, García Meza received a maximum sentence of thirty years in prison. When the verdict was read on 6 May 1993, a month before the elections, the nation spent a moment in silent tribute to the consolidation of democratic institutions, and President Jaime Paz Zamora declared a public holiday to celebrate final closure to a sordid chapter in Bolivia's history.[8]

In office, Sánchez de Lozada worked to turn symbols of a new Bolivia into reality. His Plan de Todos—a plan for all Bolivians—had as its centerpiece a scheme to sell controlling stock in former state enterprises to private investors and hold the balance of the assets gained in a privately run pension plan to benefit all Bolivians over the age of sixty-five.[9] Goni also promised to empower the poor by channeling federal money back into local communities to give them increased control over local matters. Later, he told the *New York Times* that, perhaps because as a child in the United States he had always felt like an outsider, he had a special desire to improve the conditions of indigenous Bolivians.[10]

Managing his majority in Congress with consummate skill, Sánchez de Lozada pushed through nearly all of his Plan de Todos. Education reforms began to dismantle the centralized state bureaucracy, and the revenue-sharing plan sent funds directly to local communities—bold strokes that attacked a system of centralized administration that dated back to colonial times.[11] By the end of Goni's term in office, all of the important government-owned enterprises had been privatized, and the pension plan was in place.[12]

Now, Hugo Banzer, a dinosaur from the old Bolivia who has since become an important symbol of the new, finally has his chance. Banzer appears to want (as did Víctor Paz in his final term) to ensure his place in history. With $180 million from the World Bank in hand, he presented a plan in September 1998 to attack Bolivia's culture of corruption through legal reforms, media campaigns, and financial disclosure requirements for public officials, and created a "people's ombudsman" to hear citizens' complaints.[13] Banzer also pledged to end the illicit trafficking of coca/cocaine in Bolivia by 2002, the year he leaves office. During 1998, his government destroyed an unprecedented 11,600 hectares of coca and Banzer reversed the normal lines of pressure by challenging the consuming nations to match his resolve. At ceremonies closing the 1998 eradication campaign, Banzer reminded visiting international dignitaries (among them the U.S. ambassador) that the coca his government had destroyed could instead have appeared on the world market as seventy-seven tons of finished cocaine. Despite the loss of unofficial revenues that seventy-seven tons of cocaine might have produced and the vagaries of El Niño, Bolivia's GDP grew more than 4 percent in 1998 for the sixth consecutive year, and inflation remains in single digits.[14]

Bolivia has come far since the dark days under García Meza. Few nations have begun in quite such desperate straits, and few have accomplished more in less time under a democratic regime.[15] Granado argues that basic reforms to Bolivia's social structure were accomplished by the 1952 revolution, and that essential legal, economic, and institutional correctives have now been achieved since the return of democracy. The remaining task, Granado believes, is to continue to alter fundamental Bolivian values, rituals, and mores through education and experience in self-rule; to provide opportunities for local association and empowerment that will develop the *taste* for democracy.[16] But systems of culture and power interact in complex ways, and Bolivia's structures of wealth and power continue to belie claims that the country's historical devils are dead.

Most Bolivians remain desperately poor, and many of the gains made by the 1952 revolution have been reversed. The per capita GDP stood at $764 in 1998, well below the regional average of $2,389. In 1997 Bolivia slipped two places, to 113th, in the United Nations human development index; and in 1998 fell an additional three slots to 116th among the 174 nations listed. According to UN nutrition figures, the average Bolivian received only 2,160 calories per day in 1998, 600 calories a day beneath the world average and above only Haiti in the hemisphere. Bolivia's perennial problem of properly feeding its people was exacerbated in 1998 by a drought that affected the poorest regions of the country. As a result of El Niño, Bolivian potato production fell 35 percent, wheat fell 28 percent, and corn fell 26 percent. Bolivia, where the potato originated, will have to import seed potatoes from Holland in 1999. And there are ever more mouths to fill; Bolivia's projected population at the close of 1998 was 8 million, up from 6.3 million in 1993. Such growth makes the comment of a prominent Bolivian economist particularly true: "You don't eradicate centuries of structural social inequities with 4 percent growth rates."[17]

Bolivia's democracy continues to consolidate in spite of the ongoing poverty and widening economic disparities, but these distortions threaten its survival. Public confidence remains low. In a recent public opinion poll, most Bolivians responded that conditions are bad, are getting worse, and that their leaders have no solutions. Democracy cannot thrive in a negative-sum game. Sánchez de Lozada tackled legacies of colonialism and dismantled inefficient state enterprises, but his reforms came too fast, were too confusing, and thus were too threatening to truly empower most Bolivians. His pension plan seemed a particularly cruel joke in a country where the life span of the average campesino is a decade below the mandated entitlement age of sixty-five, particularly when it came at the expense of what many Bolivians consider the national patrimony. "Before the reforms," one Bolivian observed, "the Bolivian government owned industries and the people were poor. Now the people are still poor, but they see the government having sold out to foreigners."[18]

Banzer's antidrug plan provides little to motivate individual farmers except force. To save money and to remove the incentive for coca producers to take compensation payments and apply them to new plantings, during 1998 Banzer phased out payments to producers who voluntarily eradicated their coca. With little incentive to cooperate with the government campaign, coca producers defended their livelihood, and violence in the Chapare flared. Despite a recent drop in coca prices, the income of a coca farmer remains two to four times greater than that of the average Bolivian peasant producer, and Banzer's plan fails to address this simple economic fact. As Banzer turns to coercion and military action, he endangers a tradition of dialogue that has kept Bolivia relatively free of the drug-related violence that has wracked Peru, Columbia, or, for that matter, the United States.[19]

In November 1998 the newly created public ombudsman, Ana María Romero de Campero, displayed photos of burned houses and fields, looted stores, and peasant women and children with frightened faces and charged that the army and antinarcotics police were terrorizing the Chapare. Her charges coincided with embarrassing revelations earlier that month that in the 1970s, Banzer cooperated with other South American military dictators in Operation Condor to repress political opponents. Old skeletons in Banzer's political closet began to stir, leaving the former dictator on the defensive, despite his apparent twenty-year commitment to democracy. One Bolivian commented that "a murderer doesn't become innocent by converting to Democracy."[20]

Another disturbing feature of Bolivia's restored democracy is what a Bolivian newspaper called "the bleaching of Bolivian politics."[21] The faces of Bolivia's leaders are whiter and more European than at any time since the 1952 revolution. The new political elite is increasingly technocratic, educated and trained in the United States and Europe, and less connected to Bolivia's masses than the old postrevolutionary populist políticos, or even the military. Political scientists Catherine Conaghan and James Malloy suggest that instead of uncritically lauding Bolivia's return to democracy, it might be more useful to see Bolivia as a bolder version of the general problems facing contemporary democracies. "Might not [Bolivia] tell us something about the dilemmas of postmodern political development?" they ask. What do conventional democratic practices like elections mean under a technocratic oligarchy?[22]

Political elitism and stagnant social and economic conditions doomed Bolivia's liberal, quasi-constitutional regime a half century ago. It would be a tragedy of immense proportions were they to do the same to Bolivia's current neoliberal, democratic experiment, not least because failure would reinforce a very old Bolivian myth: "We complete nothing in this country. . . . We dislike conclusions. In our hearts we expect things to turn out badly. And why not? Doesn't our history confirm it?"[23]

That demon of history is yet to die. And while only Bolivians can inter it, the United States can assist. In fact, because of the continuing realities of U.S. power and of Bolivia's position on the periphery of the emerging global system, the United States *must* assist if Bolivia is to complete the tasks essential to fully consolidate its democracy. But before the United States can become a true partner to Bolivia, it has demons of its own to exorcise. Most U.S. citizens strongly reject the adjective "imperialist" when applied to their nation. Yet it is important to realize that in Bolivia, U.S. power has made U.S. policy imperious if not technically imperial. The United States as a great power views Bolivia as too peripheral and too weak to be treated as an equal. Bolivia thus becomes a place for a great power to experiment and impose. U.S. policy in Bolivia is the product of a cumbersome, bureaucratic system that responds to many pressures—few of them Bolivian. Aid is supposed to help Bolivia escape poverty and dependency, but in practice it seems designed to enhance the influence of the United States, keep Bolivia safely docile, and provide job security for the aid and antidrug bureaucracies that have grown like Topsy in Washington.

Policy analysts can now more fully see distortions in U.S. policy toward Latin America that predate cold war national security preoccupations. Eldon Kenworthy describes an America/Américas myth that makes the Western Hemisphere a *"tabula rasa* on which God (Providence, History) demonstrates civilization's advance," with the United States at the vanguard. Viewed through American eyes, the other nations of the hemisphere are junior partners in a common mission characterized by progress, individual liberty, and freedom of association, and in which success is measured by material advances.[24] Lars Schoultz discusses the darker side of the myth—an underlying North American contempt rooted in lingering racism that causes policies and attitudes to fluctuate between imposition and neglect and that places Latin America both literally and figuratively "beneath the United States."[25]

"Difference is not deficiency," Kenworthy adds. "Differences can lead to toleration, even curiosity, rather than to judgment and corrective action." A touch of such humility might enable Americans to better understand that the United States cannot solve Bolivia's problems, and, as with coca-cocaine, is sometimes their source. Bolivia is not America in the making, or its antithesis. Bolivia is Bolivia, and the momentous changes that the country has made in recent years deserve U.S. support without imposition or control. Never has there been a time so opportune or so appropriate for Bolivia and the United States to transcend the patron-client features that have consistently limited true partnership to this point. If they do so, the next chapter in the far from completed story of their relationship will be more satisfying to both partners than have been the chapters recorded thus far.

Notes

Preface

1. Los Kjarkas, "El Destino de mi pueblo," Discos Heriba.
2. Fernando Diez de Medina, *Franz Tamayo: hechicero del Ande, retrato al modo fantástico,* 2d ed. (La Paz, 1944), 18, 23, cited in Fredrick Pike, *United States and the Andean Republics: Peru, Bolivia, and Ecuador* (Cambridge, Mass., 1977), 78.
3. Alcides Arguedas, *Pueblo Enfermo* (1909; reprint, La Paz, 1979); Alma Guillermoprieto, *Heart That Bleeds: Latin America Now* (New York, 1994), 206.
4. Eric Lawlor, *In Bolivia* (New York, 1989), 11.
5. Eldon Kenworthy analyzes the continuing power of these myths and their impact on inter-American relations in *America/Américas: Myth and the Making of U.S. Policy toward Latin America* (University Park, Pa., 1995), particularly chap. 2. For discussions of the interrelationship of systems of culture and systems of power in international relations, see Akira Iriye, "A Round Table: Explaining the History of American Foreign Relations—Culture," *Journal of American History* 77.1 (1990): 99–107; and Akira Iriye, "Culture and Power: International Relations as Intercultural Relations," *Diplomatic History* 3.2 (1979): 115–17.
6. Lester Langley draws this distinction in his introduction to the series of which this book is a part. See Lester Langley, *America and the Americas* (Athens, Ga., 1989), xvi–xvii. A recent and lengthy exchange on the listserver for Latin American historians (H-LATAM@h-net.msu.edu) revealed that there is little consensus on the meaning of the word *America,* thus my attempt to define how I use it in this work.
7. Clifford Geertz, *Interpretation of Cultures* (New York, 1973), 5.
8. For a discussion of Geertz's value to historians, see Ronald G. Waters, "Signs of the Times: Clifford Geertz and Historians," *Social Research* 47 (Autumn 1980): 537–56.
9. Among the books that have influenced my understanding of this basic presupposition and its impact on the international relations of the United States are Louis Hartz, *The Liberal Tradition in America* (New York, 1955); Seymour

Martin Lipset, *American Exceptionalism: A Double-Edged Sword* (New York, 1996); Robert A. Packenham, *Liberal America and the Third World* (Princeton, 1973); Fredrick Pike, *The United States and Latin America: Myths and Stereotypes of Civilization and Nature* (Austin, 1992); David Potter, *People of Plenty: Economic Abundance and the American Character* (Chicago, 1954); Alexis de Tocqueville, *Democracy in America*, ed. J. P. Mayer (reprint, New York, 1969); Frederick Jackson Turner, *The Frontier in American History* (reprint, New York, 1962); Walter Prescott Webb, *The Great Frontier* (Austin, 1964); and William Appleman Williams, *The Tragedy of American Diplomacy*, rev. ed. (New York, 1961).

10. Pike, *United States and the Andean Republics*, 1–23.

11. Pike, *United States and the Andean Republics*, 18, quoting Glen C. Dealy, "The Tradition of Monistic Democracy in Latin America," *Journal of the History of Ideas* 35 (1974): 640.

12. June Nash, *We Eat the Mines and the Mines Eat Us* (New York, 1979), 6–10, 322.

13. See Jean Pierre Lavaud, "Hacia una interpretación de la inestabilidad política en Bolivia, 1952–1980," *Estado y Sociedad* (La Paz) 3.4 (1987); James Malloy, *Bolivia, the Uncompleted Revolution* (Pittsburgh, 1970); Christopher Mitchell, *Legacy of Populism in Bolivia: From the MNR to Military Rule* (New York, 1977); Laurence Whitehead, "The State and Sectional Interests in the Bolivian Case," *European Journal of Political Research* 3 (1975): 115–46; and Kenneth Lehman, "U.S. Foreign Aid and Revolutionary Nationalism in Bolivia" (Ph.D. diss., University of Texas, Austin, 1992).

14. Dependency theory literature is broad and multifaceted, but for the uninitiated, a good analytical and historical introduction is Fernando Henrique Cardoso and Enzo Faletto, *Dependency and Development in Latin America* (Berkley, 1979); or Louis A. Pérez Jr., "A Round Table: Explaining the History of American Foreign Relations—Dependency," *Journal of American History* 77.1 (1990): 133–42. Criticisms of dependency theory and the shift of emphasis to a "culture of dependency" are perhaps most categorically stated in two books by Lawrence E. Harrison: *Underdevelopment Is a State of Mind* (Lanham, Md., 1985), and *The Pan-American Dream* (New York, 1997). A clear statement of the neoconservative position and its critique of dependency theory can be found in Peter L. Berger, *The Capitalist Revolution* (New York, 1986), particularly chap. 6.

Acknowledgments

1. Butch Cassidy's sister claimed that Butch was not killed in Bolivia and that he returned to the United States from South America and lived out his life peacefully. See Lula Parker Betenson (as told to Dora Flack), *Butch Cassidy My Brother* (Provo, 1975), 172–73, 184–86, 195. Evidence that the bandit pair were killed in Bolivia in 1911 is circumstantial—I found no reference to it in the mission records. Eric Lawlor provides a brief summary of the evidence he found in *In Bolivia,* 203–4.

Chapter 1: Most Different of Neighbors

1. Eldon Kenworthy, *America/Américas: Myth in the Making of U.S. Policy toward Latin America* (University Park, Pa., 1995), 16; and Pike, *United States and the Andean Republics,* 1. This chapter is extensively footnoted for those who would like to explore the colonial history of Bolivia in greater detail.

2. Sources for the early history of Bolivia include Herbert S. Klein, *Bolivia: The Evolution of a Multi-ethnic Society,* 2d ed. (New York, 1992), 33–34; Roberto Querejazu Calvo, *Chuquisaca, 1539–1825* (Sucre, 1987), 17–21; and Humberto Vázquez Machicado, José de Mesa, and Teresa Gisbert, *Manuel de historia de Bolivia* (La Paz, 1983), 108–9.

3. James B. Richardson III, *People of the Andes* (New York, 1994), 126–29.

4. This pattern is described in John V. Murra, *The Economic Organization of the Inka State* (Greenwich, Conn., 1980).

5. For a brief review of precontact history, see Klein, *Bolivia,* 13–25; and Nathan Wachtel, "The Mitimas of the Cochabamba Valley: The Colonization Policy of Huayna Capac," in *Inca and Aztec States, 1400–1800* (New York, 1982).

6. On the early history of Potosí, see Gwendolin Ballantine Cobb, "Potosí, a South American Mining Frontier," in *Greater America: Essays in Honor of Herbert Eugene Bolton* (Berkeley, 1945); R. C. Padden, introduction to *Tales of Potosí,* by Bartolomé Arzóns de Orsúla y Vela (Providence, 1975); and Pedro Querejazu, introduction, and Laura Escobari, "Potosí: Social Dynamics, Labor, and Mining Technology," in *Potosí: Colonial Treasures and the Bolivian City of Silver,* ed. Pedro Querejazu and Elizabeth Ferrer (New York, 1997).

7. For discussions of Toledo's "reforms," see Steve J. Stern, *Peru's Indian Peoples and the Challenge of Spanish Conquest* (Madison, 1982), 76–92; and John How-

land Rowe, "The Incas under Spanish Colonial Institutions," *Hispanic American Historical Review* [hereafter *HAHR*] 37 (1957): 155–56. On the local impact of the Toledan reforms, see Ann Zulawski, "Frontier Workers and Social Change: Pilaya y Paspaya (Bolivia) in the Early Eighteenth Century," in *Migration in Colonial Spanish America*, ed. David J. Robinson (Cambridge, 1990), 115. Figures are from Padden, introduction to *Tales of Potosí*, xxiii. These figures may represent only one-third of the actual silver revenues; see Cobb, "Potosí, a South American Mining Frontier," 48–49. Figures on the workforce come from Jeffrey A. Cole, *The Potosí Mita, 1573–1700* (Stanford, 1985), 9.

8. See, especially, Karen Spalding, "Indian Rural Society in Colonial Peru: The Example of Huarochiri" (Ph.D. diss., Berkeley, 1967), chap. 2; and Rowe, "The Incas under Spanish Colonial Institutions," 162–63.

9. On the mita, see Peter Bakewell, *Miners of the Red Mountain: Indian Labor in Potosí, 1545–1650* (Albuquerque, 1984); Enrique Tandeter, *Coercion and Market: Silver Mining in Colonial Potosí, 1692–1826* (Albuquerque, 1993); and Cole, *The Potosí Mita*.

10. Tandeter, *Coercion and Market*, 15, 36–38, 167–68, 176.

11. Spalding, "Indian Rural Society in Colonial Peru," 321, 326–28, 338; Rowe, "The Incas under Spanish Colonial Institutions," 162–63.

12. Magnus Mörner, *The Andean Past: Land, Societies, and Conflicts* (New York, 1985), 50.

13. Pike, *United States and the Andean Republics*, 28–30.

14. Gwendolin B. Cobb, "Supply and Transportation for the Potosí Mines, 1545–1640," *HAHR* 29.1 (1949): 34.

15. Tandeter, *Coercion and Market*, 27, 28, 35; Zulawski, "Frontier Workers and Social Change," 116.

16. This argument is most forcefully made by Carlos Sempat Assadourian in *El sistema de la economía colonial: mercado interno, regiones, y espacio económico* (Lima, 1982). Bakewell has studied entrepreneurship and free-market mining mechanisms and notes that there were greater opportunities for entrepreneurs in the colonies than in Spain itself. Peter Bakewell, *Silver and Entrepreneurship in Seventeenth-Century Potosí* (Albuquerque, 1988), 172–74.

17. Mörner, *The Andean Past*, 76, 86; Robert H. Jackson, *Regional Markets and Agrarian Transformation in Bolivia: Cochabamba, 1539–1960* (Albuquerque, 1994), 41; Klein, *Bolivia*, 64–69; Kenneth Andrien, *Crisis and Decline: The Viceroyalty of Peru in the Seventeenth Century* (Albuquerque, 1985), chap. 1.

18. John Murrin, "Beneficiaries of Catastrophe: The English Colonies in America," in *The New American History*, rev. and exp. ed., ed. Eric Foner (Philadelphia, 1997), 22.

19. Murrin, "Beneficiaries of Catastrophe," 26. Fred Anderson, *A People's Army: Massachusetts Soldiers and Society in the Seven Years' War* (New York, 1984); Bernard Bailyn, *The Ideological Origins of the American Revolution*, enl. ed. (Cambridge, Mass., 1992); T. H. Breen, *Tobacco Culture: The Mentality of the Great Tidewater Planters on the Eve of Revolution* (Princeton, 1985); and Robert A. Gross, *The Minutemen and Their World* (New York, 1976), all help explain, from different angles, how and why the colonists turned against England.

20. Hartz, *Liberal Tradition*, 69; Lester Langley, *The Americas in the Age of Revolution* (New Haven, 1996), 195. On the class nature of the revolution, see, for example, Gary B. Nash, *The Urban Crucible: Social Change, Political Consciousness, and the Origins of the American Revolution* (Cambridge, Mass., 1979); Sung Bok Kim, "Impact of Class Relations and Warfare in the American Revolution: The New York Experience," *Journal of American History* 69.2 (1982): 326–46; Arthur M. Schlesinger, "The Revolution as Class Conflict," *Political Science Quarterly* 34.1 (1919): 63–75; and Franklin J. Jamison, *The American Revolution Considered as a Social Movement* (Boston, 1963).

21. Cecilia Kenyon, "Republicanism and Radicalism in the American Revolution," *William and Mary Quarterly* 19.2 (1962): 168.

22. Langley, *Americas in the Age of Revolution*, 147. A recent study elucidates this process further, although it alters some traditional views of Spanish weakness. See Herbert S. Klein, *The American Finances of the Spanish Empire: Royal Income and Expenditures in Colonial Mexico, Peru, and Bolivia, 1680–1809* (Albuquerque, 1998).

23. Mörner, *The Andean Past*, 87–89. Klein shows that much of the surplus generated by Potosí was already being diverted through Buenos Aires, or going to pay administrative costs there. See Klein, *American Finances of the Spanish Empire.*

24. For varying interpretations of the causes of the Túpac Amaru rebellion, see Vázquez Machicado et al., *Manuel de historia de Bolivia*, 253–58; Kendall W. Brown, *Bourbons and Brandy: Imperial Reform in Eighteenth-Century Arequipa* (Albuquerque, 1986), 198–210; Scarlett O'Phelan Godoy, *Rebellions and Revolts in Eighteenth Century Peru and Upper Peru* (Cologne, 1985), 258, 279; Jurgen Golte, *Repartos y rebelliones: Tupac Amaru y las contradicciones de la eco-*

nomía colonial (1980), 177–78; and Rowe, "The Incas under Spanish Colonial Institutions," 167–69.

25. Klein, *Bolivia,* 75; Leon Campbell, "Recent Research on Andean Peasant Revolts, 1750–1820," *Latin American Research Review* 14.1 (1971): 7–11; Vázquez Machicado et al., *Manuel de historia de Bolivia,* 258. Creoles and Indians had very different ideas of what independence from Spain meant. In this regard, see Nicholas A. Robins, *El Mesianismo y la rebelión indígena: La Rebelión de Oruru en 1781* (La Paz, 1997).

26. On the Oruro story, see Oscar Cornblit, *Power and Violence in the Colonial City: Oruro from the Mining Renaissance to the Rebellion of Túpac Amaru, 1740– 1782* (Cambridge, 1995), 137–60; Robins, *El Mesianismo y la rebelión indígena;* Boleslao Lewin, *Túpac Amaru, el rebelde* (Buenos Aires, 1943), 295–97; Lillian Estelle Fisher, *The Last Inca Revolt, 1780–1783* (Norman, 1966), 150; T. Wittman, *Andean Nations in the Making* (Budapest, 1970), 180; and Vázquez Machicado et al., *Manuel de historia de Bolivia,* 265–67.

27. On Túpac Katari, see Vázquez Machicado et al., *Manuel de historia de Bolivia,* 262–64; O'Phelan Godoy, *Rebellions and Revolts,* 244–55; Campbell, "Recent Research on Andean Peasant Revolts," 11; and Mörner, *The Andean Past,* 95.

28. Klein, *Bolivia,* 78.

29. Tandeter, *Coercion and Market,* chap. 5.

30. Enrique Tandeter, "Crisis in Upper Peru, 1800–1805," *HAHR* 71.1 (1991): 51–53, 68.

31. For key sources in English on the independence process in Bolivia, see the Bibliographical Essay.

32. Charles Harwood Bowman, *Vicente Pazos Kanki: un boliviano en la libertad de America* (La Paz, 1975), 28, 38. Pazos Kanki spent several years in the United States and was involved in the Amelia Island incident off the coast of Spanish Florida. The incident revealed that the desire of the United States to take Florida outweighed any sympathy it might have had for Latin American independence movements. Pazos Kanki later wrote a history of the United States in Spanish. See *The Devil Is Dead: Democracy in Bolivia* (La Paz, 1989), 14.

33. This last-minute shift of allegiance is explored by Charles W. Arnade, *The Emergence of the Republic of Bolivia* (Gainesville, 1957), 100–15. Luís Peñaloza and Wittman look at some of the involved economic interests involved. See Luís Peñaloza Cordero, *Nueva historia económica de Bolivia,* vol. 3 (La Paz, 1983), 19–23; and Wittman, *Andean Nations in the Making,* 157–82.

34. Gerhard Masur, *Simón Bolívar* (Albuquerque, 1969), 392–97; J. B. Trend, *Bolí-*

var and the Independence of Spanish America (Caracas, 1951), 154–58. A copy of his message can be found in *Latin America, Conflict and Creation: A Historical Reader,* ed. E. Bradford Burns (Englewood Cliffs, N.J., 1993), 56–59.

35. The story of the initiative toward Brazil is found in Ron L. Seckinger, "The Chiquitos Affair: An Aborted Crisis in Brazilian-Bolivian Relations," *Luso-Brazilian Review* 11.1 (1974): 19–40.

36. J. Valerie Fifer, *Bolivia: Land, Location, and Politics since 1825* (Cambridge, 1972), 16, 17.

37. Benedict Anderson, *Imagined Communities: Reflections on the Origin and Spread of Nationalism,* 2d ed. (New York, 1991), p. 7 and chap. 4. His argument that Creoles were proto-nationalists and pioneers in the creation of modern nations or "imagined communities" is not completely convincing to those who have studied Latin American independence closely.

38. Tandeter, *Coercion and Market,* 222. See also Klein, *Bolivia,* 104.

39. Joseph Barclay Pentland, *Report on Bolivia, 1827* (reprint, London, 1974), 194, 207.

40. Edmund Temple, *Travels in Various Parts of Peru* . . . , 2 vols. (reprint, New York, 1971), 1:401; Tandeter, *Coercion and Market,* 223–31.

41. Pentland, *Report on Bolivia,* 225–26.

42. Fifer, *Bolivia: Land, Location, and Politics,* 4, 28, 36.

43. Fifer, *Bolivia: Land, Location, and Politics,* 38.

44. Fifer, *Bolivia: Land, Location, and Politics,* 40–41; Herbert S. Klein, *Parties and Political Change in Bolivia, 1880–1952* (Cambridge, 1969), 4; Antonio Mitre, *Patriarcas de la Plata* (Lima, 1981), 159–60; Miller to Secretary of State Everette, 29 June 1853, U.S. Department of State, "Dispatches from United States Ministers to Bolivia, 1848–1906," microfilm, U.S. National Archives and Records Service [hereafter NA microfilm]; and U.S. House of Representatives, *Letter of the Secretary of State, transmitting a statement of the Commercial Relations of the United States with Foreign Nations: 1859* [hereafter U.S. House of Representatives, *Commercial Relations*], 428.

45. Pentland, *Report on Bolivia,* 219–20; Klein, *Bolivia,* 101–3.

46. Pentland, *Report on Bolivia,* 219, 224, 237.

47. U.S. House of Representatives, *Commercial Relations, 1856,* 717; José María Dalence, *Bosquejo estadístico de Bolivia* (1848; reprint, La Paz, 1975), 306.

48. Pentland, *Report on Bolivia,* 247.

49. José Flores Moncayo, ed., *Legislacion boliviana del indio* . . . *1825–1953* (La Paz, n.d.), 23–32.

50. William Lee Lofstrom, "The Promise and Problem of Reform: Attempted

Social and Economic Change in the First Years of Bolivian Independence"
(Ph.D. diss. Cornell University, 1972), 350. See also Pentland, *Report on Bolivia,* 259.

51. Lofstrom, "Promise and Problem of Reform," 155, 158, 168, 204, 230; Klein,
Bolivia, 109–10.

52. Thomas Millington, *Debt Politics after Independence: The Funding Conflict in
Bolivia* (Gainesville, 1992), introduction and 132–33.

53. Lofstrom, "Promise and Problem of Reform," 39, 388, 391–98, 404–5, 416,
420, 452; Klein, *Bolivia,* 105.

54. Miguel Bonifaz, *El Problema agrario-indigena en Bolivia* (Sucre, 1948), 169. For
assessments of Sucre, see Klein, *Bolivia,* 111; Lofstrom, "Promise and Problem of Reform," 597–601; Pike, *United States and the Andean Republics,* 95;
and Vázquez Machicado et al., *Manuel de historia de Bolivia,* 337–38.

55. José Fellman Velarde, *Historia de Bolivia,* vol. 2 (La Paz, 1970), 55.

56. Mörner, *The Andean Past,* 128–29; Pike, *United States and the Andean Republics,* 121–22; Klein, *Bolivia,* 116–18.

57. Lester Langley provides an interesting comparative analysis of the revolutionary legacy in the United States and Latin America that is rooted in the
observations of Tocqueville and Bolívar. See Langley, *Americas in the Age of
Revolution,* chaps. 10, 11.

Chapter 2: Most Distant of Neighbors

1. Pentland, *Report on Bolivia,* 234; Scott Hugh Shipe Jr., "The American Legation in Bolivia: 1848–1879" (Ph.D. diss., St. Louis University, 1967), 45.

2. Note from Buchanan to Appleton, 1 June 1848, doc. 388 in *Diplomatic Correspondence of the United States. Inter-American Affairs, 1831–1860,* vol. 2 (Washington, D.C., 1932), 3–5.

3. Note from Buchanan to Appleton, 1 June 1848, *Diplomatic Correspondence,*
2:4–5.

4. Letter of 4 August 1820 to William Short, in *Thomas Jefferson, Writings,* ed.
Merrill D. Peterson (New York, 1984), 1439.

5. Morrell Heald and Lawrence S. Kaplan, *Culture and Diplomacy: The American Experience* (Westport, Conn., 1977), 4, 67–90. For an interesting analysis
of the continuing power of these ideas and how they shape discourse and
the "selling" of policies, see Kenworthy, *America/Américas.*

6. Fredrick B. Pike, *The United States and Latin America: Myths and Stereotypes of Civilization and Nature* (Austin, 1992), 168.

7. Buchanan to Appleton, *Diplomatic Correspondence*, 2:4.

8. John Higham, *From Boundlessness to Consolidation: The Transformation of American Culture, 1848–1860,* reprint from the William L. Clements Library (1969), 11.

9. Appleton to Buchanan, 13 December 1848, *Diplomatic Correspondence*, 2:15; Appleton to Buchanan, 12 February 1849 and 15 February 1849, "Dispatches from U.S. Ministers to Bolivia" NA microfilm, reel 1.

10. Quote is from Bradford Burns, *Latin America: A Concise Interpretive History* (Englewood Cliffs, N.J., 1982), 116.

11. Histories of Belzú generally fall into two distinct categories: those calling him a tyrant and a demagogue and those considering him a prototypical populist hero. For a description of the lower-class support Belzú could mobilize, see Miller to Secretary of State, 28 April 1853, "Dispatches from U.S. Ministers to Bolivia," NA microfilm, reel 1.

12. For different accounts of this story, see Dana to Cass, 12 April 1857, *Diplomatic Correspondence*, 2:78–79; Fifer, *Bolivia: Land, Location, and Politics,* 238–45; Guillermo Lora, *A History of the Bolivian Labour Movement* (New York, 1977), 10–15; Antonio Mitre, "The Economic and Social Structure of Silver Mining in XIX Century Bolivia" (Ph.D. diss., Columbia University, 1977), 44–45, 63–65; Roberto Querejazu Calvo, *Bolivia y los ingleses* (La Paz, 1973), 303–9; and Vázquez Machicado et al., *Manuel de historia de Bolivia,* 372.

13. Dalence, *Bosquejo estadístico de Bolivia,* 305–6.

14. Miller to Everette, 28 April 1853, "Dispatches from U.S. Ministers to Bolivia," NA microfilm, reel 1.

15. McClung to Clayton, 24 August 1850, 22 September 1850, *Diplomatic Correspondence*, 2:4–5.

16. Dana to Marcy, 3 March 1854, *Diplomatic Correspondence*, 2:27.

17. For details on the explorations, see William Lewis Herndon and Lardner Gibbon, *Exploration of the Valley of the Amazon* (Washington, D.C., 1854); Frances Leigh Williams, *Matthew Fontaine Maury, Scientist of the Sea* (New Brunswick, 1963), 196–201; J. Valerie Fifer, *United States Perceptions of Latin America, 1850–1930: A "New West" South of Capricorn?* (Manchester, 1991), chap. 1; and Shipe, "The American Legation in Bolivia," chap. 4.

18. U.S. House of Representatives, *Commercial Relations, 1856,* 1:713.

19. Herndon and Gibbon, *Exploration of the Valley of the Amazon*, 115, 135, 150.
20. Dana to Marcy, 29 August 1854, *Diplomatic Correspondence*, 2:28–30; Fifer, *U.S. Perceptions of Latin America*, 10, 12.
21. Dana to Cass, 25 March 1857, *Diplomatic Correspondence*, 2:67–77.
22. Smith to Secretary of State, 17 August 1861, "Dispatches from U.S. Ministers to Bolivia," NA microfilm, reel 2.
23. Hall to Seward, 12 February 1864, "Dispatches from U.S. Ministers to Bolivia," NA microfilm, reel 2.
24. Hall to Seward, 13 October 1865, *Foreign Relations of the United States, 1866* [hereafter *FRUS*], 327.
25. For discussions of Melgarejo, see Fifer, *Bolivia: Land, Location, and Politics*, 103–5; Vázquez Machicado et al., *Manuel de historia de Bolivia*, 393; Klein, *Bolivia*, 135–42; Shipe, "The American Legation in Bolivia," chaps. 6–10, esp. pp. 535–37; Tristan Platt, "The Andean Experience of Bolivian Liberalism, 1825–1900: Roots of Rebellion in 19th-century Chayanta," in *Resistance, Rebellion and Consciousness in the Andean Peasant World*, ed. Steve J. Stern (Madison, 1987), 280–309; and Mitre, "Economic and Social Structure," 123–27.
26. Fifer, *Bolivia: Land, Location, and Politics*, 106–8, 134; Shipe, "The American Legation in Bolivia," 269–80, 452–53.
27. U.S. House of Representatives, *Commercial Relations, 1872*, 87; and Spenser St. James, minister to Peru, after a visit to Bolivia: 25 January 1876, FO 97/422, quoted in Joseph Smith, *Illusions of Conflict: Anglo-American Diplomacy toward Latin America, 1865–1896* (Pittsburgh, 1979), 14.
28. Hugh C. Bailey, *Hinton Rowan Helper: Abolitionist-Racist* (Tuscaloosa, 1965), 158.
29. Shipe, "The American Legation in Bolivia," 491–520, 537. See also Bailey's discussion in *Hinton Rowan Helper*, 157–65.
30. The account of the War of the Pacific given here is developed from Valentín Abecia Baldivieso, *Las Relaciones internacionales en la historia de Bolivia*, vol. 2 (La Paz, 1978); Gonzolo Bulnes *Resumen de la Guerra del Pacífico* (Santiago, 1976); Harold Eugene Davis et al., *Latin American Diplomatic History: An Introduction* (Baton Rouge, 1977), 125–33; Clements R. Markham, *The War between Peru and Chile, 1879–1882* (London, n.d.); Richard Snyder Phillips Jr., "Bolivia in the War of the Pacific, 1879–1884" (Ph.D. diss., University of Virginia, 1973); Roberto Querejazu Calvo, *La Guerra del Pacífico* (La Paz, 1983); and Vázquez Machicado et al., *Manuel de la historia de Bolivia*.

31. Abecia, *Relaciones internacionalies en la historia de Bolivia*, 32.
32. Querejazu, *La Guerra del Pacífico*, 113.
33. On U.S. diplomacy in the War of the Pacific, see J. Lloyd Mecham, *A Survey of United States–Latin American Relations* (Boston, 1965), 413–23; Smith, *Illusions of Conflict*, 59–80; Alice Felt Tyler, *The Foreign Policy of James G. Blaine* (Minneapolis, 1927), 107–27; Phillips, "Bolivia in the War of the Pacific"; and Pike, *United States and the Andean Republics*, 127–34.
34. Smith, *Illusions of Conflict*, 63.
35. Phillips, "Bolivia in the War of the Pacific," 228–29.
36. Pike, *United States and the Andean Republics*, 131.
37. Adams to Evarts, 5 August 1880, "Dispatches from U.S. Ministers to Bolivia," NA microfilm, reel 8; Adams to Evarts, 12 November 1880, *FRUS 1881*, 76; and Adams to Evarts, 17 November 1880, *FRUS 1881*, 77–78.
38. Adams to Evarts, 17 November 1880, containing a message from the Bolivian foreign minister to Evarts, and Adams to Evarts, 16 December 1880, *FRUS 1881*, 77–82.
39. Cabrera to Evarts, 18 February 1881, *FRUS 1881*, 90–93.
40. Cabrera to Blaine, 9 May 1881, *FRUS 1881*, 93–95.
41. Smith, *Illusions of Conflict*, 72; and Tyler, *The Foreign Policy of James G. Blaine*, 124–25.
42. Adams to Freylinghuysen, 2 March 1882, 16 March 1882, "Dispatches from U.S. Ministers to Bolivia," NA microfilm, reel 9.
43. *El Deber* (La Paz), 27 December 1883, quoted in Phillips, "Bolivia in the War of the Pacific," 291.
44. For assessments, see Freylinghuysen to Logan, 23 March 1883, *FRUS 1883*, 92–96; Smith, *Illusions of Conflict*, 75, 80; and Mecham, *Survey of United States–Latin American Relations*, 417–18.
45. Mitre, "Economic and Social Structure," esp. 43, 59–62, 88–96, 181–88.
46. Klein, *Parties and Political Change in Bolivia*, 14–16.
47. Estimates of freight costs come from comparing rates given in U.S. House, *Commercial Relations, 1859*, 428, with those in U.S. House, *Commercial Relations, 1895*, 129. The latter report gives a good description of rail and other transportation in Bolivia at the close of the nineteenth century.
48. A wealth of new literature is just developing on the liberal era, particularly on the impact of liberal policy on land tenure, Indian communities, class formation, and indigenous rights. See, for example, Platt, "The Andean Experience of Bolivian Liberalism," 296–318; chapters by Robert Jackson and

Erick Langer in *Liberals, the Church, and Indian Peasants: Corporate Lands and the Challenge of Reform in Nineteenth-Century Spanish America*, ed. Robert H. Jackson (Albuquerque, 1997); and Brooke Larson, *Cochabamba, 1550–1900* (Durham, N.C., 1998), particularly chap. 9.

49. On the significance of these political events, see Mitre, *Patriarcas de la Plata*, 192–93; Erick D. Langer, *Economic Change and Rural Resistance in Southern Bolivia* (Stanford, 1989), 28–35; Platt, "The Andean Experience of Bolivian Liberalism," 296–318; and Ramiro Condarco Morales, *Zarate "el temible" Willka: historia de la rebelión indígena de 1899* (La Paz, 1983).

50. Pike, *United States and Latin America*, 159.

51. Quoted in Walter LaFeber, *The New Empire* (Ithaca, 1973), 262.

52. Bailey, *Hinton Rowan Helper*, 177–95.

53. Bailey, *Hinton Rowan Helper*, 177.

54. Helper to Moonlight, 20 April 1895, "Dispatches from U.S. Ministers to Bolivia," NA microfilm, reel 16.

55. Bailey, *Hinton Rowan Helper*, 182, 195.

56. U.S. House of Representatives, *Commercial Relations, 1895;* and William Alfred Reid, *Bolivia, the Heart of a Continent* (Washington, D.C., 1919), 11, 13.

57. Howard Wolf and Ralph Wolf, *Rubber: A Story of Glory and Greed* (New York, 1936), 34, 47.

58. Excellent background on the competing territorial claims to Acre can be found in Fifer, *Bolivia: Land, Location, and Politics*, chap. 3.

59. Fifer, *Bolivia: Land, Location, and Politics*, 122–25; Sorsby to Hay, 14 January 1903, "Dispatches from U.S. Ministers to Bolivia," NA microfilm, reel 20. An interesting fictional account of Gálvez's exploits is Marcio Souza's *The Emperor of the Amazon* (New York, 1980).

60. Villazón to Bridgman, 28 July 1900, "Dispatches from U.S. Ministers to Bolivia," NA microfilm, reel 18. The story of the Bolivian Syndicate is in Fifer, *Bolivia: Land, Location, and Politics*, 123–24; Barbara Weinstein, *The Amazon Rubber Boom* (Stanford, 1983), 177; and Fellman Velarde, *Historia de Bolivia*, 3:25. See also Bridgman to Hay, 23 July 1900, 31 July 1900; and Villazón to Bridgman, 28 July 1900, "Dispatches from U.S. Ministers to Bolivia," NA microfilm, reel 18.

61. Bryan to Hay, 14 August 1902, Sorsby to Hay, 10 November 1902, enclosure to dispatch, Seeger to Hay, 20 January 1903, *FRUS 1903*, 38–39; Sorsby to Hay, 10 November 1902, "Dispatches from U.S. Ministers to Bolivia," NA microfilm, reel 20; enclosure 2, Seeger to Hay, 20 January 1903, *FRUS 1903*,

38–41; Sorsby to Secretary of State, 3 February 1903, "Dispatches from U.S. Ministers to Bolivia," NA microfilm, reel 20; Fifer, *Bolivia: Land, Location, and Politics*, 124–27.

62. Sorsby to Hay, 28 January 1903, 3 February 1903, "Dispatches from U.S. Ministers to Bolivia," NA microfilm, reel 20; Message of President of Brazil to Brazilian Congress, enclosure in Thompson to Hay, 8 May 1903, *FRUS 1903*, 33–35; Sorsby to Hay, 26 December 1903, *FRUS 1904*, 98; Fifer, *Bolivia: Land, Location, and Politics*, 127–29.

63. Weinstein, *The Amazon Rubber Boom*, 177.

64. A translated text of the Koenig letter is included in Bridgman to Secretary, 18 September 1900, "Dispatches from U.S. Ministers to Bolivia," NA microfilm, reel 18.

65. Bolivian response to the Koenig letter is in Bridgman to Secretary, 23 November 1900, and Chilean disavowal of the letter in Bridgman to Secretary, 2 October 1900, "Dispatches from U.S. Ministers to Bolivia," NA microfilm, reel 18. Text of the Agreement with Chile is found in Ames to Secretary, 28 March 1905, *FRUS 1905*, 104–5.

66. Pentland, *Report on Bolivia*, 189, 235; Sergio Almaraz Paz, *El Poder y la caída* (La Paz, 1988), 20; James Dunkerley, *Rebellion in the Veins* (London, 1984), 7, 8.

67. Sorsby to Secretary, 18 April 1906, "Dispatches from U.S. Ministers to Bolivia," NA microfilm, reel 22.

68. Margaret A. Marsh, *The Bankers in Bolivia: A Study of American Foreign Investment* (New York, 1928), 73–79.

69. Langer, *Economic Change and Rural Resistance*, 28.

70. Fifer, *Bolivia: Land, Location, and Politics*, 135.

71. Fifer, *Bolivia: Land, Location, and Politics*, 135–37; and K. E. Knorr, *World Rubber and Its Regulation* (Palo Alto, 1945), 10.

72. Wolf, *Rubber*, 74.

73. Wálter Gómez, *La Minería en el desarrollo económico de Bolivia* (La Paz, 1978), graph 19; Sorsby to Secretary, *FRUS 1907*, 1:85.

74. Pike, *United States and the Andean Republics*, 160.

75. Alcides Arguedas, *Pueblo Enfermo*, 251, 319.

76. Buchanan to Appleton, 1 June 1848, *Diplomatic Correspondence*, 2:4.

77. Pike, *United States and Latin America*, 182.

78. Accounts of Indian uprisings are found in letters: Bridgman to Secretary, 30 December 1898, 26 January 1899, 1 February 1899, and 3 February 1899, "Dispatches from U.S. Ministers to Bolivia," NA microfilm, reel 17. Quotes

come from Bridgman to Secretary, 28 March 1899, *FRUS 1899*, 105; and Bridgman to Secretary, 28 October 1901, *FRUS 1901*, 26.

79. See Pike, *United States and the Andean Republics*, 158, 160.

Chapter 3: Center, Periphery, and the Tin Nexus

1. Grauert to Moonlight, 28 June 1896, "Dispatches from U.S. Ministers to Bolivia," NA microfilm, reel 16. For more on Grauert, see Moonlight to Adee, 12 July 1896, and Bridgman to Secretary, 13 April 1900, "Dispatches from U.S. Ministers to Bolivia," NA microfilm, reel 18. Grauert apparently did not realize that after the British removed their diplomatic representative following the conflict with Belzú, U.S. ministers represented British interests in Bolivia.

2. U.S. House of Representatives, *Commercial Relations, 1895–96*, 634. For U.S. protection of British interests, see the exchange in *FRUS 1899*, 107–10; and Fifer, *Bolivia: Land, Location, and Politics*, 238–45.

3. Marsh, *Bankers in Bolivia*, 73–79.

4. Thomas McCormick, "'Every System Needs a Center Sometimes,' An Essay on Hegemony and Modern American Foreign Policy," in *Redefining the Past: Essays in Diplomatic History in Honor of William Appleman Williams*, ed. Lloyd C. Gardner (Corvallis, 1986), 196–97. The essential literature of world systems theory, which combines elements of modernization and dependency theory, includes works by Fernand Braudel and Immanuel Wallerstein. A succinct summary of world systems theory as well as a basic bibliography can be found in Thomas McCormick, "A Round Table: Explaining the History of American Foreign Relations—World Systems," *Journal of American History* 77.1 (1990): 125–32.

5. John Hewlett, *Like Moonlight on Snow: The Life of Simón Iturri Patiño* (New York, 1947), 105; Klaus E. Knorr, *Tin under Control* (Stanford, 1945), 5.

6. General information on tin comes from Marsh, *Bankers in Bolivia*, 36; Knorr, *Tin under Control*, 10–13; U.S. Department of Interior, Bureau of Mines, *Mineral Yearbook, 1939* (Washington, D.C., 1939), 671–73, 683; David J. Fox, *Tin and the Bolivian Economy* (London, 1970).

7. Production costs in Great Britain's and Holland's Far Eastern possessions were half those in Bolivia because ores were found in alluvial deposits that could be mined with gravel pumps or by dredging rivers and old riverbeds. A Bolivian who observed such an operation in British Malaya exclaimed:

"This isn't a mine. It's a laundry!" See Charles F. Geddis, *Patiño, the Tin King* (London, 1972), 228, 289. On Bolivia's struggle for a smelter, see Antonio Mitre, *El enigma de los hornos: la economía política de la fundición de estaño* (La Paz, 1993); and Sergio Almaraz Paz, *El Poder y la caída: el estaño in la historia de Bolivia*, 5th ed. (La Paz, 1980).

8. For British interests, see John Hillman, "Bolivia and British Tin Policy, 1939–1945," *Journal of Latin American Studies* 22.2 (1990): 289–325; and Knorr, *Tin under Control*, 62–63.

9. *Mineral Yearbook, 1939*, 688; and memorandum and attached report, 6 November 1936, NA, Diplomatic Branch, Central Decimal Files, Record Group 59, 824.6354/122.

10. For sources on the Bolivian tin barons, see Dunkerley, *Rebellion in the Veins*, 8–11; Herbert S. Klein, "The Creation of the Patiño Tin Empire," *Inter-American Economic Affairs* 19.2 (1965); Gómez, *La Minería en el desarrollo económico*; Almaraz Paz, *Poder y la caída*; Geddis, *Patiño the Tin King*; and Roberto Querejazu Calvo, *Llallagua: historia de una montaña* (La Paz, 1977). For information on Hochschild's role in encouraging Jewish immigration to Bolivia, see Leo Spitzer, *Hotel Bolivia: The Culture of Memory in a Refuge from Nazism* (New York, 1998), 111–13.

11. Nash, *We Eat the Mines*, esp. 208–9, 310–34; Michael T. Tausig, *The Devil and Commodity Fetishism in South America* (Chapel Hill, 1980), 207–9.

12. For a description of the *rosca*, see Almaraz Paz, *Poder y la caída*, 78, 80, 87–93; and Herbert S. Klein, *Parties and Political Change in Bolivia, 1880–1952* (Cambridge, 1969), 33–34.

13. Marsh, *Bankers in Bolivia*, 4, 37; Reid, *Bolivia, the Heart of a Continent*, 39.

14. Joseph S. Tulchin, *The Aftermath of War* (New York, 1971), v, vi; Warren I. Cohen, *Empire without Tears* (New York, 1987), 18–44; Walter LaFeber, *The American Age* (New York, 1989), 339–41.

15. Klein, *Parties and Political Change*, 77–78; Marsh, *Bankers in Bolivia*, 55–60; Fellman Velarde, *Historia de Bolivia*, 3:80, 98–99.

16. On the Kemmerer mission, see Marsh, *Bankers in Bolivia*, 95–104; Manuel E. Contreras, "Debt, Taxes, and War: The Political Economy of Bolivia c. 1920–1935," *Journal of Latin American Studies* 22.2 (1990): 279; and articles by Robert N. Seidel and Barry Eichengree in *The Money Doctors, Foreign Debts, and Economic Reforms in Latin America from the 1890s to the Present*, ed. Paul Drake (Wilmington, 1994).

17. Drake, introduction to *Money Doctors in Latin America*, xxv.

18. Marsh, *Bankers in Bolivia*, 134.

19. William Lee Lofstrom, "Attitudes of an Industrial Pressure Group in Latin America, the Asociación de Industriales Mineros, 1925–1935" (M.A. thesis, Cornell University, 1968), 56–57; Klein, *Parties and Political Change,* 108; Almaraz Paz, *Poder y la caída,* 36; Gómez, *La Minería en el desarrollo económico de Bolivia,* 66.

20. Gómez, *La Minería en el desarrollo económico de Bolivia,* 90–91; Contreras, "Debt, Taxes, and War," 265–87; Lofstrom, "Attitudes of an Industrial Pressure Group," 12; Seidel, "American Reformers Abroad," in *Money Doctors in Latin America,* 88.

21. Klein, *Parties and Political Change,* 64–87; Pike, *The United States and the Andean Republics,* 174–77.

22. For discussions, see Lofstrom, "Attitudes of an Industrial Pressure Group," 24–39, 82–87; Gómez, *La Minería en el desarrollo económico de Bolivia,* 64, 91–92; and Contreras, "Debt, Taxes, and War," 267–79.

23. Pike, *The United States and the Andean Republics,* 14.

24. Dunkerley, *Rebellion in the Veins,* 54.

25. Klein, *Parties and Political Change,* 121–45; Malloy, *Uncompleted Revolution,* 70–72; Lofstrom, "Attitudes of an Industrial Pressure Group," 62–64; Contreras, "Debt, Taxes, and War," 273, 281–83.

26. Bruce Farcau states that the 1928 Paraguayan attack was the unilateral act of one aspiring army captain, though the popular support he gained made it difficult for the Paraguayan government to repudiate his act. See Bruce W. Farcau, *The Chaco War: Bolivia and Paraguay, 1932–1935* (Westport, Conn., 1996), 12–15. Fifer, *Bolivia: Land, Location, and Politics,* 208; Bryce Wood, *The United States and Latin American Wars, 1932–1942* (New York, 1966), 21–22. For a measure of the attention the Chaco now received, see the voluminous documentation on the border conflict in *FRUS* from 1928 until the issue was finally settled in 1938.

27. Roberto Querejazu Calvo, *Historia de la Guerra del Chaco* (La Paz, 1990), 26–27.

28. Sources discussing the Chaco War include Klein, *Parties and Political Change,* chap. 6; Farcau, *The Chaco War;* Fifer, *Bolivia: Land, Location, and Politics,* 212–21; David Hartzler Zook, *The Conduct of the Chaco War* (New Haven, 1960); and José Félix Estigarribia, *Epic of the Chaco: Marshal Estigarribia's Memoirs of the Chaco War, 1932–1935,* ed. Pablo Max Insfran (Austin, 1950).

29. See Reid, *Bolivia, the Heart of a Continent,* 56; Zook, *Conduct of the Chaco War,* 62; and Fifer, *Bolivia: Land, Location, and Politics,* 205–7. Farcau depicts the Bolivian army as acutely top-heavy and inefficient (*The Chaco War,* 19).

30. William R. Garner, *The Chaco Dispute: A Study of Prestige Diplomacy* (Washington, D.C., 1966), 1; Wood, *The United States and Latin American Wars*, 20.

31. In late 1998, Bolivia opened a canal through one of those windows that connects to the Paraguay River. The new canal, which has raised the concerns of international environmentalists, will reduce the cost of transport of goods from the Bolivian east to the Atlantic by as much as one-half. *Los Tiempos* (Cochabamba, Bolivia), 20 November 1998.

32. Zook, *Conduct of the Chaco War*, 213, 241; Farcau, *The Chaco War*, 237, 240.

33. Klein, *Parties and Political Change*, 229–320, gives a lengthy account of this significant period in Bolivia's political development. See also Malloy, *Uncompleted Revolution*, 88–94.

34. For the decree canceling Standard Oil's concession, see *FRUS 1937*, 5: 277–78.

35. For differing interpretations of Toro's purposes, see Klein, *Parties and Political Change*, 260; Fellman Velarde, *Historia de Bolivia*, 3:221; and Pike, *The United States and the Andean Republics*, 252–53. Quotes are from Norweb to Hull, 16 March 1937 and 8 May 1937, *FRUS 1937*, 5:279, 287.

36. For differing perspectives on these issues, see Irwin Gellman, *Good Neighbor Diplomacy* (Baltimore, 1979), 60–61; Fellman Velarde, *Historia de Bolivia*, 3:181, 187, 190, 192, 205, 229; and Bryce Wood, *The Making of the Good Neighbor Policy* (New York, 1961), 169.

37. Norweb to Hull, 8 May 1937, *FRUS 1937*, 5:287; Norweb to Hull, 19 March 1937, *FRUS 1937*, 5:281.

38. For the German connection, see Cole Blasier, *United States, Germany, and the Bolivian Revolutionaries* (Pittsburg, 1973), 28–29; and Emmitt James Holland, "Historical Study of Bolivian Foreign Relations" (Ph.D. diss., American University, 1968), 277–78. Another perspective on these years comes in the recent book on Jewish refugees in Bolivia. Although Busch's German connections are often emphasized, he also negotiated to allow Jewish exiles from Germany to come to Bolivia (Spitzer, *Hotel Bolivia*, 110–18). The smelter rumors are reported in memorandum of conversation, 25 June 1939, NA 824.631/36.

39. Hull to Roosevelt, 15 January 1940, and enclosure, "Statement by the Interdepartmental Committee on Strategic Materials," *FRUS 1940*, 2:250; memorandum of agreement, 28 June 1940, and statement by Federal Loan Administrator Jones, 1 July 1940, *FRUS 1940*, 2:297–300; Holland, "A Historical Study of Bolivian Foreign Relations," 310.

40. Knorr, *Tin under Control*, 89–91.

41. Accounts of the formation of the International Tin Control Scheme are in Knorr, *Tin under Control,* chaps. 6–10; William L. Baldwin, *The World Tin Market: Political Pricing and Economic Competition* (Durham, N.C., 1983), chap. 4; Geddis, *Patiño, the Tin King,* chap. 19; and Gómez, *La Minería en el desarrollo económico de Bolivia,* 65–70.

42. See Barnes to Hull, 4 December 1933, NA 824.6354/87; and several memos, Norweb to Hull, 11 March 1937, 11 June 1937, *FRUS 1937,* 5:272–75; and Butler to Duggan and attached report, 6 November 1936, NA 824.6354/122.

43. See *FRUS 1939,* 1:854, 941–44; *FRUS 1940,* 2:250, 290–300; and *Mineral Yearbook, 1939,* 673–78.

44. See Pike, *The United States and the Andean Republics,* 241–42; Holland, "A Historical Study of Bolivian Foreign Relations," 303–9; and *FRUS 1939,* 5:313–22.

45. Jenkins to Hull, 4 April 1941, *FRUS 1941,* 6:468–75.

46. Blasier, *United States, Germany, and the Bolivian Revolutionaries,* 31–39.

47. See various documents in *FRUS 1941,* 6:403–12, 437; Holland, "Historical Study of Bolivian Foreign Relations," 314, 321–23; and Lawrence Heilman, "U.S. Development Assistance to Rural Bolivia, 1941–1974" (Ph.D. diss., American University, 1982), 53–54.

48. See various documents in *FRUS 1942,* 5:588–96. Wood adds that since Standard investments in Bolivia had been in the neighborhood of $17 million, the company could not have been happy with the $1.5 million it received in compensation. See Wood, *Making of the Good Neighbor Policy,* 197–98.

49. Heilman, "U.S. Development Assistance to Rural Bolivia," 55–56. For documentary sources, see *FRUS 1942,* 5:603–14.

50. Memo of conversation, 5 May 1943, *FRUS 1943,* 5:561–64.

51. Dawson to Department, 6 January 1942, *FRUS 1942,* 5:539.

52. Hillman, "Bolivia and British Tin Policy," 290, 313–15. For tin statistics, see *Mineral Yearbook, 1939,* 688; *Mineral Yearbook, 1946,* 1173.

53. Mariano Baptista Gumucio, *Guerrilleros y generales sobre Bolivia* (Buenos Aires, 1968), table 23, p. 146.

54. Dunkerley, *Rebellion in the Veins,* 11–12, 15; Malloy, *Uncompleted Revolution,* 118–19; Manuel Contreras, "La Mano de obra en la minería estanífera, aspectos cuantitativos, c. 1935–1945" (mimeo, Cochabamba, 1989). An account of the Catavi massacre can be found in Lora, *History of the Bolivian Labour Movement,* 219–22.

55. Henry Weinberg Berger, "Union Diplomacy: American Labor's Foreign Pol-

icy in Latin America, 1932–1955" (Ph.D. diss., University of Wisconsin, 1966), 211.

56. See Berger, "Union Diplomacy," 219–21; and Holland, "Historical Study of Bolivian Foreign Relations," 418–19.

57. Magruder to Duggan, 19 February 1943, *FRUS 1943*, 5:613–15.

58. For information on the coup and the U.S. response, see *FRUS 1943*, 5:533–43; and *FRUS 1944*, 7:430–32.

59. See *FRUS 1943*, 5:553, 565–66, 576–77; *FRUS 1944*, 7:477–79; and Hillman, "Bolivia and British Tin Policy," 305.

60. See Crowley to Hull, 10 January 1944, *FRUS 1944*, 7:474–75; and memo of conversation, 21 May 1944, *FRUS 1944*, 7:482–83.

61. Byrnes to Ambassador Thurston, 14 August 1945, *FRUS 1945*, 9:588.

62. McLaughlin to Hull, 16 September 1944, *FRUS 1944*, 7:487–88; Víctor Andrade, *My Missions for Revolutionary Bolivia* (Pittsburgh, 1976), 31–32.

63. Hull to McLaughlin, 20 and 21 September 1944, *FRUS 1944*, 7:489.

64. Memorandum of conversation, 6 August 1945, *FRUS 1945*, 9:584–87; Andrade, *My Missions*, 69.

65. Memorandum of conversation, 6 August 1945, *FRUS 1945*, 9:584–87.

66. Ibid.

67. For an example of U.S. counterarguments, see memorandum of conversation, 29 January 1946, *FRUS 1946*, 9:377–79.

68. See *FRUS 1941*, 6:420–21, 432–33, 445–51; and *FRUS 1942*, 5:515–17, 520–33, 536–39, 544.

69. Office memo, 30 October 1946, *FRUS 1946*, 9:399.

70. Memorandum of conversation, 5 May 1943, *FRUS 1943*, 5:561–64; Welles to Foreign Minister Anze Matienzo, 27 July 1942, *FRUS 1942*, 5:592–93.

71. Fredrick B. Pike, *FDR's Good Neighbor Policy: Sixty Years of Generally, Gentle Chaos* (Austin, 1995), 165.

72. Pike, *FDR's Good Neighbor Policy*, 14, 71, 134–35, 232; Julianne Burton, "Don (Juanito) Duck and the Imperial-Patriarchal Unconscious: Disney Studios, the Good Neighbor Policy, and the Packaging of Latin America," in *Nationalisms and Sexualities*, ed. Andrew Parker (New York, 1992), 26. The films in the series were *South of the Border with Disney* (1941), *Saludos Amigos* (1943), and *The Three Caballeros* (1945).

73. Quoted in Holland, "Historical Study of Bolivian Foreign Relations," 463.

74. Pike, *FDR's Good Neighbor Policy*, 140, 143, 353.

75. Burton "Don (Juanito) Duck," 38.

76. Stephen G. Rabe, *Eisenhower and Latin America* (Chapel Hill, 1988), 11–14; Carleton Beals, "Ecuador, Peru, and Bolivia," in *What the South Americans Think of Us* (New York, 1945), 38.

77. Pike, *FDR's Good Neighbor Policy*, 15, 274–75, 284.

Chapter 4: Bolivian Dilemma and a Pragmatic Experiment

1. For coverage of the 1952 revolution in secondary works, see the Bibliographical Essay.

2. Air Attaché's Report, dispatch 736 from La Paz, 16 April 1952, NA 724.00/4-1752.

3. See Richard W. Patch, "Bolivia, the Restrained Revolution," *Annals of the American Academy of Political and Social Science* 334 (March 1961): 123–32; and J. Calderon, *The Bolivian Coup of 1964: A Sociological Analysis* (Buffalo, 1972). With somewhat different interpretations, James Malloy, Fredrick Pike, and Christopher Mitchell agree that MNR leaders were "reluctant" revolutionaries. See Malloy, *Uncompleted Revolution*, esp. 170–72; Mitchell, *Legacy of Populism*, esp. viii and 6; and Pike, *The United States and the Andean Republics*, 280–94.

4. Andrade, *My Missions*, 5.

5. Much has been written on the political and social impact of the Chaco War. For key discussions in English, see Lora, *A History of the Bolivian Labour Movement*, 163–66; Malloy, *Uncompleted Revolution*, 64–75; Klein, *Parties and Political Change*, 199–202, 337–42; Jerry Knudson, *Bolivia, Press and Revolution, 1932–1964* (Lanham, Md., 1986), 13–19, 36, 39; Mitchell, *Legacy of Populism*, 16–17; and Dunkerley, *Rebellion in the Veins*, 27.

6. La Paz to State Department, *FRUS 1944*, 7:472; Andrade, *My Missions*, 28.

7. Jorge Dandler and Juan Torrico explore the paternal pact between Andean peasants in Ayopaya near Cochabamba and President Villarroel in "From the National Indigenous Congress to the Ayopaya Rebellion: Bolivia, 1945–1947," in *Resistance, Rebellion and Consciousness*, 334–78. On labor, see Klein, *Parties and Political Change*, 375–76; Lora, *History of the Bolivian Labour Movement*, 234–36; and Mitchell, *Legacy of Populism*, 23.

8. See documents in *FRUS 1946*, 11:342–58, for the escalating U.S. involvement as Villarroel's government began to crumble.

9. Flack to Byrnes, 22 July 1946, *FRUS 1946*, 11:359–60.

10. Memorandum of conversation, 18 June 1948, *FRUS 1948*, 2:330–32.

11. See "Survey of Communism in Bolivia," 29 March 1950, NA 724.001/3-3050.

12. Klein portrays this as a time of true MNR radicalization while Mitchell argues that links to labor remained tenuous and interested the MNR only to the degree that they could be used to manipulate workers to the party's benefit. See Klein, *Parties and Political Change,* chap. 12; and Mitchell, *Legacy of Populism,* 17–25.

13. See Maleady to Secretary of State, 7 May 1951, NA 724.00/5-751; Maleady to Secretary of State, 8 May 1951, NA 724.00/5-851; memorandum of conversation, 9 May 1951, NA 724.00/5-951; and Acheson to La Paz, 7 May 1951, NA 724.00/5-751.

14. "Bolivia," Policy Statement, 7 August 1950, NA 611.24/8-750, p. 13.

15. See International Tin Study Group, *Statistical Yearbook, 1949* (The Hague, 1949), 48–64; memorandum of conversation, 15 June 1951, *FRUS 1951,* 2:1152–55; and U.S. Senate, Preparedness Subcommittee of the Committee on Armed Services, *Tin 1951,* sixth report, 82d Cong., 1st sess., 1951.

16. Text of press release sent in telegram 343, Guachalla to Foreign Minister, 27 October 1951, Archives of the Ministry of Foreign Relations in La Paz [hereafter Bolivian Foreign Ministry Archives] CL-351. For Symington's views, see U.S. Senate, Hearings before Preparedness Subcommittee of the Committee on Armed Services, 82d Cong., 1st sess., 24 July 1951.

17. Almaraz Paz, *Poder y la caída,* 244.

18. Detailed Bolivian accounts of the negotiations are found in the telegraph transcripts contained in bound volumes CL-352 and CL-353 from 1952 at the Bolivian Foreign Ministry archives.

19. See discussions of the revolutionary movement in Malloy, *Uncompleted Revolution,* chap. 8; Mitchell, *Legacy of Population,* 26–33; and Dunkerley, *Rebellion in the Veins,* 37.

20. *Time,* 21 April 1952.

21. Dispatch 696, "Bolivian Dilemma," 2 April 1952, NA 824.00/4-252.

22. Carter Goodrich, "Bolivia in Time of Revolution," in *Beyond the Revolution: Bolivia since 1952,* ed. James Malloy and Richard Thorn (Pittsburgh, 1971), 19. Other sources dealing with Bolivia's social conditions at the time of the revolution include Jonathan Kelley and Herbert S. Klein, *Revolution and Rebirth of Inequality* (Berkeley, 1981), 68–69, 70–77; and Paul Robert Turovsky, "Bolivian Haciendas, before and after the Revolution" (Ph.D. diss., UCLA, 1980), 76.

23. Key documents include Bolivia, Ministerio de Hacienda y Estadística, Dirección General de Estadística y Censos, *Censo Demográfico, 1950* (La Paz, 1955); and United Nations, *Report of the United Nations Mission of Technical Assistance* [commonly referred to as the Keenleyside Report] (New York, 1951).

24. Dispatch 696, "Bolivian Dilemma," 2 April 1952, NA 824.00/4-252.

25. Dispatch 725, "First Post-revolution Impressions," 14 April 1952, NA 724.00/4-1452.

26. Carlos Navia Rivera, *Los Estados Unidos y la revolución nacional: entre el pragmatismo y el sometimiento* (Cochabamba, 1984), 113. See dispatch 723 from La Paz, 12 April 1952, NA 724.00/4-1252; and dispatch 702 from Buenos Aires, 12 April 1952, NA 724.00/4-1252.

27. Blasier, "The United States and the Revolution," in *Beyond the Revolution: Bolivia since 1952*, ed. James M. Malloy and Richard S. Thorn (Pittsburgh, 1971), 69–72.

28. Cited in Knudson, *Bolivia, Press and Revolution*, 290. See also Klein, *Bolivia*, 234.

29. Milton S. Eisenhower, *The Wine Is Bitter: The United States and Latin America* (New York, 1963), 68.

30. *La Nación*, 6 November 1952, in Saturnino Rodrigo, *Diário de la revolución* (La Paz, 1955), 31–32.

31. Dispatch 7 to Eden, 9 January 1953, British Foreign Office, 3.71/103626. See also Foreign Minister Wálter Guevara's report, dispatch 644, 11 April 1953, NA 724.00/4-1153.

32. Telegram 223, Dulles to Embassy in Bolivia, 12 March 1953, *FRUS 1952–54*, 4:522–23; and telegram 53, Andrade to Foreign Ministry in La Paz, 12 March 1953, Bolivian Foreign Ministry Archives, CL-354.

33. Telegram 274, Sparks to Secretary of State, 13 March 1953, *FRUS 1952–54*, 4:524–25.

34. Telegram 46, Guevara to Embassy in Washington, 20 March 1953, Bolivian Foreign Ministry Archives, CL-354; and telegram 66, Andrade to Foreign Ministry in La Paz, 26 March 1953, Bolivian Foreign Ministry Archives, CL-354.

35. *Ultima Hora*, 16 April 1953, carried Galarza's speech. Commentary on Galarza's speech is found in Joint Weekly Summary, 17 April 1953, NA 724.00(W)/4-1753; dispatch 680 from La Paz, 23 April 1953, NA 824.00/4-2343; and memorandum of conversation, Jackson, Galarza, Fishburn, and Hudson, 23 April 1953, NA 824.00/4-2353.

36. Joint Weekly Summary, 10 April 1953, NA 724.00(W)/4-1053.

37. *Ultima Hora,* 14 April 1953. Anti-U.S. sentiment is summarized in dispatch 699 from La Paz, "Anti-U.S. Campaign Stepped Up in Labor Circles," 30 April 1953, NA 611.24/4-3053. Paz's May Day speech is covered in *Ultima Hora,* 2 May 1953, 4. See also the review of President Paz's May Day speech included in office memorandum, Hudson to Cabot, Mann and Atwood, 11 May 1953, NA 611.24/5-453.

38. Diary entry, 6 January 1953, Dwight David Eisenhower Library, Abilene, Kansas [hereafter DDE Library], Eisenhower Diary, "December 1952 to 19 August 1953," folder 4.

39. Dispatch 518 from La Paz, "Communist Infiltration into the Bolivian Government," 2 February 1953, NA 724.001/2-253; cable A-122, Dulles to Embassy in La Paz, 10 February 1953, NA 724.001/2-253.

40. Dispatch 518 from La Paz, "Communist Infiltration into the Bolivian Government," 2 June 1953, NA 724.001/2-253.

41. For comparisons of U.S. policies in Bolivia and Guatemala, see Cole Blasier, *The Hovering Giant: U.S. Responses to Revolutionary Change in Latin America* (Pittsburgh, 1976); and Kenneth Lehman, "Revolutions and Attributions: Making Sense of Eisenhower Administration Policies in Bolivia and Guatemala," *Diplomatic History* 21.2 (1997): 185–213.

42. Blasier, *Hovering Giant,* 222–26; Harold Molineu, *U.S. Policy toward Latin America: From Regionalism to Globalism* (Boulder, 1986), 217–22.

43. M. Eisenhower, *The Wine Is Bitter,* 67.

44. Richard Immerman, *The CIA in Guatemala: The Foreign Policy of Intervention* (Austin, 1982), 13. See Stephen Schlesinger and Stephen Kinzer, *Bitter Fruit: The Untold Story of the American Coup in Guatemala,* 2d ed. (New York, 1983), chap. 6, on the United Fruit Company's public relations campaign, and pp. 106–7 for a discussion of the company's impressive connections at the highest levels of the Truman and Eisenhower administrations.

45. Dispatch 699 from La Paz, 30 April 1953, NA 611.24/4-3053.

46. Office memorandum, Hudson to Atwood, 30 April 1953, NA 824.00/4-3053.

47. U.S. Department of State, *Department of State Bulletin* 29-734 (20 July 1953): 82; and *Department of State Bulletin* 29-749 (2 November 1953): 854.

48. This argument is fleshed out in Lehman, "Revolutions and Attributions."

49. Telegram 87 of 8 May 1953, telegram 95 of 27 May 1953, and telegram 98 of 9 June 1953, Guevara to Embassy in Washington, Bolivian Foreign Ministry Archives, CL-354.

50. For a firsthand account from the key UN adviser to these measures, see Arthur Karasz, "Experiment in Development: Bolivia since 1952," in *Free-*

dom and Reform in Latin America, ed. Fredrick B. Pike (Notre Dame, 1967), 270–71.

51. Dispatch 806 from La Paz, 24 June 1953, NA 724.00/6-2453; dispatch from La Paz, 27 June 1953, NA 724.00/6-2753; and Joint Weekly Summary, 6 July 1953, NA 724.00 (W)/7-653.

52. George Jackson Eder, *Inflation and Development in Latin America: A Case History of Inflation and Stabilization in Bolivia* (Ann Arbor, 1968), 593.

53. Pike, *The United States and the Andean Republics,* 291–92.

54. Mitchell, *Legacy of Populism,* 80.

55. Almaraz Paz, *Poder y la caída,* 123.

56. This argument is spelled out more completely in Lehman, "Revolutions and Attributions," 201–13. Forms of it are also presented in G. Earl Sanders, "The Quiet Experiment in American Diplomacy," *Americas* 33.1 (1976): 25–49; and Richard W. Patch, "Bolivia: U.S. Assistance in a Revolutionary Setting," in *Social Change in Latin America Today* (New York, 1960), 108–76.

Chapter 5: The Limits of Pragmatism and the Disintegration of a Special Partnership

1. The U.S. edition of *Time* carried the story but not the quote, which was apparently added to the international edition at the last minute as filler. Details on the rioting can be found in NA 724.00 and NA 611.24 for late February and early March 1959; and in *Hispanic American Report* 13.3 (May 1959): 162.

2. Gilbert in Cochabamba to Washington, 3 March 1959, NA 724.00/3-359; letter from K. L. Knickerbocker, Dean of the University of Tennessee, to Herter, 18 March 1959, NA 724.00/3-1859.

3. Andrade, *My Missions,* 198.

4. Evidence of Andrade's role can be found in NA 724.00 and NA 611.24. For example, see memorandum of conversation, 28 February 1959, NA 724.00/2-2859. *El Diário,* 1 March 1959, has Andrade's quote.

5. Office memorandum, Bennett to Cabot, 23 November 1953, NA 724.00/11-2353.

6. In March 1954, Paz told miners that Communists posed a more dangerous and subtle threat to the revolution than the old rosca because they endangered U.S. aid. See Joint Weekly Summary, 2 April 1954, NA 724.00 (W)/4-254.

7. Immerman, *The CIA in Guatemala*, 155–60; Schlesinger and Kinzer, *Bitter Fruit*, 147–58. Telegram 62, Castrillo to Guevara, 28 June 1954, Bolivian Foreign Ministry Archives, CL-548, shows Bolivian reluctance to support U.S. initiatives.

8. For further elaboration and documentation, see Kenneth Lehman, "U.S. Foreign Aid and Revolutionary Nationalism," 523–53.

9. Interview with Wálter Guevara Arze, La Paz, 25 May 1990.

10. Joint Weekly Summary, 9 July 1954, NA 724.00 (W)/7-954.

11. Dispatch 243, memorandum of conversation with Lechín, 2 December 1954, NA 824.062/12-254.

12. For Bolivia's development plan, see Bolivia, Ministry of Foreign Affairs, *Memorandum II, Economic Development of the Republic of Bolivia* (La Paz, 1954). For the rationale behind the plan, see the statement by Paz in an interview with James Wilkie and Edna Monzon de Wilkie, 6 July 1966, in Lima, Peru, quoted in James W. Wilkie, *Bolivian Foreign Trade* (Buffalo, 1971), 1–2. The development theme in the MNR program is well described by Richard Thorn, "The Economic Transformation," in *Beyond the Revolution: Bolivia since 1952*, 157–216.

13. Thomas Zoumaras, "The Path to Pan-Americanism: Eisenhower's Foreign Economic Policy toward Latin America" (Ph.D. diss., University of Connecticut, 1987), 156 and chap. 3; and Burton I. Kaufman, *Trade and Aid: Eisenhower's Foreign Economic Policy, 1953–1961* (Baltimore, 1982), 29–33.

14. Letter, Yoe to Powell, 22 October 1954, NA, Record Group [hereafter RG] 469, Restricted Subject File, box 2.

15. Cornelius Zondag, *The Bolivian Economy, 1952–1965* (New York, 1966), 112, 121.

16. See Melvin Burke, "Does 'Food for Peace' Assistance Damage the Bolivian Economy?" *Inter-American Economic Affairs* 25.1 (1971): 5, 18; Eder, *Inflation and Development in Latin America*, 35–39; Richard Gordon Frederick, "United States Aid to Bolivia, 1952–1972" (Ph.D. diss., University of Maryland, 1977), 45; Zondag, *Bolivian Economy*, 62; James W. Wilkie, *The Bolivian Revolution and U.S. Aid since 1952* (Los Angeles, 1969), 14; and Committee on Government Operations (McClellan Committee), *Report on Administration of U.S. Foreign Aid Programs in Bolivia*, 86th Cong., 2d sess. (Washington, D.C., 1960) [hereafter McClellan Report], 4–9, 15–17.

17. Letter, Drew to Sparks, 11 April 1955, NA, General Records of the Department of State, RG 59, Records of the Assistant Secretary of State, Roy Richard Rubottom, 1956–1961 [hereafter Rubottom LOT].

18. Dispatch 583 from La Paz, 24 June 1955, *FRUS 1955–57*, 7:514–15.

19. Frederick, "United States Aid to Bolivia," 47.

20. Confidential supplement to the Milton Eisenhower Report (n.d.), DDE Library, Ann Whitman Files, Name Series, box 13, folder 1.

21. Dispatch 417, "Bolivian Highlights, 1953," 13 January 1954, NA 724.00/1-1354.

22. Louis Hartz, *The Liberal Tradition in America* (New York, 1955), 306.

23. Eder, *Inflation and Development in Latin America*, 87. For State Department concerns about Eder, see Sanders to Rubottom, 4 December 1956, Rubottom LOT; and office memos, Briggs to Rubottom, 4 and 7 December 1956, Rubottom LOT. See also the commentary on Eder's role in Laurence Whitehead, *The United States and Bolivia, a Case of Neo-Colonialism* (London, 1969), 11–17.

24. Covered in Eder, *Inflation and Development in Latin America*, 435–39, 448–52. Interesting insights also come from Robert Alexander, who observed the events firsthand. See Robert J. Alexander, *The Bolivian National Revolution* (Westport, Conn., 1958), 213–20.

25. Jon V. Kofas, "The Politics of Austerity: The IMF and U.S. Foreign Policy in Bolivia, 1956–1964," *Journal of Developing Areas* 29 (January 1995): 220; Gómez, *La Minería en el desarrollo económico de Bolivia*, tables 7 and 19.

26. Telegram 86, Embassy in Washington to Foreign Ministry in La Paz, 25 September 1958, Bolivian Foreign Ministry Archives.

27. See Figures from Gómez, *La Minería en el desarrollo económico de Bolivia*, table 19, p. 218; Thorn, "Economic Transformation," appendix table 6, 378–79; and James W. Wilkie, *Bolivian Foreign Trade*, tables 1 and 7, and pp. 25–26. For Bolivian protests of the lead-zinc tariffs, see telegrams 67 and 73, Embassy in Washington to La Paz, 28 May 1957 and 3 June 1957, Bolivian Foreign Ministry Archives.

28. Memorandum of conversation, 18 September 1958, document BL-12, *FRUS 1958–60*, microfilm.

29. Memorandum of conversation, Roosevelt and Peñaranda, 5 May 1943, *FRUS 1943*, 5:563.

30. Philip W. Bonsal, *Cuba, Castro, and the United States* (Pittsburgh, 1971), 26–27; Mario Lazo, *Dagger in the Heart* (New York, 1968), 176–79.

31. A collection of Bonsal's letters revealing his advocacy can be found in Rubottom LOT, and NA, Office of the Assistant Secretary of State for Inter-American Affairs [hereafter ARA] Files, LOT 62D429, "Bonsal Letters," in *FRUS: 1958–60*, microfilm. James Wilkie has shown that the United States

provided little economic support for development until the 1960s. See Wilkie, *The Bolivian Revolution and U.S. Aid since 1952*, 41–45.

32. Memorandum of conversation, 11 February 1959, NA 824.00-TA/2-1159.

33. Statement by R. R. Rubottom to House Foreign Affairs Committee, Subcommittee on Latin America, 3 June 1958, Rubottom LOT. Nixon's visit is covered as well in *Department of State Bulletin* 38.989 (9 June 1958), and 38.992 (30 June 1958).

34. See Mitchell, *Legacy of Populism*, chap. 4; and Malloy, *Uncompleted Revolution*, 269–78. Both cover this process in excellent detail but give little attention to external factors.

35. J. Fred Rippy, "Bolivia: An Exhibit of the Problems of Economic Development in Retarded Countries," *Inter-American Economic Affairs* 10.3 (1956): 61–74.

36. Kenneth Iverson, "The *Servicio* in Theory and Practice," attached to letter, Donavan to Dickens, NA, RG 469, AID, Mission to Bolivia, Office of Director, Oscar Powell, 1950–1954, box 3, Memoranda, Chief of IIAA Mission.

37. McClellan Report, 17–18; and "U.S. Technical Assistance and Development Aid Program, Bolivia," February 1957, DDE Library, Citizen Advisors on Mutual Security Program, box 16, Bolivia.

38. Dispatch 845 from La Paz, 22 April 1959, NA 724.00/4-2259.

39. Allan R. Richards, *Administration—Bolivia and the United States* (Albuquerque, 1961), 22–27.

40. Memo, Briggs to Rubottom, 25 June 1958, NA 724.5-MSP/6-2558. Further discussion of the debate between the ICA and embassy officials can be found in Lehman, "U.S. Foreign Aid and Revolutionary Nationalism," 634–38.

41. Telegram 557, UN Ambassador Lodge to Secretary of State, 20 January 1959, NA 724.00/1-2059; and U.S. State Department, Bureau of Intelligence and Research, Intelligence Report 7943, 5 February 1959, on the Bolivian Situation and Soviet Bloc Overtures. See also telegram 82 from Washington, 9 September 1958, Bolivian Foreign Ministry Archives; and letter from Bonsal to Siracusa, NA, ARA Files, LOT 62D429, "Bonsal Letters," in *FRUS: 1958–60*, microfilm.

42. Knudson, *Bolivia, Press and Revolution*, 343–44; *El Diário*, 6 January 1958.

43. On the importance of the *pulperías* to miners, see Nash, *We Eat the Mines*, 91–92. Eder defined the worker wage as $1 a day, arguing that if the miners demanded $b6,000, then the exchange rate of the peso would have to be six

thousand to the dollar on grounds that "there was no way to escape this equation unless Comibol produced more tin or dismissed half its workers" (Eder, *Inflation and Development*, 132).

44. Guevara volunteered this information in an interview in La Paz, 23 May 1990. The story is corroborated by telegrams of 6 January 1959 from Washington and 18 January 1959 from La Paz found in the Bolivian Foreign Ministry Archives.

45. Confidential memo to R. R. Rubottom, 5 October 1959, NA, Rubottom LOT.

46. For this story, see dispatch 734: "The *Time* Article and the Bolivian Reaction: Preliminary Views," 1 March 1959, NA 611.24/3-959; *El Diário*, 1 March 1959; and memorandum from police mission, 4 December 1959, NA 611.24/ 12-459.

47. *El Diário*, 3 March 1959, carries the president's speech. Siles's comment comes in dispatch 767, Embassy to Washington, 24 March 1959, NA 611.24/ 3-2459.

48. Dispatch 740, 10 March 1959, NA 724.00/3-1059. The quote is from dispatch 734 from La Paz, 9 March 1959, NA 611.24/3-959.

49. "Report by the Vice President on Latin American Trip," 11 March 1955, DDE Library, Ann Whitman Files, NSC Series, box 6, 240th Meeting of the NSC.

50. "Report by the Vice President on His Trip to South America," 23 May 1958, DDE Library, Ann Whitman Files, NSC Series, box 10, 366th Meeting of the NSC.

51. See Stephen G. Rabe, *Eisenhower and Latin America* (Chapel Hill, 1988), chaps. 6–8; Zoumaras, "Path to Pan-Americanism," chaps. 10–12; Kaufman, *Trade and Aid*, 200; and Cole Blasier, "The Elimination of United States Influence," in *Revolutionary Change in Cuba*, ed. Carmelo Mesa-Lago (Pittsburgh, 1971), 52–56.

52. See memoranda: 26 March 1959, NA 724.5 MSP/3-2659; 18 May 1959, NA 611.24/5-1859; 19 May 1959, NA 724.00/5-1959; 20 May 1959, NA 611.24/ 5-2059; and 23 July 1959, NA 724.00/7-2359. James W. Wilkie, "U.S. Foreign Policy and Economic Assistance in Bolivia, 1948–1976," in *Modern-Day Bolivia*, ed. Jerry Ladman (Tempe, 1982), 85, gives assistance figures.

53. "Report by the Vice President on His Trip to South America," 23 May 1958.

54. Whitehead, *The United States and Bolivia;* and Calderon, *The Bolivian Coup of 1964*, 108.

55. *Hispanic American Report* 14 (1961): 157; *El Diário*, 13 January 1960, 23 March

1960, 6 October 1960, 16 December 1960, 22 December 1960, and 22 January 1961.

56. *El Diário*, 2 January 1961; *Hispanic American Report* 13 (1961): 473, 551, 636, 728, 911, and 14 (1962): 157. See also telegram 132 from Washington, 2 November 1960, Bolivian Foreign Ministry Archives, CL-368, which reports on the offer to the foreign minister.

57. Text of the letter and Paz's response are in the *Department of State Bulletin* 44.1146 (June 12, 1961): 920–23.

58. *Hispanic American Report* 14 (1961): 538; *El Diário*, 16 January 1961, 7 June 1961, and 20 June 1961.

59. Dispatch 72, La Paz to Washington, 31 August 1959, NA 824.00/8-3159.

60. *Hispanic American Report* 14 (1961): 65, and ibid., 727.

61. See telegram, Andrade in Washington to La Paz, 5 October 1959, Bolivian Foreign Ministry Archives, CL-369.

62. Catavi's ores now contained less than 1 percent tin. Labor problems compounded the difficulties: in 1951, twenty-four thousand workers produced 34,600 tons of tin; but in 1961, twenty-seven thousand workers (down from thirty-six thousand workers in 1956) produced 15,000 tons. See Melvin Burke, *The Corporación Minera de Bolivia (COMIBOL) and the Triangular Plan: A Case Study in Dependency* (Meadville, Pa., Latin American Issues no. 4, 1987), 8–15; and Strom to Department of State, 16 August 1960, BL-33, *FRUS 1958–60*, microfilm.

63. *Hispanic American Report* 14 (1961): 62.

64. Secretary to Embassy, 15 September 1960, and Secretary to Embassy, 22 November 1960, documents BL-33, BL-34, and BL-40, *FRUS 1958–60*, microfilm.

65. On negotations, see telegrams, Washington to La Paz, 25 April 1961, 8 June 1961, and 10 June 1961, Bolivian Foreign Ministry Archives, CL-369.

66. Mitchell, *Legacy of Populism*, 85.

67. *El Diário*, 20 June 1962 and 1 July 1962.

68. As a labor specialist in the State Department, Stephansky visited Bolivia in 1958 and afterward sent a memo to his superiors on the need for development assistance. See memo, Stephansky to Rubottom, 18 June 1958, RG 59, ASS-IIA, Roy Richard Rubottom, Subject File 1957-9 LOT 60D553, box 8.

69. Thorn, "Economic Transformation," 194–99, 172, table 5; Gómez, *Minería en el desarrollo económico de Bolivia*, 46.

70. *Hispanic American Report* 17 (June 1964): 547–48; Dunkerley, *Rebellion in the Veins*, 108.

71. *El Diário,* 31 March 1963 and 1 April 1963.

72. Bolivia, Dirección Nacional de Informaciones, *Visita del Presidente Víctor Paz Estensorro a los Estados Unidos* (La Paz, 1963), 10; *Department of State Bulletin* 49.1273 (November 18, 1963): 788. A letter from President Johnson to President Paz on 29 November 1963 notes that Paz was the last official visitor received by Kennedy before the assassination. President Lyndon B. Johnson to President Victor Paz Estenssoro, 29 November 1963, Lyndon Baines Johnson Library [hereafter LBJ Library], National Security File, Latin America, Bolivia.

73. *El Diário,* 21 November 1963.

74. Robert A. Packenham, *Liberal America and the Third World* (Princeton, 1973), 80. See his discussion of Kennedy's development policies, 59–85.

75. *Hispanic American Report* 14 (1961): 727.

76. Described by Malloy, *Uncompleted Revolution,* 291–310; and Mitchell, *Legacy of Populism,* 84–90.

77. *Hispanic American Report* 14 (1961): 1025; Dunkerley, *Rebellion in the Veins,* 108; *El Diário,* 15, 16, and 17 September 1961.

78. *Hispanic American Report* 16 (1963): 800; *El Diário,* 9 September 1963. For debate over worker responsibility for COMIBOL losses, see Burke, *COMIBOL and the Triangular Plan,* 39–52. While the workforce was reduced under the Triangular Plan, COMIBOL's wage bill actually increased due to a growing number of high-paid above-ground technicians and professionals. The attack on rank-and-file workers was as much political as economic in motive.

79. Blasier, "The United States and the Revolution," 97. Observers of internecine conflicts in the MNR noted that Lechín was prominently absent from memorial services for Kennedy in late November, whereas normally he would have sat at the president's right hand. *El Diário,* 26 November 1963.

80. *El Diário,* 2, 3, 6, and 7 December 1963.

81. *El Diário,* 7 December–18 December 1963; and *Hispanic American Report* 16 (1963): 1182.

82. *El Diário,* 20 January 1963.

83. *El Diário,* 7 December 1963.

84. *El Diário,* 9 March, 24 April, 30 September, and 9 October 1963.

85. Dunkerley, *Rebellion in the Veins,* 115; *El Diário,* 22 February 1964.

86. Gary Prado Salmón, *Poder y fuerzas armadas, 1949–1982* (La Paz, 1987), 147.

87. William H. Brill, *Military Intervention in Bolivia: The Overthrow of Paz Estenssoro and the MNR* (Washington, D.C., 1967), 29.

88. On Mann, see Ralph Nicholas Hoffman Jr., "Latin American Diplomacy: The Role of the Assistant Secretary of State, 1957–1969" (Ph.D. diss., Syracuse University, 1969), 19–21, 319, 340. For larger shifts under Johnson, see Packenham, *Liberal America and the Third World*, 85–96; Stephan G. Rabe, "Controlling Revolutions: Latin America, the Alliance for Progress and Cold War Anti-Communism," in *Kennedy's Quest for Victory: American Foreign Policy, 1961–1963*, ed. Thomas G. Paterson (New York, 1989), 112–17; and William O. Walker, "Mixing the Sweet with the Sour: Kennedy, Johnson, and Latin America," in *The Diplomacy of the Crucial Decade: American Foreign Relations during the 1960s*, ed. Diane B. Kunz (New York, 1994), 67–69.

89. *El Diário,* 8 June 1964. *El Diário,* long critical of the MNR regime, endorsed the shift in an editorial on 11 June 1964.

90. Telegram, Rusk to La Paz, 16 January 1964; telegram, Rusk to La Paz and attachments, 21 April 1964; and draft memo, Third Progress Report on Bolivian Internal Defense Plan, 23 April 1964, LBJ Library, National Security File, Latin America, Bolivia.

91. "Bolivia—Pre-election Contingency Plan," 20 March 1964, drafted 20 March and approved 9 April 1964, LBJ Library, National Security File, Latin America, Bolivia.

92. Telegram, La Paz to Secretary of State, 8 May 1964, LBJ Library, National Security File, Country File, Bolivia. The army officer's name was blacked out of the memo, but because of his position and the length of the blacked-out name, it appears to have been Ovando.

93. Quoted in Blasier, "United States and the Revolution," 98.

94. Mitchell, *Legacy of Populism*, 94–96; and Brill, *Military Intervention in Bolivia*, 35. On elections, *Hispanic American Report* 17 (1964): 442, notes that only two minor parties ran candidates, who were allegedly financed by the MNR to provide token opposition. See Prado, *Poder y fuerzas armadas*, 140–41.

95. For different interpretations of Ovando's role, see Brill, *Military Intervention in Bolivia*, 35; and Mitchell, *Legacy of Populism*, 94–95. Brill, who interviewed Barrientos, believes Ovando did not throw his support to the coup until late; Mitchell believes Ovando was a co-conspirator all along, a position Ovando confirmed to *El Diário,* 7 November 1964.

96. Dunkerley, *Rebellion in the Veins*, 119; Brill, *Military Intervention in Bolivia*, 44–45; *El Diário,* 26 and 29 October 1964, 3 and 7 November 1964.

97. Malloy, *Uncompleted Revolution*, 8–11, 341.

98. Sergio Almaraz Paz, *Réquiem para una república*, 4th ed. (La Paz, 1988), 17–19.

99. Almaraz Paz, *Réquiem para una república*, 16.
100. A position implicitly taken by Laurence Whitehead (*United States and Bolivia*) and Sergio Almaraz Paz (*Réquiem para una república*), to cite two of the more persuasive and careful arguments along those lines.
101. Packenham, *Liberal America and the Third World*, 20, the points fleshed out in chaps. 3 and 4.
102. See the discussion by Alan Knight, "Social Revolution: A Latin American Perspective," *Bulletin of Latin American Research* 9.2 (1990): 175–202.
103. Packenham, *Liberal America and the Third World*, 173; see his discussion of MNR and aid to Bolivia in a footnote on 172–73.
104. Rabe, "Controlling Revolutions," 107; Walker, "Mixing the Sweet with the Sour," 63.

Chapter 6: The National Security State and the Limits of Hegemony

1. *El Diário*, 5 November 1964, 1.
2. Charles D. Corbett, *The Latin American Military as a Socio-Political Force: Case Studies of Bolivia and Argentina* (Miami, 1972); William H. Brill, *Military Intervention in Bolivia: The Overthrow of Paz Estenssoro and the MNR* (Washington, D.C., 1967), 16–17; Rex A. Hudson and Dennis M. Hanratty, eds., *Bolivia: A Country Study* (Washington, D.C., 1991), 226.
3. See Lehman, "U.S. Foreign Aid and Revolutionary Nationalism," 183–84, for a more detailed discussion based on primary sources. See also Malloy, *Uncompleted Revolution*, 181–84; Prado, *Poder y fuerzas armadas*, 40–53; Lora, *History of the Bolivian Labour Movement*, 284–85; and Knudson, *Bolivia, Press and Revolution*, 305–10.
4. State Department memorandum, Siracusa to Bernbaum, 2 February 1956, *FRUS 1955–57*, 7:539.
5. Lehman, "U.S. Foreign Aid and Revolutionary Nationalism," 613–17.
6. "Outlook for Bolivia," document BL-1, *FRUS 1958–60*, vol. 5, microfiche supplement, outlines some of the history of the agreements. For a more detailed account, see Lehman, "U.S. Foreign Aid and Revolutionary Nationalism," 626–28.
7. See Prado, *Poder y fuerzas armadas*, 83–100; Mitchell, *Legacy of Populism*, 72; Hudson and Hanratty, eds., *Bolivia: A Country Study*, 226–27; and Embassy

to Department of State, 14 May 1960, document BL-31, *FRUS 1958–60,* vol. 5, microfiche supplement.

8. Prado, *Poder y fuerzas armadas,* 101–3; Whitehead, *United States and Bolivia,* 24. By 1962 the army was turning away thousands of youths who desired to enlist. Conference memo, La Paz, 4 May 1962, NA 724.00/5-462, cited in Robert O. Kirkland, "United States Assistance to the Bolivian Military, 1958–1964" (paper presented at the Middle Atlantic Conference on Latin American Studies, Trenton, N.J., March 1998).

9. See Brill, *Military Intervention in Bolivia,* 15–18, 31–32; and James V. Kohl, "National Revolution to Revolution of Restoration: Arms and Factional Politics in Bolivia," *Inter-American Economic Affairs* 39.1 (1985): 28–29. Statistics come from Rabe, "Controlling Revolutions," 117; and Thorn and Malloy, *Beyond the Revolution,* appendix, table 9, 390–91.

10. Gary Prado Salmón, *The Defeat of Che Guevara: Military Response to Guerilla Challenge in Bolivia* (New York, 1990), 123.

11. Prado, *Defeat of Che Guevara,* 24.

12. For different perspectives on the role of Fox, see Almaraz Paz, *Réquiem para una república,* 20; Brill, *Military Intervention in Bolivia,* 27; Dunkerley, *Rebellion in the Veins,* 113–15; Whitehead, *United States and Bolivia,* 15–16; and *El Diário,* 29 October 1964.

13. Memo, Siracusa to Bernbaum, 2 February 1956, *FRUS 1955–57,* 7:537.

14. Prado, *Poder y fuerzas armadas,* 153.

15. Brill, *Military Intervention in Bolivia,* 50.

16. Thorn, "Economic Transformation," 201; and L. Enrique García Rodriguez, "Structural Change and Development Policy in Bolivia," in *Modern-Day Bolivia,* ed. Jerry Ladman (Tempe, 1982), 168, 171, and 178.

17. Brill, *Military Intervention in Bolivia,* 49–50; and Malloy, *Uncompleted Revolution,* 146–47.

18. *New York Times,* 3 May 1969, 8.

19. Key sources on Ché Guevara's Bolivian operation include Prado, *Defeat of Che Guevara;* Daniel James, introduction to *Complete Bolivian Diaries of Ché Guevara* (New York, 1969); Martin Ebon, *Che: The Making of a Legend* (New York, 1969); and Jon Lee Anderson, *Ché Guevara, a Revolutionary Life* (New York, 1997), chap. 29. The jeep belonged to "Tanya," the German Argentine revolutionary Haydee Tamara Bunke Bider, who was later rumored to be an agent of the KGB sent to keep Ché's operation under close observation and perhaps even to sabotage it. See *New York Times,* 15 July 1968.

20. Dunkerley, *Rebellion in the Veins*, 153; Felix I. Rodriguez and John Weisman, *Shadow Warrior: The CIA Hero of a Hundred Unknown Battles* (New York, 1989), 129.

21. Prado, *The Defeat of Che Guevara*, 115, 155–56, 182–83, 245; Rodriguez and Weisman, *Shadow Warrior*, 143–56; Anderson, *Ché Guevara*, 727–43; James, introduction to *Complete Bolivian Diaries of Ché Guevara*, 50–59; and *New York Times*, 28 March 1967–15 October 1967. During the summer of 1997, when this manuscript was in preparation, Ché again received international media attention when his body was exumed and sent to Cuba.

22. Ricardo Rojo, *My Friend Che* (New York, 1968), 27–28; Anderson, *Ché Guevara*, 100–109; Ebon, *Che*, 23–34.

23. Anderson notes that "perhaps the most crucial single question about the life of Ernesto Ché Guevara to remain unanswered" is: "Who decided he should go to Bolivia; when and why was that decision made?" Ché himself said that "Bolivia will be sacrificed for the cause of creating conditions for revolution in the neighboring countries. We have to create another Vietnam in the Americas with its center in Bolivia" (Anderson, *Ché Guevara*, 680, 703).

24. Lawlor, *In Bolivia*, xi.

25. James M. Malloy and Eduardo Gamarra, *Revolution and Reaction: Bolivia, 1964–1985* (New Brunswick, 1988), 103.

26. See Mitchell, *Legacy of Populism*, 97–99; Malloy, *Uncompleted Revolution*, 46–49; and Kohl, "National Revolution to Revolution of Restoration," 25.

27. Malloy and Gamarra, *Revolution and Reaction*, 36.

28. John H. Magill, *Labor Unions and Political Socialization* (New York, 1974), 32–34. See also Burke, *COMIBOL and the Triangular Plan*.

29. Malloy, *Uncompleted Revolution*, 145–46.

30. Dunkerley, *Rebellion in the Veins*, 148–49; James, introduction to *Bolivian Diaries of Ché Guevara*, 22.

31. Prado, *Poder y fuerzas armadas*, 168, 224–30.

32. Prado, *Defeat of Che Guevara*, 16.

33. Prado, *Defeat of Che Guevara*, 216–19; *New York Times*, 16 and 22 July 1968.

34. *New York Times*, 17, 18, and 25 August 1968. See also Laurence Whitehead, "Bolivia's Conflict with the United States," *World Today* 26 (April 1970): 171. A *New York Times* correspondent stated: "Indications were that the Bolivian government has taken the Arguedas statements seriously and that relations between the United States and this country are entering a complicated pe-

riod" (*New York Times*, 19 August 1968). Arguedas reappeared in late 1998, charged with heading a band of kidnappers in Bolivia (*Los Tiempos*, 13 October 1998).

35. Waltraud Queiser Morales, *Bolivia: Land of Struggle* (Boulder, 1992), 183.

36. *New York Times*, 3 May 1969, 8. See also Whitehead, "Bolivia's Conflict with the United States," 170; and Dunkerley, *Rebellion in the Veins*, 156. Although it was not open knowledge at the time of Barrientos's death, the U.S. Senate's MacKay Commission later revealed that Gulf paid off Bolivian officials to the tune of $1.8 million, some of which went to buy Barrientos's helicopter. See Morales, *Bolivia, Land of Struggle*, 90.

37. Mitchell, *Legacy of Populism*, 107; Dunkerley, *Rebellion in the Veins*, 157; Prado, *Poder y fuerzas armadas*, 248–49.

38. Whitehead, "Bolivia's Conflict with the United States," 173–74.

39. *New York Times*, 6 February 1969, 9.

40. In the late 1950s, 40 percent of U.S. aid went straight to budget support. In 1965, $6 million went to budget support; by 1967 that figure had fallen to $1 million, and by 1968 assistance for that purpose was nil. See Whitehead, "Bolivia's Conflict with the United States," 174; and, for a more extended discussion, Wilkie, *The Bolivian Revolution and U.S. Aid since 1952*.

41. Mitchell, *Legacy of Populism*, 109–10; Whitehead, "Bolivia's Conflict with the United States," 174; Dunkerley, *Rebellion in the Veins*, 164. For the text of the Revolutionary Manifesto of the Armed Forces, see Prado, *Poder y fuerzas armadas*, 250–54.

42. Morales, *Bolivia, Land of Struggle*, 183; Dunkerley, *Rebellion in the Veins*, 166; Burke, *COMIBOL and the Triangular Plan*, 39; and Prado, *Poder y fuerzas armadas*, 260.

43. Whitehead, "Bolivia's Conflict with the United States," 173; Mitchell, *Legacy of Populism*, 108.

44. Raul Barrios Morón, *Bolivia y los Estados Unidos: democrácia, derechos humanos, y narcotráfico, 1980–1982* (La Paz, 1989), 32.

45. Mitchell, *Legacy of Populism*, 112–14; Dunkerley, *Rebellion in the Veins*, 166, 170–73; Whitehead, "Bolivia's Conflict with the United States," 175–76; Prado, *Poder y fuerzas armadas*, 312–13.

46. Dunkerley, *Rebellion in the Veins*, 174–77.

47. Prado, *Poder y fuerzas armadas*, 296. His strengths when compared with Ovando, Dunkerley notes, were his honesty, approachability, and a certain common touch on which he failed to capitalize (*Rebellion in the Veins*, 179).

48. Klein, *Bolivia*, 253–54; Dunkerley, *Rebellion in the Veins*, 195–96; René Zavaleta, "Bolivia—Military Nationalism and the Popular Assembly," *New Left Review* 73 (May–June 1972): 58–82.

49. *New York Times*, 17 October 1970, 17 November 1970. See also Dunkerley, *Rebellion in the Veins*, 185.

50. Dunkerley, *Rebellion in the Veins*, 129; Nash, *We Eat the Mines*, 232. For a brief discussion of *Yahwar Mallcu*, originally filmed in Quechua and only later subtitled in Spanish, see *New York Times*, 27 December 1969, 5.

51. *New York Times*, 23 September 1970, 13; 25 January 1971, 56.

52. Barrios Morón, *Bolivia y los Estados Unidos*, 30; Dunkerley, *Rebellion in the Veins*, 185.

53. Memo, Siracusa to Bernbaum, 2 February 1956, *FRUS 1955–57*, 7:539.

54. Malloy and Gamarra, *Revolution and Reaction*, 38.

55. P. Samuel Huntington, *Political Order in Changing Societies* (New Haven, 1968), 196; quoted in James M. Malloy and Sylvia Borzutsky, "The Praetorianization of the Revolution," in *Modern-Day Bolivia*, ed. Jerry Ladman (Tempe, 1982), 48.

56. On the coup, see Dunkerley, *Rebellion in the Veins*, 199; Mitchell, *Legacy of Populism*, 117–18; Prado, *Poder y fuerzas armadas*, 324–25; and James V. Kohl, "Bolivia Begins the Seventies," *New Politics* 10 (Fall 1973), 48.

57. *New York Times*, 30 August 1971, 3, looks at the role played by Major Robert J. Lundin, an adviser at the Bolivian air force school who had frequent contacts before the rebellion with Banzer and allowed the rebels to use his own radio to communicate with the U.S. embassy. For other evidence of U.S. support for Banzer, see Prado, *Poder y fuerzas armadas*, 324–25; Barrios Morón, *Bolivia y los Estados Unidos*, 30–31, 35; and Kohl, "Bolivia Begins the Seventies," 55–57. In all, the United States extended $63 million in aid through the regime's first year in power.

58. Dunkerley, *Rebellion in the Veins*, 203.

59. Paulo R. Schilling, *El expansionismo brasileño* (Mexico, 1978), 71.

60. For Banzer's Brazilian connections, see Dunkerley, *Rebellion in the Veins*, 183, 198–99, 206; Ruth Needleman, "Bolivia: Brazil's Geopolitical Prisoner," *North American Congress on Latin America, Report on the Americas* [hereafter *NACLA Report*] 8.2 (February 1974): 25; and Gustavo V. Dans, *"Brasil a la ofensiva: la estratégia continental del imperialismo* (Lima, n.d.), 53.

61. Kohl, "Bolivia Begins the Seventies," 51; Morales, *Bolivia, Land of Struggle*, 184.

62. London, Economist Intelligence Unit, Ltd., *Quarterly Economic Review* (4th quarter, 1972), 1, 11; Dunkerley, *Rebellion in the Veins*, 209–12.

63. Mitchell, *Legacy of Populism*, 121.

64. Juan L. Cariaga, "The Economic Structure of Bolivia after 1964," in *Modern-Day Bolivia*, ed. Jerry Ladman (Tempe, 1982), 147.

65. Mitchell says the MNR collaboration with Banzer was "a betrayal of whatever ideals the party still retained"; Malloy and Gamarra comment that Paz joined with Banzer as a measure of his continuing realism. See Mitchell, *Legacy of Populism*, 125; and Malloy and Gamarra, *Revolution and Reaction*, 81–82.

66. Prado, in *Poder y fuerzas armadas*, 369–74, describes his own role in the failed coup.

67. Ministerio de Planamiento y Coordinación, *Informe Anual al CEPCIES, 1975*, and *Resumen: Plan Operativo, 1977*, 24. See also Dunkerley, *Rebellion in the Veins*, 223, 226; and Mitchell, *Legacy of Populism*, 123.

68. Klein, *Bolivia*, 259–60.

69. Mitchell, *Legacy of Populism*, 128; Dunkerley, *Rebellion in the Veins*, 226; Jerry Ladman, "The Political Economy of the 'Economic Miracle' of the Banzer Regime," in *Modern-Day Bolivia*, ed. Ladman (Tempe, 1982), 332. See the "Manifesto" of the *autogolpe* in Ladman, *Modern-Day Bolivia*, 385–88.

70. Morales, *Bolivia, Land of Struggle*, 121, 46; Malloy and Gamarra, *Revolution and Reaction*, 106; Juan Antonio Morales, "The Bolivian External Sector after 1964," in *Modern-Day Bolivia*, ed. Jerry Ladman (Tempe, 1982), 226.

71. Cariaga, "The Economic Structure of Bolivia after 1964"; Salvador Romero Pittari, "The Role of the State in the Rural-Urban Configuration," in *Modern-Day Bolivia*, ed. Jerry Ladman (Tempe, 1982), 175, 188, 315. For further discussion of Bolivia's growing inequities after the revolution, see Jonathan Kelley and Herbert S. Klein, *Revolution and Rebirth of Inequality: A Theory Applied to the National Revolution in Bolivia* (Berkeley, 1981).

72. For economic assessments, see Dunkerley, *Rebellion in the Veins*, 220, 225–27; Morales, "The Bolivian External Sector after 1964," 212; Ladman, "The 'Economic Miracle' of the Banzer Regime," 326–27; and *Quarterly Economic Review* (1977, 4th quarter), 20.

73. Prado, *Poder y fuerzas armadas*, 463.

74. Heilman, "U.S. Development Assistance to Rural Bolivia," 248–58; Robert Alexander, "Labor"; Wilkie, "U.S. Foreign Policy and Economic Assistance in Bolivia," 72–73, 105.

75. Dunkerley, *Rebellion in the Veins*, 238.

76. *Quarterly Economic Review* (4th quarter, 1977), 18; "Bolivia, the Will of the People," *Latin America Political Report* 12.4 (27 January 1978). On the last days of the *banzerato*, see Dunkerley, *Rebellion in the Veins*, 237–39; Ladman, "The 'Economic Miracle' of the Banzer Regime," 334–36; Whitehead, "Failed Democratization," 59–62; and Prado, *Poder y fuerzas armadas*, 423.

77. Ladman, "The 'Economic Miracle' of the Banzer Regime," 337.

78. The court annulled the elections on grounds that the final vote count exceeded the already inflated number of registered voters by fifty thousand (Ladman, "The 'Economic Miracle' of the Banzer Regime," 339). See Dunkerley, *Rebellion in the Veins*, 246–48, for examples of voter fraud.

79. Prado, *Poder y fuerzas armadas*, 499.

80. Ladman, "The 'Economic Miracle' of the Banzer Regime," 337.

81. Jerry Ladman, "Failure to Redemocratize," in *Modern-Day Bolivia*, ed. Ladman (Tempe, 1982), 353–54; and Dunkerley, *Rebellion in the Veins*, 263.

82. Whitehead, "Failed Democratization," 63–64; Malloy and Gamarra, *Revolution and Reaction*, 120.

83. Ladman, "Failure to Redemocratize," 354–55; Dunkerley, *Rebellion in the Veins*, 265.

84. *Presencia*, 9 November 1979.

85. Dunkerley, *Rebellion in the Veins*, 268–70.

86. *New York Times*, 13 August 1980, 12.

87. Morales, *Bolivia, Land of Struggle*, 126; Clare Hargreaves, *Snowfields: The War on Cocaine in the Andes* (New York, 1992), 102–8; Dunkerley, *Rebellion in the Veins*, 299–305.

88. Instituto de Estudios Políticos para América Latina y África [hereafter IEPALA], *Narcotráfico y política: militarismo y mafia en Bolivia* (Madrid, 1982), 60–61, 69; Ladman, "Failure to Redemocratize," 358–61; Dunkerley, *Rebellion in the Veins*, 270–72; *New York Times*, 13 August 1980, 12.

89. Dunkerley, *Rebellion in the Veins*, 280; Morales, *Bolivia, Land of Struggle*, 125–26.

90. Dunkerley, *Rebellion in the Veins*, 284; *New York Times*, 5 June–19 June 1980.

91. Based on notes taken from *El Mundo* (Santa Cruz, Bolivia), 15 June–15 July 1980; Dunkerley, *Rebellion in the Veins*, 287–89; *New York Times*, 9 July 1980, 14; 12 July 1980, 4.

92. Whitehead, "Failed Democratization," 67.

93. *El Mundo*, 18 and 19 July 1980, 5 August 1980; Dunkerley, *Rebellion in the Veins*, 288–308; *New York Times*, 14 August 1980, 1; 15 August 1980, 6.

94. Morales, *Bolivia, Land of Struggle,* 126–30; Dunkerley, *Rebellion in the Veins,* 299–305; Barrios Morón, *Bolivia y los Estados Unidos,* 71; *New York Times,* 7 August 1980, 7; 10 February 1981, 10.
95. *New York Times,* 26 July 1980, 1; Barrios Morón, *Bolivia y los Estados Unidos,* 65–69, 123. García Meza was excluded from an Andean Pact summit and Bolivia was declared a nonfunctioning member.
96. Gregorio Selser, *Bolivia: el cuartelazo de los cocadolares* (Mexico, 1982), 195–96. The story was covered in the *60 Minutes* segment about Arce Gómez. Bail of $3 million was set on the captured trafficker, but was lowered to $1 million when top officials in the Bolivian military vouched for his character. As soon as the bail was posted, the man disappeared. See Hargreaves, *Snowfields,* 76.
97. Scott B. McDonald, *Dancing on a Volcano: The Latin American Drug Trade* (New York, 1988), 57.
98. Hargreaves, *Snowfields,* 108–10; IEPALA, *Narcotráfico y política,* 53–54, 62; Dunkerley, *Rebellion in the Veins,* 320–22; *New York Times,* 14 August 1980, 13, 31 August 1980, 1.
99. Memo, Siracusa to Bernbaum, 2 February 1956, *FRUS 1955–57,* 7:539.

Chapter 7: Frontier Myths, Cocaine Dependency, and Limits to the American Dream

1. Herndon and Gibbon, *Exploration of the Valley of the Amazon,* 103.
2. Fifer, *U.S. Perceptions of Latin America,* 1; Herndon and Gibbon, *Exploration of the Valley of the Amazon,* 161–63.
3. Fifer, *U.S. Perceptions of Latin America,* 25–28.
4. Pike, *The United States and Latin America,* 15. Pike provides an excellent extended discussion of the ideas presented in this paragraph.
5. Pike, *The United States and Latin America,* 127, 135.
6. Fifer, *Bolivia: Land, Location, and Politics,* 118–20. See also J. Valerie Fifer, "The Empire Builders: A History of the Bolivian Rubber Boom and the Rise of the House of Suárez," *Journal of Latin American Studies* 2 (1970): 113–46.
7. Fifer, *U.S. Perceptions of Latin America,* 5.
8. Fifer, *Bolivia: Land, Location, and Politics,* 198–202; Lawlor, *In Bolivia,* 191–93.
9. Lesley Gill, *Peasants, Entrepreneurs, and Social Change: Frontier Development in Lowland Bolivia* (Boulder, 1987), 32; Richard Thorn, "Economic Transformation," 164–65.

10. Dwight B. Heath et al., *Land Reform and Social Revolution in Bolivia* (New York, 1969), 290–91, 324–27, 332–35; Raymond E. Crist and Charles M. Nissley, *East from the Andes* (Gainesville, 1973), 130; G. Richard Fletcher, "Santa Cruz: A Study of Economic Growth in Eastern Bolivia," *Inter-American Economic Affairs* 29.2 (1975): 23.

11. U.S. Agency for International Development, *Report of Santa Cruz Area Development Mission* (September 1954), 12–16, cited in Lawrence Heilman, "U.S. Development Assistance to Rural Bolivia," 128–29. An early experimental project under the auspices of the United Nations to help highlanders relocate to Santa Cruz tended to confirm this assessment by failing spectacularly. See Heath et al., *Land Reform and Social Revolution in Bolivia*, 290–91, 347–48; and Crist and Nissley, *East from the Andes*, 135–36.

12. The Bolivian government successfully attracted large colonies of Japanese, Okinawans, and Russian and Canadian Mennonites to Santa Cruz.

13. Alexander, *The Bolivian National Revolution*, 176; Crist and Nissley, *East from the Andes*, 137–38.

14. The U.S.-funded agricultural *servicio* devoted 50 percent of its funds to Santa Cruz during the 1950s, with 90 percent of its loan funds going to commercial farmers and only 10 percent to peasants and colonists. See Heilman, "U.S. Development Assistance to Rural Bolivia," 97–98; and Dunkerley, *Rebellion in the Veins*, 95.

15. *Un Transplante humano, el proyecto de colonización "Alto Beni" de Bolivia* (La Paz, 1965), 5, quoted in Heilman, "U.S. Development Assistance to Rural Bolivia," 116.

16. Allyn Maclean Stearman, "The Highland Migrant in Lowland Bolivia: Multiple Resource Migration and the Horizontal Archipelago," *Human Organization: Journal of the Society for Applied Anthropology* 37.2 (1978): 182; Gill, *Peasants, Entrepreneurs, and Social Change*, 50–59, 180–83; Ladman, "The 'Economic Miracle' of the Banzer Regime," 330–31.

17. For discussions of the rise in highlanders' colonization of the east, see Javier Albó, *Bodas de plata o réquiem por una reforma agraria* (La Paz, 1979), 23; Roberto Vilar, "El trabajador temporal y la agro-industria," in *Cambios en el agro y el campesinado boliviano* (La Paz, 1982), 176; E. Boyd Wennergren and Morris D. Whitaker, "Investments in Access Roads and Spontaneous Colonization," *Land Economics* 52.1 (1976): 88–92; Stearman, "The Highland Migrant in Lowland Bolivia," 182; Hernán Zeballos Hurtado, "From the Uplands to the Lowlands" (Ph.D. diss., University of Wisconsin at Madison, 1975), 203.

18. René Bascopé Aspiazu, *La Veta blanca: coca y cocaina en Bolivia* (La Paz, 1982). A good discussion and evaluation of Bascopé's thesis can be found in James Painter, *Bolivia and Coca: A Study in Dependency* (Boulder, 1994), 26–27. Lesley Gill provides case studies to support his thesis in *Peasants, Entrepreneurs, and Social Change*, 183–93.

19. See Hargreaves, *Snowfields*, 3; and McDonald, *Dancing on a Volcano*, 10.

20. Alison L. Spedding, "Cocataki, Taki-Coca: Trade, Traffic, and Organized Peasant Resistance in the Yungas of La Paz," in *Coca, Cocaine, and the Bolivian Reality*, ed. Madeline Barbara Léons and Harry Sanabria (Albany, 1997), 118–19.

21. Hargreaves, *Snowfields*, 31; Painter, *Bolivia and Coca*, table 1.8, p. 20.

22. See IEPALA, *Narcotráfico y política*, vol. 2: *Bolivia, 1982–1985* (Cochabamba, 1985), 128–29; and Kevin Healy, "The Boom within the Crisis: Some Recent Effects of Foreign Cocaine Markets on Bolivian Rural Society and Economy," in *Coca and Cocaine: Effects on People and Policy in Latin America*, ed. Deborah Pacini and Christine Franquemont (Ithaca, 1986), 112–25. Painter, *Bolivia and Coca*, 9–21, includes a careful discussion of coca benefits to peasant producers.

23. Sidney W. Mintz, "The Forefathers of Crack," *NACLA Report* 22.6 (1989): 32.

24. Healy, "The Boom within the Crisis," 128–30.

25. Humberto Fajardo Sainz, *La Herencia de la coca: pasado y presente de la cocaina*, 3d ed. (Santa Cruz, 1993), 149, 162.

26. The quote is found in Peter Andreas and Coletta Youngers, "U.S. Drug Policy and the Andean Cocaine Industry," *World Policy Journal* 6.3 (1989): 530.

27. This quote is in Andrew Weil, "New Politics of Coca," *New Yorker*, 15 May 1995, 71. For the cultural place of coca, see Alison Spedding, "The Coca Field as a Total Social Fact," in *Coca, Cocaine, and the Bolivian Reality*, ed. Madeline Barbara Léons and Harry Sanabria (Albany, 1997), 47–70; and William E. Carter and Maricio Mamani, *Coca en Bolivia* (La Paz, 1986).

28. James Dunkerley, *Political Transition and Economic Stabilisation: Bolivia, 1982–1989* (London, 1990), 45–46.

29. *Basuco* is a mixture of cocaine paste and tobacco smoked in a cigarette or *pitillo*. It is highly addictive and increasingly prevalent in urban Bolivia and among those working in the maceration pits where coca paste is made.

30. For a discussion of these inequities, see Linda Farthing, "Social Impacts Associated with Antidrug Law 1008," in *Coca, Cocaine, and the Bolivian Reality*, ed. Madeline Barbara Léons and Harry Sanabria (Albany, 1997), 253–70.

31. Pentland, *Report on Bolivia, 1827*, 213. For more on early coca production, see Healy, "The Boom within the Crisis," 101; Mario de Franco and Ricardo Godoy, "The Economic Consequences of Cocaine Production in Bolivia: Historical, Local, and Macroeconomic Perspectives," *Journal of Latin American Studies* 24 (May 1992): 379; Painter, *Bolivia and Coca*, 1–7; Herbert S. Klein, "Coca Production in the Bolivian Yungas in the Colonial and Early National Periods," in *Coca and Cocaine: Effects on People and Policy in Latin America*, ed. Deborah Pacini and Christine Franquemont (Ithaca, 1986), 53–64; and Maria Luisa Soux, *La Coca liberal* (La Paz, 1993). Archaeological evidence shows coca has probably been used since about 2500 B.C. (Weil, "The New Politics of Coca," 71–72).

32. U.S. House of Representatives, Consular Reports, *Reports from the Consuls of the United States . . . October, November, December, 1885* (Washington, D.C., 1886), 15–18.

33. Painter, *Bolivia and Coca*, 2; Steven B. Duke and Albert C. Gross, *America's Longest War: Rethinking Our Tragic Crusade against Drugs* (New York, 1993), 66–68; Kevin Healy, "Coca No Es Cocaina" (paper presented at the 1995 Meeting of the Latin American Studies Association, Washington, D.C., 28–30 September 1995), 8. The first advertisements for Coca Cola showed a coca leaf.

34. Dispatch 402, La Paz to State Department, and response, 4 April 1950, NA 824.53/4-450.

35. Madeline Barbara Léons and Harry Sanabria, "Coca and Cocaine in Bolivia: Reality and Policy Illusion," in *Coca, Cocaine, and the Bolivian Reality*, ed. Léons and Sanabria (Albany, 1997), 21; Painter, *Bolivia and Coca*, 1–8.

36. U.S. House of Representatives, International Narcotics Control Study Missions to Latin America and Jamaica, "Report of the Select Committee on Narcotics Abuse and Control," 98th Cong., 1st sess. (Washington, D.C., 1984), 49–52; Painter, *Bolivia and Coca*, 78; Dunkerley, *Rebellion in the Veins*, 318; Hargreaves, *Snowfields*, 112.

37. Barrios Morón, *Bolivia y los Estados Unidos*, 106–7. For the transcript of the interview with Arce Gómez on *60 Minutes*, see Selser, *Bolivia: el cuartelazo de los cocadolares*, 190–98.

38. Dunkerley, *Rebellion in the Veins*, 330–37; Morales, *Bolivia, Land of Struggle*, 127.

39. Morales, *Bolivia, Land of Struggle*, 147–49; James Dunkerley, *Bolivia 1980–1981: The Political System in Crisis* (London, 1982), 33; Luis E. Breuer, "Hy-

perinflation and Stabilization: the Case of Bolivia, 1984–1986" (Ph.D. diss., University of Illinois, 1989), 77–84; Baldwin, *The World Tin Market*, 3.

40. *New York Times*, 15 August 1981, 1; Barrios Morón, *Bolivia y los Estados Unidos*, 151–84; Dunkerley, *Rebellion in the Veins*, 342–43.

41. Healy, "The Boom within the Crisis," 109–10; Malloy and Gamarra, *Revolution and Reaction*, 171–72; Dunkerley, *Rebellion in the Veins*, 347.

42. Kenneth Jamison, "Austerity Programs under Conditions of Political Instability," in *Paying the Costs of Austerity*, ed. Howard Handelman and Werner Baer (Boulder, 1989), table 4.1.

43. See Dunkerley, *Political Transition*, 3, 14–15; Malloy and Gamarra, *Revolution and Reaction*, 165–68.

44. Discussions of the packages are in Breuer, "Hyperinflation and Stabilization," 88–113; and James Dunkerley and Rolando Morales, "The Crisis in Bolivia," *New Left Review* 155 (January/February 1986): 89.

45. For discussions of and statistics on the crisis, see Breuer, "Hyperinflation and Stabilization," 80, 106, 116, 124; Healy, "The Boom within the Crisis," 108; Dunkerley and Morales, "The Crisis in Bolivia," 90; Hudson and Hanratty, eds., *Bolivia: A Country Study*, 186; Morales, *Bolivia, Land of Struggle*, 157–58; and Jennifer L. Bailey and Torbjorn L. Knutson, "Bolivia's Response to Economic Chaos," *World Today* 43.1 (January 1987): 48.

46. Dunkerley, *Political Transition*, 20. See also Morales, *Bolivia, Land of Struggle*, 185–86, 193.

47. Hudson and Hanratty, eds., *Bolivia: A Country Study*, 209, 261; Guillermo Bedregal Gutiérrez and Ruddy Viscarra Pando, *La Lucha boliviana contra la agresión del narcotráfico* (La Paz, 1989), 223–25.

48. Based on data in Painter, *Bolivia and Coca*, tables 1.2, 1.8. For the implications of the day the price hit $800, see Hargreaves, *Snowfields*, 30.

49. Healy, "The Boom within the Crisis"; and IEPALA, *Narcotráfico*, 2:159ff.

50. U.S. House of Representatives, *Latin American Study Missions concerning International Narcotics Problems* (Washington, D.C., 1985), 79–81.

51. Malloy and Gamarra, *Revolution and Reaction*, 189–94, quotation on 194.

52. For an interesting series of essays on Paz's career, see *Víctor Paz: su presencia en la historia revolucionaria de Bolivia*, ed. Guillermo Bedregal Gutiérrez (La Paz, 1987). In 1978, Paz told a reporter in the United States that he was "too old to serve as president again." A year later he was a candidate (*Albuquerque Journal*, 22 January 1978, A10).

53. Morales, *Bolivia, Land of Struggle*, 102; Eduardo A. Gamarra, "Crafting Po-

litical Support for Stabilization: Political Pacts and the New Economic Policy in Bolivia," in *Democracy, Markets, and Structural Reform in Latin America,* ed. William C. Smith et al. (New Brunswick, 1993), 108–10; Juan Antonio Morales and Jeffrey Sachs, "Bolivia," in *Developing Country Debt and Economic Performance,* ed. Jeffrey D. Sachs (Chicago, 1989), 238–39.

54. The Paz quote is from Carlos D. Mesa Gisbert, "Cincuenta años por los caminos del poder," in *Víctor Paz: su presencia en la historia revolucionaria de Bolivia,* ed. Guillermo Bedregal Gutiérrez (La Paz, 1987), 172–74. The Sachs quote is from Lawrence Wechsler, "Bolivia Goes East," *NACLA Report* 25.1 (July 1991): 28–29. Good discussions of the role of Sachs, who later advised Poland and Russia, can be found in Robert E. Norton, "Jeff Sachs—Doctor Debt," and Catherine M. Conaghan, "Reconsidering Jeffrey Sachs and the Bolivian Economic Experiment," both in *The Money Doctors, Foreign Debts, and Economic Reforms in Latin America from the 1890s to the Present,* ed. Paul Drake (Wilmington, 1994), 231–66. Wechsler provides a more critical analysis.

55. Conaghan, "Reconsidering Jeffrey Sachs and the Bolivian Economic Experiment," 249.

56. Quoted in Baldwin, *The World Tin Market,* 5.

57. Conaghan, "Reconsidering Jeffrey Sachs and the Bolivian Economic Experiment," 250. For analyses of the results of the NEP from different perspectives, see Conaghan, 242–50; Malloy and Gamarra, *Revolution and Reaction,* 199; Dunkerley, *Political Transition,* 31, 35; Morales and Sachs, "Bolivia," 188; Breuer, "Hyperinflation and Stabilization"; and Latin American Regional Reports—Andean Group [hereafter LARR-AG], 23 May 1991.

58. Morales, *Bolivia, Land of Struggle,* 159–160; Washington Estellano, "From Populism to the Coca Economy in Bolivia," *Latin American Perspectives* 83.21 (1994): 39; John Crabtree et al., *The Great Tin Crash: Bolivia and the World Market* (London, 1987), 3–7; Hudson and Hanratty, eds., *Bolivia: A Country Study,* 105; Painter, *Bolivia and Coca,* 7; *NACLA Report,* 28. By 1987 Bolivia was importing forty-eight pounds of food per person from international aid organizations; in 1970 the figure had been two pounds. See Michael J. Gilgannon, "Drugs, Debt, and Dependency," *America* 159.12 (29 October 1988), 312.

59. U.S. House of Representatives, *Latin American Study Missions,* 84–85. Painter, *Bolivia and Coca,* chap. 4, provides an excellent discussion of the costs and benefits of the coca-cocaine trade to Bolivia.

60. Painter, *Bolivia and Coca*, 7, 15, 16; U.S. House of Representatives, *U.S. Narcotics Control Programs in Peru, Bolivia, Columbia, and Mexico: An Update* (Washington, D.C., 1989), 77, 91.

61. Painter, *Bolivia and Coca*, 54–55; Breuer, "Hyperinflation and Stabilization," 234; Conaghan, "Reconsidering Jeffrey Sachs and the Bolivian Economic Experiment," 256; Andreas and Youngers, "U.S. Drug Policy and the Andean Cocaine Industry," 542–43.

62. U.S. House of Representatives, *The Role of the U.S. Military in Narcotics Control Overseas* (Washington, D.C., 1986), 26, 36; Hudson and Hanratty, eds., *Bolivia: A Country Study*, 210.

63. U.S. House of Representatives, *Report of the Delegation to Latin America of the Committee on Armed Services* (Washington, D.C., 1986), 26; U.S. House of Representatives, *Cocaine Production in the Andes* (Washington, D.C., 1989), 96; Hargreaves, *Snowfields*, 152–56; Hudson and Hanratty, eds., *Bolivia: A Country Study*, 661–62.

64. U.S. House of Representatives, *Role of the U.S. Military in Narcotics Control Overseas*, 22; Conaghan, "Reconsidering Jeffrey Sachs and the Bolivian Economic Experiment," 257.

65. Eduardo Gamarra, "U.S.-Bolivia Counternarcotics Efforts during the Paz Zamora Administration, 1989–1992," in *Drug Trafficking in the Americas*, ed. Bruce Bagley and William O. Walker (New Brunswick, 1994), 225–26; Bedregal and Viscarra, *La Lucha boliviana contra la agresión del narcotráfico*, 569–605.

66. Hudson and Hanratty, eds., *Bolivia: A Country Study*, 259; U.S. House of Representatives, *Narcotics Review in South America* (Washington, D.C., 1988), 68; *Presidential Certifications regarding International Narcotics Control* (Washington, D.C., 1988), 35–36, 49; *Narcotics Control Recommendations for the Andean Region, 1987–1991* (Washington, D.C., 1991), 47–49.

67. U.S. Senate, *Narcotics Related Foreign Aid Sanctions: An Effective Foreign Policy?* (Washington, D.C., 1987), 8–12.

68. Andreas and Youngers, "U.S. Drug Policy and the Andean Cocaine Industry," 553.

69. Farthing, "Social Impacts Associated with Antidrug Law 1008"; Painter, *Bolivia and Coca*, 79–80; Hudson and Hanratty, eds., *Bolivia: A Country Study*, 258–61.

70. Luis Verdesoto and Gloria Ardaya Salinas, *Entre la presión y el consenso: escenarios y previsiones para la relación Bolivia–Estados Unidos* (La Paz, 1993),

167–69; U.S. Department of State, "Secretary Schultz Visits Latin America," *Department of State Bulletin* 88.2139 (October 1988): 2, 15–19.

71. Estellano, "From Populism to the Coca Economy in Bolivia," 34.

72. For biographical material on Paz Zamora and details on his policies, see Dunkerley, *Rebellion in the Veins*, 154, 189, 258, 284; *New York Times*, 7 August 1989, 3; and *Wall Street Journal*, 23 August 1991, 10 June 1992, and 29 March 1993.

73. *Wall Street Journal*, 23 August 1991, 29 March 1993.

74. Gamarra, "U.S.-Bolivia Counternarcotics Efforts during the Paz Zamora Administration," 221–24; Peter Andreas, "Our Man in La Paz," *NACLA Report* 25.1 (1991): 19; U.S. Senate, *Narcotics Related Foreign Aid Sanctions: An Effective Foreign Policy*, 15–20 , 31, 37–40. For an interesting sampling of Gelbard's public statements, see the chronological summary in Verdesoto and Ardaya, *Entre la presión y el consenso*, 169–223. Paz Zamora admitted in a newspaper interview that he heaved a sigh of relief when Gelbard left in mid-1992.

75. Raphael F. Perl, "United States Andean Drug Policy: Background and Issues for Decisionmakers," *Journal of Interamerican Studies and World Affairs* 34.3 (1992): 13–17.

76. Gamarra, "U.S.-Bolivia Counternarcotics Efforts," 225.

77. Painter, *Bolivia and Coca,* 21; Gamarra, "U.S.-Bolivia Counternarcotics Efforts," 220, 227–30; Coletta Youngers, *A Fundamentally Flawed Strategy*, WOLA, Issue Brief 4 (Washington, D.C., 1991). Newspapers reported later that Bolivia was the top recipient of aid in the hemisphere, with 61 percent going to the military. Verdesoto and Ardaya, *Entre la presión y el consenso*, 191.

78. Gamarra, "U.S.-Bolivia Counternarcotics Efforts," 244.

79. Léons and Sanabria, "Coca and Cocaine in Bolivia," 26; Painter, *Bolivia and Coca,* chap. 6, 136, 142–43; Verdesoto and Ardaya, *Entre la presión y el consenso,* 197.

80. Gamarra, "U.S.-Bolivia Counternarcotics Efforts," 231–32. Hargreaves has some interesting speculation on what might have been behind the decision; see *Snowfields,* 163–65, 168–75.

81. Quoted in Andreas and Youngers, "U.S. Drug Policy and the Andean Cocaine Industry," 531. See also Hargreaves, *Snowfields,* 15–22.

82. Hargreaves, *Snowfields,* 166–68; Gamarra, "U.S.-Bolivia Counternarcotics Efforts," 229–34; "Enter the Green Berets," *NACLA Report* 22.6 (1989): 33; and Painter, *Bolivia and Coca,* 97–98.

83. *New York Times,* 20 September 1992; Gamarra, "U.S.-Bolivia Counternarcotics Efforts," 244–45; LARR-AG, 30 July 1992; and *Latin America News Update* [hereafter *LANU*], January 1995.

84. Gamarra, "U.S.-Bolivia Counternarcotics Efforts," 237–42; Painter, *Bolivia and Coca,* 94–95, 98–103, 142; *Latin American Weekly Report* [hereafter *LAWR*], 9 July 1992. One study comments that the idea of "using the military for the police function of illicit drug suppression was so clearly counter-productive that it is evident that it emanated from anger not reason." See Donald J. Mabry, "The U.S. Military and the War on Drugs," in *Drug Trafficking in the Americas,* ed. Bruce Bagley and William O. Walker (New Brunswick, 1994), 54.

85. Verdesoto and Ardaya, *Entre la presión y el consenso,* 211–23, 231.

86. Healy, "Coca No Es Cocaina," 19; Weil, "New Politics of Coca," 78–79; and "Coca: The Real Green Revolution," *NACLA Report* 22.6 (1989): 28.

87. LARR-AG, 28 January 1993.

88. LARR-AG, 8 April 1993.

89. LARR-AG, 7 October 1993.

90. *LAWR,* 24 March 1994; and Weil, "New Politics of Coca," 79.

91. U.S. Department of State, *International Narcotics Strategy Report* (March 1995), 72.

92. *LAWR,* 28 July 1994, 4 August 1994.

93. *LAWR,* 10 March 1994, 28 April 1994, 12 May 1994.

94. *LAWR,* 15 and 22 September 1994. The forum and resulting agreements are discussed in LARR-AG, 13 October 1994; *LANU,* November 1994, 23–24; and Weil, "New Politics of Coca," 80.

95. *LAWR,* 24 November 1994; Léons and Sanabria, "Coca and Cocaine in Bolivia," 32.

96. *LAWR,* 2 February 1995, 24 November 1994, 1 December 1994.

97. Eduardo Gamarra, "Fighting Drugs in Bolivia," in *Coca, Cocaine, and the Bolivian Reality,* ed. Madeline Barbara Léons and Harry Sanabria (Albany, 1997), 252; *LAWR,* 13 April 1995; *Wall Street Journal,* 24 February 1995; LARR-AG, 9 March 1995.

98. *New York Times,* 24 March 1989, 4.

99. *LAWR,* 27 October 1994.

100. *LAWR,* 23 May 1996, 18 July 1996, 22 August 1996.

101. *LAWR,* 5 and 26 October 1995, 9 November 1995.

102. *U.S. Department of State Dispatch* 7.24 (10 June 1996), 310–13.

103. Waltraud Queiser Morales, "Militarizing the Drug War in Bolivia," *Third*

World Quarterly 13.2 (1992): 366. Figures are from LaMond Tullis, "Bolivian and Colombian Policy Options on Illicit Drugs" (paper prepared for the annual meeting of the Latin American Studies Association, Washington, D.C., 28–30 September 1995), 1; *LAWR*, 1 July 1997; LARR-AG, 4 November 1997.

104. In the midst of his dilemma, Goni in late 1995 turned to higher powers, and in a visit to the Vatican appealed to Pope John Paul II to approach the United States and ask it to reconsider its increasing demands and constantly shrinking assistance (*LAWR*, 26 October 1995).

105. Francisco E. Thoumi, " Illegal Drugs Policy Failure in the Andes" (paper prepared for the annual meeting of the Latin American Studies Association, Washington, D.C., 28–30 September, 1995), 14.

106. Tullis, "Bolivian and Colombian Policy Options on Illicit Drugs," 12.

107. Hargreaves, *Snowfields*, 184–87. See also Kevin Healy, "The Coca-Cocaine Issue in Bolivia: A Political Resource for all Seasons," in *Coca, Cocaine, and the Bolivian Reality*, ed. Madeline Barbara Léons and Harry Sanabria (Albany, 1997).

108. Kevin Jack Riley, "*Snow Job?*" *The Efficacy of Source Country Cocaine Policies* (Rand Institute, 1993), 87, 140–45.

109. *LANU*, May 1994, 20.

110. A good brief study in this regard is Peter Andreas, "Coca Denial," *NACLA Report* 25.1 (July 1991): 14–15.

Epilogue

1. Cited in Verdesoto and Ardaya, *Entre la presión y el consenso*, 75, 76.

2. Ibid.

3. Kenworthy, *America/Américas*, 164–65.

4. Javier del Granado, *The Devil Is Dead: Democracy in Bolivia* (La Paz, 1989).

5. *Los Tiempos*, 2 July 1997.

6. Guillermoprieto, *Heart That Bleeds*, 196.

7. *New York Times*, 24 March 1989, 4; 10 June 1992, D16; 16 July 1995, 10; 19 September 1993, 9.

8. *New York Times*, 22 April 1993, 8; *LAWR*, 6 May 1993.

9. *Wall Street Journal*, 15 August 1995, 1; *Forbes* 155.6 (13 March 1995): 47; *Oil and Gas Journal* 93.32 (7 August 1995): 43. Goni was at pains to distinguish

between his plan of "capitalization" and the Paz Zamora administration's aborted plans to privatize those same enterprises. According to Sánchez de Lozada, Paz Zamora's plan would have provided a one-time infusion of funds to the state, and how that windfall would be used depended heavily on the government in power. Goni's plan leaves a long-term trust fund for Bolivia's elderly.

10. *New York Times,* 16 July 1995, 10.

11. After leaving office, Sánchez de Lozada admitted that education "could have been better attended to." The political costs of tackling the powerful teachers' union and the few short-term payoffs of educational reform limited his efforts. Interview published in the *Miami Herald,* 29 July 1997.

12. On privatization and the pension plan, see *LAWR,* 6 April 1995 and 18 May 1995; *New York Times,* 16 July 1995, 10; 25 May 1995; and *LAWR,* 29 June 1995. There was strong nationalist opposition to privatizing the railroad because it went to a Chilean company, thus accentuating the sense of suffocation Bolivians already felt at the hands of their neighbor to the west. Opposition for privatizing the smelting and refining company arose because old nationalists remembered the struggle Bolivia had gone through to get them, and for YPFB because it had stood as symbol of national patrimony and nationalist resistance to foreign control since the Standard Oil nationalization in 1937. See *LAWR,* 28 December 1995; *Oil and Gas Journal* 94.8 (19 February 1996): 29; *Wall Street Journal,* 15 August 1995, 1; and LARR-AG, 16 November 1995.

13. *Miami Herald,* 28 September 1998. In 1996, the Berlin-based advocacy group Transparency International rated Bolivia the second most corrupt nation in the world. In 1998, Bolivia "rose" to seventeenth from the bottom. *Los Tiempos,* 24 September 1998.

14. See *LAWR,* 26 June and 23 September 1997; LARR-AG, 27 January 1998; *Los Tiempos,* 17, 25, and 27 April, 9 June, and 17, 20, and 22 December 1998. Growth rates for 1998 were announced by ECLA (the United Nations Economic Commission for Latin America) and covered in *Los Tiempos,* 18 December 1998.

15. The *Washington Times* published a laudatory report on Bolivia prepared by its advertising department on 23 March 1998 that made exactly this point.

16. Granado, *The Devil Is Dead,* 53–55, 74, 153–55, 166, 197–227, 232–63.

17. The quote is from "Bolivia Falls Short: When Even an Economic Miracle Isn't Enough," *New York Times,* 12 July 1998. Statistics in this paragraph

come from *LAWR*, 11 August and 15 December 1998; LARR-AG, 17 June 1997, and 28 July 1998; and *Los Tiempos*, 6 August, 9 September, 6 October, 23 and 24 October, 15 and 18 December 1998.

18. "Newly Elected Ex-Dictator Vows to Wage War on Drugs in Bolivia," *Washington Post*, 4 August 1997.

19. *LAWR*, 8 September 1998; *Los Tiempos*, 17, 20, and 22 December 1998.

20. For a good summary of the problems facing Banzer by late 1998, see *Los Tiempos*, 20 December 1998. For the ombudsman's charges, see *Los Tiempos*, 26 November 1998. The Operation Condor story grows out of the inquest of Spanish judge Baltasar Garzón into the Pinochet regime. See multiple entries in *Los Tiempos*, 21 October 1998 through the end of the year; and *LAWR*, 3 November 1998. The quote is from the *Bolivian Times* (La Paz), 5 November 1998. In December, Banzer was declared persona non grata in the Chapare as peasant producers took a cue from Mexican leftists who made a similar declaration during Banzer's trip to Mexico earlier that month. See *Los Tiempos*, 10, 11, and 21 December 1998.

21. *Bolivian Times*, December 1998.

22. Catherine M. Conaghan and James M. Malloy, *Unsettling Statecraft: Democracy and Neoliberalism in the Central Andes* (Pittsburgh, 1994), 221.

23. Lawlor, *In Bolivia*, 11.

24. Kenworthy, *America/Américas*, chap. 2, esp. p. 18.

25. Lars Schoultz, *Beneath the United States: A History of U.S. Policy toward Latin America* (Cambridge, Mass., 1998).

Bibliographical Essay

Little has been written on U.S.-Bolivian relations. In Spanish, the only longitudinal study is a short book by Julio Sanjinés Goitia, *148 años de relaciones diplomáticos, Bolivia-EE.UU* (1996). Fredrick Pike's *United States and the Andean Republics: Peru, Bolivia, and Ecuador* (1977) remains the best general account in English, and in many ways the present volume is an elaboration of themes suggested in Pike's earlier and broader work. Because almost all of the story told in this book is found in bits and pieces elsewhere, I have cited sources extensively throughout and will not list many of the sources that appear in the endnotes. Rather I will confine the balance of this essay to general works pertaining to Bolivia's international relations, and particularly to U.S.-Bolivian relations.

Those who seek a broader and deeper introduction to Bolivian history than this book provides should consult Herbert S. Klein, *Bolivia: The Evolution of a Multi-ethnic Society*, 2d ed. (1992); Waltraud Queiser Morales, *Bolivia, Land of Struggle* (1992); and Rex A. Hudson and Dennis M. Hanratty, eds., *Bolivia: A Country Study* (1991). All contain extensive bibliographies. Klein's is annotated and complements this bibliographical survey by being particularly strong on early Bolivian history and on social and ethnohistorical accounts. Klein supplements his own bibliography in an article entitled "Recent Trends in Bolivian Studies," *Latin American Research Review* 31.1 (Winter 1996): 162–69. A good concise general study in Spanish is Humberto Vázquez Machicado, José de Mesa, and Teresa Gisbert, *Manuel de historia de Bolivia* (1983).

Bolivia's international relations have been defined to an exceptional extent by the country's geopolitical isolation. Most useful is J. Valerie Fifer's fascinating little book, *Bolivia: Land, Location, and Politics since 1825* (1972). Eduardo Arze Cuadros, *La Economía de Bolivia: ordenamiento territorial y dominación externa, 1492–1979* (1979), gives a Bolivian nationalist rejoinder to Fifer's occasionally bleak assessment of Bolivia's geopolitical viability, and in addition provides a great deal of useful statistical information. Julio Pozzo Medina, *Geopolítica y geoestrategia* (1984) looks at Bolivia's geopolitics from a military perspective.

Bolivia as a geopolitical entity was shaped by the nature of its independence. Key works in English include Charles W. Arnade, *The Emergence of the Republic of Bolivia* (Gainesville, 1957), which focuses on Bolivia's Creole elite and their late conversion to independence; Timothy E. Anna, *The Fall of the Royal Government of Peru* (1979), which provides the convoluted context for the story Arnade tells; and William Lee Lofstrom's dissertation, "The Promise and Problem of Reform: Attempted Social and Economic Change in the First Years of Bolivian Independence" (1972), which focuses on postindependence reforms and the reasons they failed. Thomas Millington, *Debt Politics after Independence: The Funding Conflict in Bolivia* (1992), gives an interesting interpretation of the economic causes of those failures. The dream and ultimate failure of a Peruvian-Bolivian union is told in Philip Taylor Parkerson's dissertation, "Subregional Integration in Nineteenth Century South America: Andres Santa Cruz and the Peru-Bolivia Confederation, 1835–1839" (1979). Parkerson's and Lofstrom's works have been published in Spanish: Lofstrom, *El Mariscal Santa Cruz en Bolivia* (1983); and Parkerson, *Andres de Santa Cruz y la confederación Peru-Bolivia, 1935–1939* (1984).

An interesting account of the independence period in Spanish, because the subject spent time in the United States, is the story of revolutionary figure Vicente Pazos Kanki: Charles Harwood Bowman, *Vicente Pazos Kanki: un boliviano en la libertad de America* (1975). Useful because it gives attention to the underclasses and not just the Bolivian Creole elite or Colombian liberators is René Danilo Arze Aguirre, *Participación popular en la independencia de Bolivia* (1979).

Valentín Abecia Baldivieso has written a two-volume account of Bolivia's international relations that focuses mainly on Bolivia's five surrounding neighbors: *Las Relaciones internacionales en la historia de Bolivia* (1978). With much the same focus is the two-volume account by diplomat Jorge Escobari Cusicanqui, *Historia diplomática de Bolivia*, 4th ed. (1982); and the most recent such work by historian Eduardo Arze Quiroga, *Las Relaciones internacionales de Bolivia, 1825–1990* (1991). Roberto Querejazu Calvo, *Bolivia y los ingleses* (1973), looks at relations with Great Britain from a Bolivian perspective; Joseph Barclay Pentland, *Report on Bolivia, 1827* (reprint ed., 1974); Edmund Temple, *Travels in Various Parts of Peru . . .* , 2 vols. (1833, reprint, 1971); and Lardner Gibbon's fascinating account of his semiofficial visit to Bolivia for the United States in the early 1850s, *Exploration of the Valley of the Amazon* (1854), all give an outsider's perspective on Bolivia and its early prospects. The best sources in English on U.S.-Bolivian relations during the period before the War of the Pacific are Scott Hugh Shipe's dissertation, "The American Legation in Bolivia: 1848–1879" (1967); and the bound volume *Diplomatic Correspondence of the United States. Inter-American Affairs, 1831–1860*, vol. 2 (1932).

A great deal has been written on the War of the Pacific but with Bolivia as a peripheral player. Besides the general accounts on international relations listed above, Roberto Querejazu Calvo, *La Guerra del Pacífico* (1983), and a dissertation by Richard Snyder Phillips, "Bolivia in the War of the Pacific, 1879–1884" (1973), focus on Bolivia. The domestic political consequences of the war are best described in Herbert S. Klein, *Parties and Political Change in Bolivia, 1880–1952* (1969).

Bolivians have written a great deal on their desire to restore access to the sea, although U.S. writers have paid scant attention to the matter. Exceptions include Ronald Bruce St. Johns, "Hacia el Mar: Bolivia's Quest for a Pacific Port," *Inter-American Economic Affairs* 31 (Winter 1977): 41–73; E. James Holland, "Bolivian Relations with Chile and Peru: Hopes and Realities," in *Modern-Day Bolivia*, ed. Jerry Ladman (1982); and a recent study prepared for the Department of State by William L. Krieg: *Bolivia's Quest for the Sea* (1993). Walter Guevara Arze, longtime MNR foreign minister, like St. Johns and Holland, tells the story of Banzer's failed initiative in the mid-1970s: *Radiografía de la negociación del gobierno de las fuerzas armadas con Chile* (1988). An answer in English to Chilean claims is Juan Siles Guevara, *Bolivia's Right to the Pacific Ocean* (1980).

International tin relations is a complex story; many of the key sources are included in the notes for Chapter 3. Standing out are Wálter Gómez, *La Minería en el desarrollo económico de Bolivia* (1978); Klaus E. Knorr, *Tin under Control* (1945); Antonio Mitre, *El enigma de los hornos: la economía política de la fundición de estaño: el proceso boliviano a la luz de otras experiencias* (1993); and two articles by John Hillman in the *Journal of Latin American Studies*: "Bolivia and the International Tin Cartel" (20.1 [1988]: 83–100) and "Bolivia and British Tin Policy, 1939–1945" (22.2 [1990]: 289–315). A volume written and published by the Latin America Bureau in London explains the causes and consequences of the 1985 tin crash: John Crabtree et al., *The Great Tin Crash: Bolivia and the World Market* (1987). A host of other excellent studies discuss the domestic impacts of mining on Bolivia. Examples include Herbert S. Klein, "The Creation of the Patiño Tin Empire," *Inter-American Economic Affairs* 19.2 (1965): 3–24; Charles F. Geddis, *Patiño, the Tin King* (1972); Manuel Contreras's dissertation, "The Formation of Technical Elites in Latin America: Mining, Engineering, and the Engineering Profession in Bolivia" (1990); Guillermo Lora, *A History of the Bolivian Labour Movement* (1977); June Nash, *We Eat the Mines and the Mines Eat Us* (1979), and the account of Domitila Barrios de Chungara, *Let Me Speak! Testimony of Domitila, a Woman of the Bolivian Mines* (1978).

On the economic ramifications of growing U.S. investments in Bolivia after World War I, Margaret A. Marsh gives a very interesting and critical contemporary account in *The Bankers in Bolivia: A Study of American Foreign Investment* (1928). Several essays on Bolivia and the Kemmerer mission to Bolivia are included in *The Money Doctors, Foreign Debts, and Economic Reforms in Latin America from the 1890s to the Present*, ed. Paul Drake (1994). See also Manuel E. Contreras, "Debt, Taxes, and War: The Political Economy of Bolivia c. 1920–1935," *Journal of Latin American Studies* 22.2 (1990): 265–87. Recently Jayne Spencer wrote a dissertation on "Oil, Politics, and Economic Nationalism in Bolivia, 1899–1942: The Case of Standard Oil Company of Bolivia" (1996).

There is much in the literature on the Chaco War. Key sources on the war in English are David Hartzler Zook, *The Conduct of the Chaco War* (1960); and Bruce W. Farcau, *The Chaco War: Bolivia and Paraguay, 1932–1935* (1996). On the U.S. role in the peace talks, see William R. Garner, *The Chaco Dispute: A Study of Prestige Diplomacy* (1966); Bryce Wood, *The United States and Latin American Wars, 1932–1942* (1966); and Leslie B. Rout, *Politics of the Chaco Peace Conference, 1935–1939* (1970). On Bolivia's German connections prior to and during World War II, see Cole Blasier, *United States, Germany, and the Bolivian Revolutionaries* (1973); and several of the chapters in Jerry Knudson, *Bolivia, Press and Revolution, 1932–1964* (1986). Another interesting, detailed account of prewar and wartime relations is E. James Holland's dissertation, "Historical Study of Bolivian Foreign Relations" (1968).

The 1952 revolution is so central to Bolivia's history and to U.S.-Bolivian relations that the serious student of Bolivia in the United States should be familiar with several excellent published accounts of the revolution in English. Robert J. Alexander, *The Bolivian National Revolution* (1958), portrays it, in midcourse, as a heroic attempt to remake and modernize Bolivia; James Malloy, *Bolivia, the Uncompleted Revolution* (1970), looks at why the task remained unfinished; and Christopher Mitchell, *Legacy of Populism in Bolivia: From the MNR to Military Rule* (1977), portrays it as a failed revolution, limited by the vision and program of its leaders. Several of the key students of the revolution in the United States contributed to *Beyond the Revolution: Bolivia since 1952*, ed. James M. Malloy and Richard S. Thorn (1972), which contains an excellent essay on the United States and the MNR by Cole Blasier.

These key works all touch on the role of the United States from their authors' distinct vantage points, but several published accounts focus on U.S. assistance to the revolutionary government. Fundamental is the enlightening memoir of

Bolivian ambassador to the United States Víctor Andrade, *My Missions for Revolutionary Bolivia* (1976). G. Earl Sanders, "The Quiet Experiment in American Diplomacy," *Americas* 33.1 (1976): 25–49, postulates possible U.S. motives; and Carlos Navia Rivera, *Los Estados Unidos y la revolución nacional: entre el pragmatismo y el sometimiento* (1984), suggests Bolivia's dilemma.

Supporting U.S. aid programs are two articles by Richard W. Patch: "Bolivia, the Restrained Revolution," *Annals of the American Academy of Political and Social Science* 334 (1961): 123–32; and "Bolivia: U.S. Assistance in a Revolutionary Setting," in *Social Change in Latin America Today* (1960). Several studies touch on U.S. assistance programs to rural Bolivia: Dwight B. Heath et al., *Land Reform and Social Revolution in Bolivia* (1969); Raymond E. Crist and Charles M. Nissley, *East from the Andes* (1973); Lawrence Heilman's dissertation, "U.S. Development Assistance to Rural Bolivia, 1941–1974" (1982); and Lesley Gill, *Peasants, Entrepreneurs, and Social Change: Frontier Development in Lowland Bolivia* (1987). Many examinations of aid are critical from a variety of angles: James W. Wilkie, *The Bolivian Revolution and U.S. Aid since 1952* (1969), assesses statistically how aid slowed and eventually stalled the revolution without providing sufficient developmental impulse to shore up the MNR; George Jackson Eder provides a fascinating candid account of his role in stabilization and why he believes aid fed MNR corruption in *Inflation and Development in Latin America: A Case History of Inflation and Stabilization in Bolivia* (1968); Richard Gordon Frederick's dissertation, "United States Aid to Bolivia, 1952–1972," examines aid's counterproductive features; and Melvin Burke, *The Corporación Minera de Bolivia (COMIBOL) and the Triangular Plan: A Case Study in Dependency* (1987), explores the mixed economic legacy and underlying political agenda of the Triangular Plan. A general assessment of the economic legacy of the MNR-U.S. partnership is Cornelius H. Zondag, *The Bolivian Economy, 1952–1965* (1966).

Several recent dissertations use newly released U.S. documents to more fully describe U.S. policy and the nature and purpose of aid: Thomas Zoumaras, "The Path to Pan-Americanism: Eisenhower's Foreign Economic Policy toward Latin America" (1987); Naoki Kamimura, "The United States and the Bolivian Revolutionaries, 1943–1954: From Hostility to Accommodation to Assistance" (1991); and Kenneth Lehman, "U.S. Foreign Aid and Revolutionary Nationalism in Bolivia: The Pragmatics of a Patron-Client Relationship" (1992). On a similar track is Glen Rotchin, *The Clientelist State and International Patronage: The Case of Revolutionary Bolivia, 1952–1964* (1994). Still lacking is a good study rooted equally in Bolivian sources. Even Navia Rivera's excellent *Los Estados*

Unidos y la revolución nacional, cited above, relies heavily on U.S. sources. A problem has been that Bolivian Foreign Ministry archives are disorganized and incomplete, though there have been recent improvements on both counts.

The anomoly of U.S. assistance to a revolutionary nationalist regime in Latin America—particularly in light of U.S. policies in Guatemala, Cuba, and elsewhere—has led to a number of analytical comparative accounts. The standard is still Cole Blasier, *The Hovering Giant: U.S. Responses to Revolutionary Change in Latin America* (1976); but more recent analyses using released archival material include book chapters in Bryce Wood, *The Dismantling of the Good Neighbor Policy* (1985); and Martha L. Cottam, *Images and Intervention: U.S. Policies in Latin America* (1994); an article: Kenneth Lehman "Revolutions and Attributions: Making Sense of Eisenhower Administration Policies in Bolivia and Guatemala, *Diplomatic History* 21.2 (1997): 185–213; and several dissertations: John Stephen Zunes, "Decisions on Intervention: United States Responses to Third World Nationalist Governments, 1950–1957" (1990); Jennifer Leigh Bailey, "Dependent Revolution: The United States and Radical Change in Bolivia and Cuba" (1990); and James Forshee Siekmeier, "Fighting Economic Nationalism: U.S. Aid and Development Policy toward Latin America, 1953–1961" (1993).

Several works touch on the role of the United States as they examine the collapse of the MNR government in 1964. Gregorio Selser, *La CIA en Bolivia* (1970); J. Calderón, *The Bolivian Coup of 1964: A Sociological Analysis* (1972); and Laurence Whitehead, *The United States and Bolivia, a Case of Neo-Colonialism* (1969), suggest U.S. support for the military coup. William H. Brill, *Military Intervention in Bolivia: The Overthrow of Paz Estenssoro and the MNR* (1967); and Sergio Almaraz Paz, *Réquiem para una república,* 4th ed. (1988), emphasize Bolivia's internal problems, though they agree on little else.

The key secondary sources that guided me through the military years are James Dunkerley, *Rebellion in the Veins* (1984), fascinating reading for any Boliviaphile who can remember those years; James M. Malloy and Eduardo Gamarra, *Revolution and Reaction: Bolivia, 1964–1985* (1988), an analysis by two political scientists of military rule and its failure to bring stability; Gary Prado Salmón, *Poder y fuerzas armadas, 1949–1982* (1987), the most balanced look at military rule from within that institution; and, finally, the collection of essays by Bolivian and U.S. political scientists and economists on a variety of themes relating particularly to the Banzer years found in *Modern-Day Bolivia,* ed. Jerry Ladman (1982). Laurence Whitehead, "Bolivia's Conflict with the United States," *World Today* 26 (April 1970): 167–77; and James V. Kohl, "Bolivia Begins the Seventies," *New Politics* 10 (Fall 1973): 48–58, focus on U.S. relations with the leftist military regime of the late 1960s and early 1970s.

The thirtieth anniversary of the defeat of Ché Guevara in Bolivia and the discovery of his body have generated a spate of recent books, all touching on Ché's Bolivian experiences: Jon Lee Anderson, *Ché Guevara, a Revolutionary Life* (1997); Jorge G. Castaneda, *Compañero: The Life and Death of Che* (1997); and Paco Ignacio Taibo, *Guevara, Also Known as Che* (1997). Especially important on the Bolivian campaign are Gary Prado Salmón, *The Defeat of Che Guevara: Military Response to Guerrilla Challenge in Bolivia* (1990); Harry Villegas, *Pombo: A Man of Che's Guerrilla: With Che Guevara in Bolivia* (1997); and Ché's own diary, which both gives the flavor of the campaign and hints at the reasons for its ultimate failure: Ernesto Guevara, *The Bolivian Diary of Ernesto Che Guevara* (1994).

Narcotráfico y política: militarismo y mafia en Bolivia, edited by Instituto de Estudios Políticos para América Latina y África (1982); and Gregorio Selser, *Bolivia: el cuartelazo de los cocadolares* (1982), detail the rise of García Meza. Increasingly, from that point, coca-cocaine preoccupied those writing about Bolivia. For interesting details, see Dunkerley, *Rebellion in the Veins;* and Clare Hargreaves, *Snowfields: The War on Cocaine in the Andes* (1992). Raul Barrios Morón, *Bolivia y los Estados Unidos: democrácia, derechos humanos, y narcotráfico, 1980–1982* (1989); and Guillermo Bedregal Gutiérrez and Ruddy Viscarra Pando, *La Lucha boliviana contra la agresión del narcotráfico* (1989), give a Bolivian perspective on the matter. The best economic analyses of the impact of the coca-cocaine trade on Bolivia are James Painter, *Bolivia and Coca: A Study in Dependency* (1994); and Mario de Franco and Ricardo Godoy, "The Economic Consequences of Cocaine Production in Bolivia: Historical, Local, and Macroeconomic Perspectives," *Journal of Latin American Studies* 24 (May 1992): 379.

A multidisciplinary perspective on coca-cocaine in Bolivia can be found in *Coca and Cocaine: Effects on People and Policy in Latin America*, ed. Deborah Pacini and Christine Franquemont (1986); and *Coca, Cocaine, and the Bolivian Reality*, ed. Madeline Barbara Léons and Harry Sanabria (1997). In addition to his contributions to both those edited volumes, Kevin Healy has written other articles on coca-cocaine from the perspective of the Bolivian peasant; see, for example, "Coca, the State, and the Peasantry in Bolivia, 1982–1988," *Journal of Interamerican Studies and World Affairs* 30.2–3 (1989): 105–26; and "The Political Ascent of Bolivia's Peasant Coca Leaf Producers," *Journal of Interamerican Studies and World Affairs* 33.1 (1991): 87–121. The best studies of U.S.-Bolivian coca relations are several articles by Eduardo Gamarra, including his contribution to *Coca, Co-*

caine, and the Bolivian Reality, and "U.S.-Bolivia Counternarcotics Efforts during the Paz Zamora Administration, 1989–1992," in *Drug Trafficking in the Americas,* ed. Bruce Bagley and William O. Walker (1994). Gamarra also wrote *Entre la droga y la democracia: la cooperación entre Estados Unidos–Bolivia y la lucha contra el narcotráfico* (1994). Studies focusing on implementation of U.S. drug policies include Jaime E. Malamud Goti, *Smoke and Mirrors: The Paradox of the Drug Wars* (1992); and Sewell H. Menzel's dissertation, "Implementing U.S. Anti-drug Policy in the Andes: A Comparative Study of Bolivia, Peru, and Colombia" (1993). For a complete bibliography on coca-cocaine studies relating to Bolivia, see *Coca, Cocaine, and the Bolivian Reality.*

Key discussions of recent Bolivian neoliberal policies include Juan Antonio Morales and Jeffrey Sachs, "Bolivia," in *Developing Country Debt and Economic Performance,* ed. Jeffrey D. Sachs (1989); the articles on Sachs by Robert E. Norton and Catherine Conaghan in *Money Doctors in Latin America,* ed. Paul W. Drake (1994); a dissertation by Luis E. Breuer, "Hyperinflation and Stabilization: The Case of Bolivia, 1984–1986" (1989); the essay by Eduardo Gamarra in *Democracy, Markets, and Structural Reform in Latin America,* ed. William C. Smith et al. (1993); and Catherine M. Conaghan and James M. Malloy, *Unsettling Statecraft: Democracy and Neoliberalism in the Central Andes* (1994). Richard Bauer provides an early assessment of Sánchez de Lozada's reforms in *The Bolivian Formula: From State Capitalism to Capitalisation* (1997). Of interest because the author, a Bolivian, attempts to apply Tocquevillian analysis to Bolivia's new democracy is Javier del Granado, *The Devil Is Dead: Democracy in Bolivia* (1989). A valuable Bolivian analysis of U.S.-Bolivian relations in the context of the transition to democracy, the drug wars, and neoliberal reforms is Luis Verdesoto and Gloria Ardaya Salinas, *Entre la presión y el consenso: escenarios y previsiones para la relación Bolivia–Estados Unidos* (1993).

There is another layer to U.S.-Bolivian relations that this volume scarcely touches. Because Bolivia is so different and distant it has always drawn a strange mixture of adventurers, business speculators, humanitarian reformers, missionaries, and dropouts from the United States. Besides the account by Lieutenant Gibbon on his early foray into the Amazon (William Lewis Herndon and Lardner Gibbon, *Exploration of the Valley of the Amazon* [1854]), other tales by adventurers to Bolivia include Charles Johnson Post, *Across the Andes: A Tale of Wandering Days among the Mountains of Bolivia and the Jungles of the Upper Amazon* (1912); and Julian Duguid, *Green Hell: Adventures in the Mysterious Jungles of Eastern Bolivia* (1931).

More needs to be written on the role of humanitarians, nongovernment agencies, and missionaries. Peter C. Wagner, a missionary himself, gives a brief account of missionary activity in *The Protestant Movement in Bolivia* (1970). Gerald Colby and Charlotte Dennett provide an interesting if occasionally hysterical account of connections between U.S. oil interests, right-wing dictators such as Banzer in his first dispensation, and the Wycliffe Bible Translators in *Thy Will Be Done: The Conquest of the Amazon: Nelson Rockefeller and Evangelism in the Age of Oil* (1995). Images of Bolivia seen through the eyes of Austrian Jews who came to Bolivia, many of whom eventually moved on to the United States, can be found in Leo Spitzer, *Hotel Bolivia: The Culture of Memory in a Refuge from Nazism* (1998).

A number of new guides with such titles as *Doing Business in Bolivia* (1998) and *Cracking Latin America: A Country-by-Country Guide to Doing Business in the World's Newest Emerging Markets* (1994) have appeared in the last decade to encourage those who would like to spur Bolivia along the path to modernization and make a few dollars in the process. A countercultural perspective is presented in Mark Jacobs, *Stone Cowboy: A Novel* (1997), a fictional account of three alienated Americans who find redemption of sorts in an exotic Bolivian purgatory. The novel is excellent, and Jacobs knows Bolivia, but he gives a rather bleak and unidimensional depiction of its people—of more than passing interest since in his other life Jacobs is a U.S. Foreign Service officer. From a reverse angle, Bolivian scholar Mariano Baptista Gumucio, in *Latinoamericanos y norteamericanos* (1987), provides a creatively formatted and thought-provoking look at the cultural gulf between the United States and Bolivia.

The list given here is barely suggestive, but in conjunction with the more exhaustive bibliographical essay in Klein's *Bolivia: The Evolution of a Multi-ethnic Society*, it should give the interested reader a toehold on the fascinating and multifaceted story of Bolivia.

Index